Improving
Teacher Education
Resources and
Recommendations

Myles I. Friedman
Patricia S. Brinlee
Patricia B. Dennis Hayes

LONGMAN

New York and London

IMPROVING TEACHER EDUCATION
Resources and Recommendations

Longman Inc., New York
Associated companies, branches,
and representatives
throughout the world.

Developmental Editor: Lane Akers
Editorial and Design Supervisor: Joan Matthews
Cover Design: Dan Serrano
Manufacturing and Production Supervisor: Robin B. Besofsky
Composition: Kingsport Press
Printing and Binding: BookCrafters Inc.

Library of Congress Cataloging in Publication Data

Friedman, Myles I   1924–
    Improving teacher education.

    Includes index.
    1. Teachers, Training of. 2. Teachers, Training of—Evaluation. I. Brinlee, Patricia S., joint author. II. Hayes, Patricia B. Dennis, joint author. III. Title.
LB1715.F73   370'.7'1   79–25458
ISBN 0–582–28150–4

Manufactured in the United States of America

9 8 7 6 5 4 3 2 1

Sources

For the quotation on page 5: From Charles E. Silberman, *Crisis in the Classroom: The Remaking of American Education.* New York: Random House, Inc. Copyright © 1971 by Random House, Inc. Reprinted by permission of the publisher.

For the poem on page 6: From J. S. Bossard, *Parent and Child.* Philadelphia: University of Pennsylvania Press. Copyright © 1956 by University of Pennsylvania Press. Reprinted by permission of the publisher.

For the quotation on page 11: From P. A. Olson, L. Freeman, J. Bowman, and J. Peipes (Eds.). *The University Can't Train Teachers: A Symposium of School Administrators Discuss School-Based Undergraduate Education for Teachers.* Lincoln: University of Nebraska Press. Copyright © 1972 by University of Nebraska Press. Reprinted by permission of the publisher.

For the quotations on pages 12–13 and 136: From A. W. Combs, *The Professional Education of Teachers: A Perceptual View of Teacher Preparation.* Boston: Allyn and Bacon, Inc. Copyright © 1965 by Allyn and Bacon, Inc. Reprinted by permission of the publisher.

For the quotation on page 13: From J. Myron Atkin, "Institutional Self-Evaluation Versus National Professional Accreditation or Back to the Normal School?" *Educational Researcher,* 7, 1978, 3–7. Reprinted by permission of the author.

For the quotation on pages 27 and 29: From Jackson, P. W. "Old Dogs and New Tricks." In L. J. Rubin (Ed.), *Improving Inservice Education: Proposals and Procedures for Change.* Boston: Allyn and Bacon, Inc. Copyright © 1971 by Allyn and Bacon, Inc. Reprinted by permission of the publisher.

For the quotation on page 65: From "The Student NEA Looks at Accreditation." An overview of accreditation and certification with guidelines for student involvement to improve teacher education. A partnership project between the Student National Educational Association and the National Education Association. Washington, D.C.: National Education Association, 1975. Reprinted by permission of the publisher.

For the quotations on pages 66 and 142: From the Study Commission on Undergraduate Education and the Education of Teachers, *Teacher Education in the United States: The Responsibility Gap.* Lincoln: University of Nebraska Press. Copyright © 1976 by University of Nebraska Press. Reprinted by permission of the publisher.

For the illustration on page 69: From L. W. Anderson, "Student Involvement in Learning and School Achievement." *California Journal of Educational Research, 2,* 1975, 53–62. Reprinted by permission of the author.

For the quotation on page 83: From John M. Thomas and Warren G. Bennis (Eds.). *The Management of Change and Conflict.* Baltimore: Penguin Books, Inc. Copyright © 1972 by Penguin Books, Inc. Reprinted by permission of the author.

For the quotation on page 87: From Lortie, D.C. *School Teacher: A Sociological Study.* Chicago: University of Chicago Press. Copyright © 1975 by University of Chicago Press. Reprinted by permission of the publisher.

For the quotation on page 88: From B. M. Harris, E. W. Bessent, and K. E. McIntyre, *In-Service Education: A Guide to Better Practice.* Englewood Cliffs, N.J.: Prentice-Hall. Copyright © 1969 by Prentice-Hall, Inc. Reprinted by permission of the publisher.

For the quotation on page 137: From B. O. Smith, S. B. Cohen, and A. Pearl, *Teachers for the Real World.* Washington, D.C.: The American Association for Colleges of Teacher Education, 1969. Reprinted by permission of the publisher.

For the quotation on page 138: From J. B. Conant, *The Education of American Teachers.* New York: McGraw-Hill. Copyright © 1963 by McGraw-Hill Book Company. Reprinted by permission of the publisher.

For the quotations in chapter 10: From *Standards for State Approval of Teacher Education.* National Association of State Directors of Teacher Education and Certification, 1973. Printed by NASDTEC, 5th ed., further revision of U.S. circular no. 351, proposed minimum standards for state approval of teacher preparing institutions. Salt Lake City, Utah: NASDTEC. Reprinted by permission of the publisher.

For the list on page 152: Adapted from *NTE Common Examinations Bulletin.* Copyright © 1971, 1974 by Educational Testing Service. All rights reserved. Reprinted by permission.

For the illustration on page 153: From "Harvard's Report on the Core Curriculum." Washington, D.C.: *The Chronicle of Higher Education,* March 6, 1978, 15–18. Reprinted by permission of the publisher.

For the illustration on page 154: From "Berkeley Faculty Votes to Raise Standards, Restore Requirements." Washington, D.C.: *The Chronicle of Higher Education,* April 3, 1978, Vol XVI, No. 6, p. 11. Reprinted by permission of the publisher.

For the quotation on page 163: From Jackson, P. W. "Old Dogs and New Tricks." In L. J. Rubin (Ed.). *Improving Inservice Education: Proposals and Procedures for Change.* Boston: Allyn and Bacon. Copyright © 1971 by Allyn and Bacon, Inc. Reprinted by permission of the publisher.

For the quotation on page 170: From Richard A. Schmuck, P. J. Runkel, J. H. Arends, and R. I. Arends, *The Second Handbook of Organization Development in the Schools.* Palo Alto, Calif.: Mayfield. Copyright © by Mayfield Publishing Company. Reprinted by permission of the author.

For the quotations on pages 175 and 183: From *Discrepancy Evaluation* by Malcolm Provus. Berkeley, Calif.: McCutchan Publishing Corporation. Copyright © 1971 by McCutchan Publishing Corporation. Reprinted by permission of the publisher.

For the quotation on page 235: From C. E. Bogie and D. W. Bogie, "Teachers' Preferences toward Alternate Systems of Salary Increment." *Education, 99* (2), 1978, 215–220. Reprinted by permission of the author.

For the quotation on page 240: From Robert Glaser and A. J. Nitko, "Measurement in Learning and Instruction." In R. L. Thorndike (Ed.), *Educational Measurement,* 2d ed. Washington, D.C.: American Council on Education, 1971. Reprinted by permission of the author.

For the questionnaire on pages 260–261: Patricia A. Brinlee, "Inservice Questionnaire." Informal instrument of the Job-Related Curriculum Project. College of Education, University of South Carolina. Reprinted by permission of the author.

For the material on page 268: From Ned Flanders, *Analyzing Teaching Behavior.* Reading, Mass.: Addison-Wesley, page 34. Copyright © 1970 by Addison-Wesley Publishing Company, Inc. Reprinted by permission of the publisher.

For the form on page 269: From William J. Gephart, R. B. Ingles, and G. Suretsky, *The Evaluation of Teaching.* Occasional paper 18. National Symposium for Professors of Educational Research, 1974. Reprinted by permission of the author.

For the form on page 272: "Michigan State University Teacher Evaluation Sheet." East Lansing: Michigan State University. Reprinted by permission of the publisher.

For the material on pages 273–274: From M. Hildebrand, Robert C. Wilson, and E. R. Dienst, *Evaluating University Teaching.* Berkeley, California: Center for Research and Development in Higher Education, 1971. Reprinted by permission of the author.

For the rating scale on pages 273–279: "Course and Teacher Rating Scale," informal instrument of the College of Education, University of South Carolina, Columbia. Developed by Dr. Joseph P. Ryan. Copyright © by the College of Education, University of South Carolina. Reprinted by permission of the publisher.

For the material on pages 280–281: "Ohio Observational Record" (original edition), and "Ohio Teaching Record" (experimental edition). Columbus: Ohio State University. Reprinted by permission of the publisher.

Contents

Sources . . . . *iii*
Foreword by Leon M. Lessinger. . . . . *ix*
Acknowledgments . . . . *xi*
Introduction . . . . *xiii*

SECTION 1   IMPROVING TEACHER EDUCATION
PROGRAMS **3**

PART I   ORIENTATION AND METHOD   4
1. Teacher Education Today: Relic or Relevant   4
2. A Model for Solving Problems in Teacher Education. . .   15

PART II   IDENTIFYING PROBLEMS IN TEACHER
EDUCATION   24
3. Identifying the "Musts" of Teaching   24
4. Identifying the "Shoulds" of Teaching.   42
5. Building Support for Change   76
6. Identifying Inservice Training Problems   87
7. Evaluating at the Problem Identification Stage   98

PART III   DESIGNING TEACHER EDUCATION
PROGRAMS   105
8. Determining the "Whats" and "Hows" of the Teacher
   Education Program   105
9. The Professional Core Component   119
10. Teaching Specializations   134
11. The General Education Component.   148
12. Designing Inservice Teacher Training Programs   161
13. Evaluating at the Program Design Stage   171

PART IV   TESTING AND ACHIEVING SOLUTIONS IN
TEACHER EDUCATION   177
14. Evaluating at the Program Installation Stage   177
15. Evaluating at the Program Operation Stage   185
16. Evaluating at the Program Effectiveness Stage   200
17. Program Efficiency: An Optional, Final Consideration . .   210

SECTION 2 IMPROVING TEACHER COMPETENCIES 215

18. Identifying Problems in Professional Growth 216
19. Designing Programs for Professional Growth 228
20. Testing and Achieving Solutions in Professional Growth . 236
21. Characteristics of Exemplary Teacher Education Programs. 245

APPENDIXES 252

A. Observational Data Sources, Teacher Report Data Sources, Competency List Information. 252
B. General Survey Form 254
C. Data Collection Instruments 255
D. Source Competency Lists 256
E. Questionnaire 260
F. Open-Ended Questionnaire for Assessing Overall Curriculum 262
G. Professional Associations 265
H. Summary of General Education Requirements at Selected Teacher Education Programs 266
I. Sample Standardized Classroom Observation Instruments . 268
J. Sample Format and Content of Observation Instruments . 269
K. Text Construction Texts 270
L. Texts for Scoring and Evaluation 271
M. Sample Instruments for Student Evaluation of Instructor Performance 272
N. Formats for Observational Records 280
O. Sample Format for Analysis of Student Problems in Practice Teaching. 283
P. Texts on Teaching for Objectives 284
Q. Texts on Interaction Analysis. 284
R. Texts for Selecting Standardized Tests. 285
S. Texts for Psychometric Aspects of Text Construction. . . 285
Bibliography *286*
Index *298*

Tables and Figures

TABLES

3.1. Applications of the Data Base 28

3.2–3.9. The Generic Teacher Job Description

3.2. Teaching as a Profession 36
3.3. Instructional Planning 37
3.4. Teaching: Implementing Instructional Plans 38
3.5. Interpersonal Skills for Teachers 39
3.6. Using Instructional Aids 40
3.7. Diagnosing Readiness for Learning 40
3.8. Achievement Test Construction and Instructional Evaluation . 41
3.9. Supportive Services 42

4.1. Data Sources for Identifying Desired Teacher Competencies . 44
4.2. Teaching as a Profession 50
4.3. Instructional Planning 52
4.4. Implementing Instructional Plans 54
4.5. Interpersonal Skills 56
4.6. Using Instructional Aids 58
4.7. Diagnosing Readiness for Learning 59
4.8. Achievement Test Construction and Instructional Evaluation . 60
4.9. Supportive Services 61
4.10. Additional Categories 62
4.11. Additional Categories 63
4.12. Additional Categories 64
4.13. Filtering the Data Base 70
11.1. Relative Emphasis on Professional Coursework in Various
Programs 155
11.2. Relative Emphasis on Supportive Coursework in Various
Professional Programs 156
11.3. Comparative Chart 158
20.1. Examples of Evaluation Instruments for Teacher Training
Programs 238

FIGURES

5.1. Organization: Readiness to Change 85
6.1. Problem Identification: Inservice Training Needs 92
8.1. Teaching as a Profession 109
9.1. Suggested Professional Core Course Sequence 123
9.2. Laboratory/Field Experiences. 130
18.1. Correspondence of Problem-Solving and Diagnostic
Prescriptive Models 222
18.2. Diagnostic Discrepancy Analysis 227
19.1. Professional Growth Requirements 231

Foreword

There are a large number of books and articles dealing with the topic of improving teacher training and education. Most discuss problems, dysfunctions, and crises. Few propose viable solutions. Fewer base their solutions on documented requirements. Fewer still base solution strategies on documented requirements *and* a case study of an actual project using those solution strategies. Professor Friedman and his associates have produced a publication which belongs in that last, select group. They present the problem and issues, show us how to solve problems of this nature, use their problem-solving model in the solution of the challenge of improving teacher training and education, detail their solutions as manifested in a legislatively funded project, and discuss their tactics and strategies in the larger framework of theory and practice.

The result, this book, is a genuine contribution to the improvement of teacher training and education. The reader is constantly supplied with *how* to work, *what* to look for, and *ways* to think and plan for action. Examples are given for reference or for adoption. The tables alone make this book a valuable tool.

Along the way, Friedman and his associates discuss important elements for making improvements. Here are a few of those presented:

- The critical nature of dealing with the value components and beliefs of decision-makers

- The requirement to evaluate critically the conformance of the program implementation with the design (How often a program is evaluated before the program is actually operational.)

- The unproductiveness of traditional approaches to the issues of teacher training and education

- The effect on education of competition for students between various elements of the university

- The impact of the separation of coursework and fieldwork

- The consequences of poor professional role models for teachers

- The confusion generated by making teacher certification virtually synonymous with graduation from an accredited program

- The importance of uncovering the continuous corrective action as weakness

- The *sine qua non* of data-based action

- The distinction and utilization of "must" behavior and "should" behavior

- The ways to accomplish change

This is a "how-to" book cast in a theoretical framework of problem solving and organizational implementation. The authors know what they are talking about; they have tested what they advocate by putting it to use to develop an exemplary program of teacher training and education. There is even a section on costs and benefits. Given the press for increased accountability and productivity, this optional section adds additional interest and credibility.

I predict widespread use of this book by board members, legislators, and other decision-makers; managers and administrators of teacher preparation institutions, in-service training and education centers; school leaders; and professors of education. What a delight it is to find a practical yet scholarly approach to improving the pre- and inservice training and education of teachers. And it is a pleasure to read.

Leon M. Lessinger

Acknowledgments

Improving Teacher Education is a product of the Job-Related Curriculum Project, a South Carolina-based effort to strengthen both the quality and the relevance of teacher preparation programs. In 1977, the faculty of the College of Education at the Columbia campus of the University of South Carolina decided there was a need to reexamine the undergraduate teacher training curriculum. A statewide needs assessment was designed to identify the current job requirements of practicing public school teachers so as to have baseline data for developing the new curriculum.

A receptive climate for the work of the project was evident among public school teachers and administrators around the state from the beginning. It was here, at the grass roots level, that many of the most useful recommendations for revising teacher education were generated. Support for the project was strong, as evidenced by the numerous letters of endorsement the project received. Teachers involved in identifying needed competencies were especially supportive of the job-related approach. Many cited their own need for additional training to refine their teaching skills and to keep pace with instructional innovations. As the discrepancies between current teacher education practices and on-the-job demands became more and more evident, the focus of the project was expanded to include inservice teacher training needs as well.

Because of the participatory approach used in designing the job-related curriculum, literally hundreds of individuals contributed information and recommendations to the project. Unfortunately, space does not permit the authors to acknowledge each of these persons by name. The authors are deeply indebted to the educators, citizens, and legislators, as well as to the various educational and community groups who participated in the development of the data base.

The financial support provided by the legislature of South Carolina made possible the continued work of the project. The authors are grateful that the current climate of concern for educational improvement in the state has been translated into reality by legislative commitment.

As we emphasize in the book, the likelihood of a project succeeding is also enhanced by administrative backing. In our case, the job-related curriculum was given this essential support by University of South Carolina President James B. Holderman and Provost Francis Borkowski. Dr. Leon Lessinger, former dean of the College of Education, also provided leadership and support for our effort.

The authors would also like to thank the faculty members of the College of Education, University of South Carolina, who coordinated and contributed to the development of the professional core courses. As a result of their assistance, the professional courses reflect a range as well as depth of expertise that would have been otherwise impossible to obtain.

The authors are also indebted to the late Dr. Steven Buebel and to Donald Mankowski, who were instrumental in conducting the initial indentification of professional skills.

The perseverance and competence of Susan Roth, our secretary, were invaluable to the completion of the book. In addition to preparing numerous drafts, she made many recommendations which improved the continuity of the manuscript.

We are especially grateful to those who reviewed the preliminary manuscript. The expertise and varying perspectives they brought to this task enabled us to make substantial improvements in the book. Reviewers included:

Dr. Lorin Anderson, Associate Professor
College of Education
University of South Carolina

Dr. Al Dorsey, Supervisor
Teacher Education
State of South Carolina
State Department of Education

Dr. Anthony LaBue, Dean
School of Education
California State University

Dr. Leon Lessinger, Professor
  and former Dean
College of Education
University of South Carolina, *and*
a former commissioner,
United States Office of Education

Dr. Robert Phelps
Congress of Faculty Associations, *and*
former Executive Secretary,
Pennsylvania State Education Association

Mr. Al Schweigert, Past Region II Representative
Elementary Administration Committee
Association of California School Administrators

Dr. Allen Warner
Director of Field Experiences
College of Education
University of Houston

Introduction

Concerns about the quality of teacher education today are widespread. Indeed, it would be hard to find anyone in the educational community, whether teacher, teacher educator, or administrator who would disagree with the contention that improvement in teacher education is needed. Much has been written about one aspect of the teacher education problem or another. Our involvement in the Job-Related Curriculum Project, however, has enabled us to use a comprehensive data-based, problem-solving approach to the solution of the many complex and interrelated issues which confront teacher education.

Improving Teacher Education is comprehensive. It deals with both preservice and inservice teacher education. We view the professional development of the teacher as a continuous process beginning with entry level preservice training and building on this base during employment to provide for continued growth and increased competency. This book analyzes the requirements of professional preparation—the competencies all teachers need to perform successfully as educational practitioners. It probes into the general education component of the teacher education program, that aspect of professional preparation which should ensure that teachers acquire a liberal education so that they may stand before our children with a broad fund of knowledge representative of the fabric of our culture. In addition, it examines teacher specialization—the acquisition of special skills and knowledge at a particular grade level and/or in a particular subject area. Also encompassed in our discussion of specializations are cognate areas which augment and broaden teacher competency, increase the flexibility of teachers' qualifications, and often make teachers more employable.

The following are the major complementary aims addressed in the text:

1. Each teacher should have a common core of skills, knowledge, and attitudes that are required to perform effectively as a teacher whatever the subject content or the special characteristics of the learner.

2. Each teacher should have an area of teaching specialization which enables him to be effective in a specific content area and/or with particular learners.

3. Each teacher should have a general education including the areas of language and communication skills, literature, the social and behavioral sciences, the fine arts and humanities, mathematics, natural science, and American culture and heritage.

4. Whenever possible, each teacher should develop expertise in an area other than his specialization in order to diversify his skills and qualifications.

Of the various areas of teacher education considered in *Improving Teacher Education,* emphasis is placed on professional preparation. Since the beginning of the teaching profession, some have contended that talent in communications and managing children plus a liberal education sufficiently qualified an individual to teach. In recent years, however, there has been a growing effort to define a fundamental set of competencies that all teachers need. A large number of competency lists has been generated. The commonalities of these lists begin to describe in performance terms the teaching profession. However, more work remains in order to define cogently the proficiencies required by the educational practitioner. In addition, instructional programs must be designed to teach these basic competencies.

Many teacher training programs have elected to teach competencies, but few have adequately prepared programs to do so. In *Improving Teacher Education,* we attempt to redress this problem. Our review of teacher education programs in the United States indicates that the competencies that many are designed to achieve are based on what Houston and Warner (1978) call wisdom-consensus rather than on a data base derived from research on the subject. According to Houston and Warner, "one of the major challenges of competency-based education is to move from the conventional wisdom-consensus model for competency specification to an empirically derived, data-based model" (pp. 117, 118). In the Job-Related Curriculum Project, the competencies identified were founded on a data base which established the skills, knowledge, and attitudes teachers are actually required to demonstrate on the job. In this way the data base provided fresh and empirical criteria for designing a teacher education program.

In the book, we describe these professional skills and how they can be translated into a comprehensive preservice training program. Although the data base has the most direct significance for the professional core, it also has important implications for the general education and area of specialization requirements for prospective teachers. Not only are the professional skills identified in the data base significant in terms of the preparation of entry level teachers, but they are also reference points for the continuing professional growth of the individual teacher and of the total school staff. Therefore, we offer recommendations for strengthening inservice programs as well.

To provide a means for implementing these recommendations, we have developed and applied a problem-solving model to address the teacher education problem. This ensures that data collection and the development of a teacher education program based on the data proceed systematically. The problem-solving model is presented in Chapter 2 and its applications are clarified in subsequent chapters where it is used to deal with specific teacher education issues. The book is organized to explicate and conform to the model. Briefly, the model is simple and consists of only three linear stages—Stage 1: Identifying Problems, Stage 2: Designing Solutions, and Stage 3: Testing and Achieving Solutions. First, problems are identified. Programs are then designed to solve these problems. Finally, the programs are implemented and tested to achieve a solution. In *Improving Teacher Education,* the model is applied to 1) improving teacher education programs, and 2) improving or augmenting the competencies of the individual teacher. Both the *process* that produces teachers and the *product—*

the educational practitioner who has acquired these competencies—are assessed. The contributions of both preservice and inservice teacher education to the professional growth process are considered.

Improving Teacher Education thus has a threefold purpose. First, it provides a problem-solving framework for comprehensively analyzing and attacking current weaknesses in both pre- and in-service teacher education. Next, it explains how this approach can be applied by providing concrete examples of procedures and products appropriate to each of the three problem-solving stages. Finally, it demonstrates the use of this approach at the macro level, for implementing comprehensive pre- and in-service programs, as well as at the micro level, for facilitating individual professional growth.

As previously mentioned, the book is organized to conform to the problem-solving model introduced in Chapter 2. Section 1 of the book, *Improving Teacher Education Programs,* focuses on the problem of developing effective instructional programs to train teachers. This section is subdivided into four parts. Part I is entitled *Orientation and Method.* Parts II, III, and IV conform to the three stages of the model. Part II is entitled *Identifying Problems in Teacher Education.* Part III is entitled *Designing Teacher Education Programs,* and Part IV, *Testing and Achieving Solutions in Teacher Education.*

Section 2, *Improving Teacher Competencies,* deals with the problem of ensuring that individuals proceeding through a teacher education program acquire the intended competencies. This section consists of three chapters, each of which conforms to a stage of the problem-solving model: *Identifying Problems in Professional Growth, Designing Programs for Professional Growth,* and *Testing and Achieving Solutions in Professional Growth.*

Improving
Teacher Education

Improving Teacher Education Programs

1

Teacher Education Today: Relic or Relevant

CONVENTIONAL TEACHER EDUCATION: CHARACTERISTICS AND CRITIQUE

During the past decade, criticisms of public education have grown to a crescendo. Much of this dissatisfaction is aimed at teacher training programs. Rapid changes in society and in technology have led to revolutionary changes in public expectations of schools in general and of teachers in particular. Many teacher training institutions have been accused of preparing teachers for students and schools that no longer exist. These institutions have lost contact with their constituency and continue to prepare teachers as they did twenty years ago. Thus, the preparation teachers receive has become less and less relevant to actual on-the-job performance requirements.

It is clear that teachers need new skills, knowledge, and attitudes if they are to perform their duties competently. Widespread student apathy, the increasing incidence of classroom violence, the apparent decline in academic achievement, the rise of drug abuse, the complexities of desegregation, and similar problems baffle even the most experienced teachers. In addition to trying to cope with these difficulties, teachers are confronted almost daily with new responsibilities, such as those associated with mainstreaming. They are expected to adapt to new environments, such as the open classroom, as well as to implement new instructional technology and classroom management techniques. Current inservice training programs are often grossly inadequate in helping them retool to meet these demands. Many beginning teachers enter the classroom full of enthusiasm, only to find their training almost certainly unrealistic and quite often obsolete. As a result, teacher drop-outs and burn-outs are becoming increasingly common.

RUMBLINGS IN BOOT CAMP: SHORTCOMINGS OF PRESERVICE TEACHER EDUCATION

In light of the upheaval in the public schools and the attendant demands on the teacher, the question may well be asked, "Why hasn't teacher education kept pace with, or even anticipated, these changes?" Unfortunately, there are no easy answers to this question. Some teacher education programs, like institutional Rip Van Winkles, are just beginning to awaken to the realities that have been apparent to outside observers for a long while. Some institutions have tried to catch up by making only minor and superficial program changes. Still others have made significant progress in revamping their programs to accommodate new requirements.

Conventional teacher education programs vary somewhat from institution to institution. Generally, however, they share the following characteristics:

1. The program does not begin until the junior year or until completion of general education requirements.

2. Specific entry requirements for the program are typically minimal.

3. Professional preparation courses generally account for fewer than a fourth of the students' total course units.

4. Courses in the area of specialization, for secondary teachers especially, are taught in relative isolation from the corresponding methods courses.

5. There is little in the way of fieldwork until the final semester, when eight to twelve weeks is set aside for student teaching.

Regardless of the exact combination of these or other program characteristics, the essence of the deficiencies of conventional programs is that "the content and procedures of teacher education frequently have no demonstrable relevance to the actual teaching task" (Sarason, 1962, p. vii). That is, neither the "what" nor the "how" of the program has been consciously thought out in terms of classroom applicability. The content of education courses often seems to have attained sacramental status, unchallenged and unchanged despite the knowledge explosion and the breakthroughs in what is known about the learning process. The procedures taught in conventional programs come in for even more devastating criticism. According to Silberman (1971), for example:

> The wasteland of teacher education, virtually unrelieved by hopeful exceptions, is the course work in "methods of teaching." . . . Some are so abstract as to have no contact with reality; what passes for theory is a mass of platitudes and

generalities. Some courses focus entirely on the "how to" of teaching, presenting a grab-bag of rules of thumb, unrelated to one another or to any conception of teaching. Still other courses are glorified bull sessions in which teacher and students exchange anecdotes. (p. 443)

Without the intense criticisms of public education of the 1960's and the accountability movement, however, it is doubtful that teacher education would be subjected to the intense scrutiny it is receiving today. The demand for accountability, while fostering a healthy assessment of program outcomes, also resulted in a rather self-serving cycle of scape goating on the part of various actors in the educational hierarchy. Thus, it seems almost inevitable that teachers and their preparation would receive at least some share of the blame for the less than satisfactory performance and behavior of public school students. As the following verse illustrates, buck passing is not a new phenomenon in education, nor is it limited to teacher education:

WHICH ONE?

THE COLLEGE PRESIDENT—
  Such rawness in a student is a shame
    But lack of preparation is to blame.
HIGH SCHOOL PRINCIPAL—
  Good Heavens, what crudity, the boy's a fool!
    The fault of course is with the Grammar School.
GRAMMAR SCHOOL PRINCIPAL—
  Oh, that from such a dunce I might be spared!
    They send them up to me so unprepared.
PRIMARY PRINCIPAL—
  Poor kindergarten block-head! And they call
    that preparation! Worse than none at all.
KINDERGARTEN TEACHER—
  Never such a lack of training did I see!
    What sort of person can the mother be?
MOTHER—
  You stupid child—but then you're not to blame,
    Your father's family are all the same.
Shall father in his own defense be heard?
No! Let the mother have the final word.
              (Bossard, 1956, p. 297)

Teacher education has long been subject to charges of preoccupation with trivialities. Quibbling over terminology, for example, seems to be a favorite pastime of teacher educators. The question of whether teaching is properly called an art or a science has received far more concern than seems warranted. Another time-honored yet unresolved, and perhaps unresolvable, question which has filled volumes of education journals is whether the undergraduate program should be called "training," "education," or "preparation." One of the more recent controversies of this sort is what to call the hoped-for result of instruction. Seemingly endless quantities of ink have been devoted to the defense, operationalization, and critique of competing labels such as behavioral objectives, instructional objectives, competency statements, and intended outcomes. These concerns should not be dismissed flippantly as they do reflect some of the philosophical tensions and technical concerns in education. They do have their place; but this place is not center stage when the educational arena is burning. Debate over questions such as these deflects attention from more relevant concerns—concerns which need to be resolved in order to clarify the purposes and procedures of teacher education.

The deficiencies in teacher education might have remained in-house squabbles if discrepancies between graduates' preparation and expected performance had not become so painfully obvious. In the past, a teacher was usually able to compensate for these deficiencies through a sort of self-directed, on-the-job training. Today this approach is no longer feasible or adequate. If colleges of education continue to accept formulas such as 3 hours of history of education + 3 hours of child development + 6 hours of methods + 6 hours of student teaching = a teacher, an increasing number of beginning teachers will find themselves unable to cope with the realities of the classroom. In this day of educational malpractice suits, teacher educators can no longer afford to ignore the rumblings in boot camp.

One of the most damning criticisms of teacher education programs is that, in many cases, the resources needed to equip teachers with the necessary skills are and have been available. The fact that these resources have not been mobilized to provide this training indicates three shortcomings on the part of those involved in teacher education: first, a sense of complacency; second, a lack of touch with the realities of the public school classroom; and third, a lack of personal commitment to public school improvement. Obviously, these three factors are interactive. As long as teacher educators could remain unaware of and uninvolved in the problem, it was easy for them to avoid the difficult search for solutions. Today, however, it is clear that the fate of teacher education programs is inextricably linked to the performance of their graduates in the real world of the classroom.

REVOLT IN THE TRENCHES: SHORTCOMINGS OF INSERVICE TEACHER EDUCATION

While deficiencies in preservice teacher education are serious, those of inservice education are even more profound in their potential impact. Clearly, it is unrealistic to assume that the beginning teacher is a finished product, however well prepared for entry to the profession he may be. The pace of societal change can only be expected to increase, thus putting even greater demands on teachers to sharpen their present skills and to develop new proficiencies. Fortunately, one of the greatest strengths of the teaching profession has been its historical commitment to the ongoing development of professional competency. The opportunities for advanced study, both of a formal and an informal nature, surpass those of perhaps any other occupation or profession. The typical "free summer" schedule, provisions for sabbatical leave, required coursework for salary increments, reserved days for inservice programs, availability of staff development materials, and increasing federal funding for Teacher Centers and similar skill-improvement programs would seem to offer ample opportunity for any teacher or faculty to increase teaching proficiency.

Yet there is perhaps no term in the educational lexicon that is met with more derision by teachers than the phrase "inservice education." Announcing an inservice program at a faculty meeting is likely to elicit a similar reaction to announcing an innoculation program to third graders. This is not to say that teachers do not acknowledge their weaknesses or that they are not interested in improving their skills. Rather, the format of the typical inservice workshop does not permit much in the way of in-depth investigation of a topic or intensive skill development. Often, the content of such sessions has been identified as important by an administrator or other nonteacher. So-called inservice training sessions are frequently used to provide a captive audience for a salesman representing commercial instructional materials. Much of what passes for inservice training is characterized by superficiality and impracticality, even when the topic is relevant.

There is also much disenchantment among teachers regarding education courses taken for certificate renewal credit. Again, the charge that such courses are not relevant to job requirements seems to be the major concern. The perceived weaknesses in all phases of continuing professional education have led to a movement to give control of inservice training to teachers themselves. This movement has significant political ramifications. Competition among college of education faculties, school districts, and teachers' associations for control of teacher education has made inservice teacher education a battlefield. Teachers' associations in particular are advocating the position that Teacher Centers and other inservice programs be staffed, designed, and administered from within the ranks of the teaching profession. The potential impact of such a movement on colleges and universities is tremendous. It has done much to shake the complacent reliance of teacher educators on retreading teachers as a major source of enrollment. Consequently, many are reassessing the relevance of existing programs and course offerings.

ISSUES AND TRENDS IN TEACHER EDUCATION

A number of issues have been generated as a result of the weaknesses in conventional pre- and inservice teacher education. Some of these concerns have long been debated within the educational community. However, their significance has escalated as the discrepancies between what is and what should be have become more and more obvious. Other issues are relatively recent in origin and represent a reaction to current conditions. Many of these issues have tended to polarize various factions concerned with teacher education. This polarization has spawned trends, some of which can only be termed divisive. Others hold much promise for improving teacher training.

One debate which has intensified in recent years concerns the apportionment of the teacher's preservice education among general education, professional education, the area of specialization, and a minor and/or electives. The traditional four year, 120-semester-hour pie can only be sliced so many ways. There have always been legitimate differences of opinion regarding the appropriate degree of emphasis on each of these components not only for the prospective teacher but for other undergraduates as well. In many colleges, however, this debate has become more vitriolic of late, as faculty retrenchment due to declining enrollments and financial difficulties has become a reality. Competition for students is now a pragmatic as well as a philosophical issue.

Not only is there rivalry among the various areas mentioned above, but there is also competition *within* each of these domains. How many courses should be required in the humanities as opposed to the sciences? Should the general education component be interdisciplinary or discipline centered? Within the area of specialization, how much concentration should be on the discipline *per se* and how much on the content the student will be expected to teach? Should the prospective teacher have a specialized or a diversified background? Can both breadth and depth be provided without jeopardizing professional training? What professional skills will the entry level teacher need and which courses will best facilitate the attainment of those competencies?

While these and similar questions have not been satisfactorily answered by most teacher education programs, a number of states now require a five-year preparation period for teachers. This practice originally developed as a way of accommodating the additional subject area concentration deemed essential for secondary teachers in the post-Sputnik years. It has now become a trend in the preparation of elementary teachers as well. In many institutions the flexibility afforded by this larger pie has resulted in more emphasis on professional courses, including a longer and more intensive period of practice teaching.

One issue underlying many of these controversies is the question of how much of a teacher's preparation should be theoretical and how much should be applied. Teaching is not the only profession confronting this issue, as witnessed by the recent call for increased emphasis on clinical experiences for prospective trial lawyers. The need for both theory and practice in any professional preparation program is obvious. Openshaw (1968) observed that

"theory without practice is sterile; practice without theory is a vicious cycle." Assuming this statement to be true, it would appear that some of our current approaches to the preparation of teachers might be characterized by both sterility and vicious cycling. (p. 197)

The crux of the problem is that theory and practice have come to be viewed as dichotomous entities rather than as a holistic unit. The solution is not, as some would have it, to exclude one or the other but rather to find a way to integrate the two.

The way in which teacher education courses have conventionally been taught has contributed to the apparent irreconcilibility of educational theory and practice. Theories were emphasized because of their explanatory power and their applicability to a wide variety of particular situations. However, because of the separation between coursework and fieldwork, teacher educators have often left it up to students to figure out how to apply the concepts covered in a course. This does not necessarily indicate that the instructors themselves were incapable of applying these theories. Rather, the diversity of the typical class in terms of subject and level specializations, potential placement, and personal characteristics, combined with the distance, both in time and place, from the students' actual "need to know," made relevant applications difficult. Even professors with extensive and recent public school experience found it hard to come up with a sufficient number and variety of examples, demonstrations, and sample products to cover every possible application of a given theory. Those who tried to do so, in fact, were likely to be charged with sinning on the side of the practical, that is, teaching only a "bag of tricks."

Another current trend in preservice training is an increased emphasis on field-based experiences. Practice teaching, which Conant (1963) called the "one indisputably essential element in professional education" (p. 142) has been lengthened and raised to the status of an internship by many institutions. In addition, the recognition that exposure to the public school classroom should begin early and continue throughout the prospective teacher's training has led to the inclusion of field experiences in many previously textbook-bound courses. A number of programs now require prospective teachers to observe extensively and participate in a wide variety of school and other youth-oriented activities.

One cautionary note should be raised: frequent exposure to classroom situations, in and of itself, cannot be expected to produce competent teachers. Actual classroom experiences will do much to alleviate the "culture shock" commonly experienced by beginning teachers. For prospective teachers to benefit measurably from fieldwork, however, it is necessary to structure and process their observations and participation. Without provisions for integrating the academic and the field components of teacher preparation, what could have been useful learning experiences remain simply experiences. Sitting in a ninth grade classroom for X number of hours will no more prepare one to be a teacher than sitting in an operating room will qualify one to be a surgeon. While this exposure may help the prospective doctor and teacher develop more realistic expectations of their future roles, we should not thereby assume proficiency in the removal of either an appendix or ignorance.

Some leading school administrators critical of conventional teacher education have recommended extending the field-based trend to its logical conclusion. Proponents of school-centered training want to take the responsibility for the professional training of teachers away from the university and give it to the school system. In *The University Can't Train Teachers* (Olson, Freeman, Bowman, and Peipes, 1972), a variety of options are considered, most of which advocate a university "hands-off" policy except for providing two or three years of liberal arts background to the prospective teacher. One spokesman sees this as an extension of skill-oriented training at other levels:

> Those of us in the school systems are saying to universities what people in industry are saying to high schools, "Look, give up any pretense you have to providing technical training; you can't do it. Just give us a kid who can read and write and who's got a reasonable general education and we will give him the training he needs to function in our setting. But, don't waste this guy's time teaching him dysfunctional courses in a dysfunctional setting." (p. 71)

According to the school-centered models, local districts rather than universities should be responsible for making certification recommendations to state departments.

Proposals such as these are an indictment of the "ivory tower" syndrome which has pervaded many teacher education programs. Yet such criticisms must not be accepted wholesale. While field-based experiences certainly promise to increase the relevance of teacher education, it does not follow that academic preparation is unnecessary or that school-based training is automatically superior to university-based programs. Indeed, the argument can be made that public schools are having a hard enough time fulfilling their present responsibilities without taking on the additional challenges of administering teacher training programs. A lesson can be learned here from experiences with performance contracting, in which various private companies contracted to take over public schools, run them according to a business or efficiency model, and guarantee gains in student achievement. On the whole, performance contracting was judged to be a failure, thus proving the adage that the ability to see flaws in a system seems to be inversely proportional to one's responsibility for correcting them.

It should also be noted that despite obvious weaknesses in conventional programs, university-based teacher educators do possess expertise in various aspects of education which practitioners may not have. Caught up in the day-to-day routine of the classroom, many public school personnel lack the time and overall perspective needed to take on the total responsibility for teacher training. Also, without massive federal support, it is difficult to envision the financial feasibility of this alternative. In many school systems, the gap between the state of the art in instruction and the practice of that art is great. Moving the locus of control of teacher training to the school district will not necessarily improve that training and may, in fact, result in more "vicious cycling" or *status quo* practice of outmoded instruction than is presently apparent.

One of the major trends in teacher education, the competency-based approach, gained prominence in the early 1970's. Murphy (1975) gives the following definition: "The word *competence* is derived from the Latin infinitive *competere,* meaning 'to be suitable.' A person is competent, therefore, if he possesses the skills suitable for performing the tasks required" (p. 50). This movement is a rejection of the "trading stamp" approach in teacher education, in which one fills up a stamp book, or transcript, with credits earned which can be redeemed for a diploma. The competency-based approach, on the other hand, may be likened to a "merit badge" system in which one is rewarded only upon demonstrating successful completion of certain predetermined tasks. Wide variations in emphasis and organization exist under the umbrella of competency-based programs. The performance orientation, however, is perhaps the most salient feature distinguishing competency-based from other programs.

While some of these programs are based on sound principles, are well designed, and appear to be effective, others are more form than substance. In many instances, these programs simply put "old wine in new bottles." There is little change in the "what" or content of instruction. And, in some cases, the differences in the "how" of instruction involve changes which are more apparent than real. For example, some institutions have merely repackaged the course content of their conventional program as self-paced modules. As students complete each module, they are certified as having achieved "competency" in the particular unit. Without a substantial increase in staff or reorganization of existing resources, the job of monitoring and certifying the performance of each student's mastery of a long list of competencies becomes virtually unmanageable. In some cases, students in competency-based programs actually experience less in the way of field experiences and peer interaction than do students in conventional courses. Thus, merit badges can replace trading stamps without any substantial change in the quality of the resulting preparation.

The humanistic approach to teacher education is yet another trend, or perhaps one should say, another approach that has recently been revitalized. Programs carrying this label emphasize the self-discovery and actualization of their participants as well as their ability to facilitate similar growth in their future students. Creativity is a prime goal. Experiential activities, problem-solving techniques, and the like are seen as means to the end of preparing teachers. Terms such as "competencies" and "trainees" are eschewed because of their supposed mechanistic connotations. One of the leading proponents of this movement, Arthur Combs (1965), gives this description of the humanistic approach:

> If we adapt this "self as instrument" concept of the professional worker to teaching, it means that teacher-education programs must concern themselves with persons rather than competencies. It means that the individualization of instruction we have sought for the public schools must be applied to these programs as well. It calls for the production of creative individuals, capable of shifting and changing to meet the demands and opportunities afforded in daily tasks. Such a teacher will not behave in a set way. His behavior will change from moment to moment, from day to day, adjusting continually and smoothly to the needs of his students,

the situations he is in, the purposes he seeks to fulfill, and the methods and materials at his command. (p. 9)

Analysis of this passage, however, reveals nothing that is inherently incompatible with competency-based or other skill-oriented programs. The kind of flexibility Combs describes is a common goal of many programs not specifically labelled as humanistic. As with other trends, the only danger seems to be that of excess. Carried to the extreme, such programs may produce teachers who understand themselves and their students but are technically underprepared.

RATIONALE FOR THE PROBLEM-SOLVING APPROACH

Inadequate conceptualization of the purposes and procedures of teacher education, or "mindlessness," to use Silberman's phrase, continues to plague teacher education despite these promising trends. As Atkin (1978) comments:

> There are few signs at present of consensus within the education profession about the characteristics of effective preparation programs. The sharp and growing political conflicts are amplified by conceptual disarray. Competency-based teacher education flowers at one institution, "humanistic" education at another. There is little agreement either on "foundations" courses, appropriate field experiences in the early years of preparation for teaching, the level of technical training that is required to teach certain skills, or on much else. (p. 6)

The tendency to look for a quick and easy solution to a complex problem has led to the bandwagon popularity of some trends and a continuing naive belief that manipulating one aspect of the teacher education program is sufficient to bring about needed changes. Consequently, some programs have increased the amount of field experiences by establishing, sometimes arbitrarily, a particular number of clock hours a prospective teacher must "put in" in the classroom. Others have increased the requirements for courses in the area of specialization. Many have tinkered with the instructional delivery system without modifying the instructional content. These specific changes are not in and of themselves wrong; rather, the problem is that they represent Band-Aid approaches to the improvement of teacher education. The reforms cited in the examples above may well produce an improvement in the prospective teacher's preparation. However, without starting from ground zero to determine what skills, knowledge, and attitudes the teacher must have to function effectively, there is no empirical assurance that any of these changes will bring about the kind of improvement desired.

The above discussion brings into focus the folly of trying to patch up an outmoded program to meet new demands. While the weaknesses of the conventional curriculum are generally recognized, the exact nature and extent of the deficiencies are largely unknown. The best way to determine what the teacher education program should encompass is to start from scratch. A comprehensive assessment of the skills, knowledge, and attitudes needed by the teacher to function effectively in today's classroom must be undertaken before any meaningful decisions can be made as to what constitutes a relevant program.

In the chapters that follow, procedures for accomplishing these tasks are provided. This problem-solving approach enables the evaluator to pinpoint specific required and desired knowledge, skills, and attitudes that have not been adequately developed by conventional teacher education programs.

As a general look at the existing state of teacher education has indicated, a great deal is lacking. In Chapter 2 a model for solving problems in teacher education is discussed. The model is a general problem-solving mechanism; however, its use is illustrated in the context of the improvement of teacher education. To complete the identification of the problem we need to establish the preferred state, that is, the goals to be pursued in teacher education. In Chapters 3 and 4 we present a method for establishing the preferred state and the teacher competencies we derived from the application of the problem-solving method. The derived teacher competencies represent the preferred teacher characteristics the teacher education program is to be designed to produce.

In Chapter 3 our approach to identifying preferred teacher characteristics is presented. At this point, the "musts" of teaching, those competencies that are required of all teachers, are identified. In Chapter 4 we focus on the "shoulds" of teaching and show how both the "musts" and "shoulds" are filtered through the constraints of accreditation agencies to arrive at a final compilation of preferred teacher characteristics.

2

A Model for Solving Problems in Teacher Education

A systematic approach to problem-solving in education is a critical need. In addition, the application of evaluation techniques to the identification and solution of problems in education is essential. In this chapter, we present a model which can be used to find solutions to problems in teacher education as well as in other areas where a problem-solving approach is needed.

Unlike many problem-solving models, the model we propose is relatively simple, consisting of only three stages with the same three components designated for each stage. Contributing to its simplicity is the fact that the model is essentially linear. That is, one proceeds in a step-by-step fashion through each of the three stages. While in a particular stage, modifications and refinements are made before proceeding to the next stage. Thus, there is no need to recycle to earlier stages of the process. Extensive feedback loops are avoided because the basic decision to be made at a given stage is whether to terminate, modify, or proceed to the next stage. When the process has been completed, the only decision that needs to be made is whether or not the problem has been solved. The systematic and practical nature of this model maximizes the probability that the problem will be solved.

The three stages of the problem-solving model are:

Stage 1	Stage 2	Stage 3
Identifying Problems	Designing Solutions	Testing and Achieving Solutions

First, problems are identified. Programs are then designed for the purpose of solving these problems. Finally, the programs are implemented and tested to achieve a solution. Within each stage activities, evaluations, and decision-making take place. A brief explanation of each stage and its component functions will clarify the process. For additional information on the model, see Friedman and Anderson (1979). More specific applications to teacher education contexts will be made throughout the book.

STAGE 1: IDENTIFYING PROBLEMS

To be more specific, a problem can be defined as a significant discrepancy between an existing degree or amount of a characteristic and a preferred degree or amount of that characteristic. "Significant," here, refers to a discrepancy that is great enough 1) to be noticeable, and 2) to elicit concern among decision-makers for action. Sometimes such a discrepancy is referred to as a need, in the sense that there is a need to reduce the discrepancy. Consequently, some educators refer to Stage 1 as "needs assessment."

To illustrate this stage of the model, let us suppose that a teacher training institution is interested in having all prospective teachers score a minimum of 85 percent on a comprehensive test of instructional content and techniques prior to student teaching. This objective represents the preferred state of a relevant characteristic. Data gathered on three hundred teachers in training indicates that only 60 percent attained the preestablished mastery score. This information represents the present or existing state of the characteristic. Further analysis reveals that only 20 percent of the students scored above 85 percent on the test. This is another way of reporting the existing state of the characteristic. In this example, a discrepancy obviously exists.

Whether or not the discrepancy is significant is subject to the interpretation of decision-makers. Decision-makers are those who are empowered to direct activities. Virtually all organizations authorize individuals and groups to make decisions which direct the activities of the organization. The model suggests that the discrepancy information be provided to decision-makers so that they can decide whether the discrepancy constitutes a problem for their organization.

Activities

The primary activities involved in problem identification are information gathering and analysis. First, information pertaining to the context of the problem is collected to determine the nature and scope of the project and the feasibility of proceeding. The nature and scope of the inquiry is focused by determining the characteristics to be examined. Feasibility is established by determining whether the resources are available to study the characteristics. In addition, it is important to identify the personnel to be involved in the process, including decision-makers, evaluators, and program development specialists.

Second, data are collected to determine the existing and preferred levels of the characteristics under consideration.

Evaluation

The evaluation component of problem-solving may be defined as the identification of existing and preferred states, the comparison of the two states, and the interpretation of the results of the comparison. Thus one identifies what is—the existing state of affairs, and what ought to be—the preferred state of affairs. Then he compares the two states and extracts meaning from the comparison. A possible problem is indicated when a discrepancy is detected between the existing and preferred states.

Decision-making

At this point, a decision must be made as to whether a discrepancy is sufficiently large to constitute a problem. If there is no discrepancy or it is decided that the discrepancy is too small to constitute a problem, there is no need to proceed further. If it is decided that a problem exists, then one proceeds to design a program to solve the problem. To move to the next stage it is important to build a support base for the program. This includes the commitment of resources and the establishment of a reward system for participating in the program.

STAGE 2: DESIGNING AND PREPARING SOLUTIONS

Activities

At this stage, the primary activities involve designing programs to solve the problem, that is, to reduce the discrepancy and making preparations to ensure that the programs will be implemented according to design specifications. The design should specify the procedures for installing, operating, and evaluating the program.

In general, a program may be diagrammed as follows:

$$\begin{array}{ccc} \text{Enabling} & \text{Enabling} & \text{Terminal} \\ \text{Activity 1} \rightarrow \text{Objective 1} \rightarrow \text{Activity 2} \rightarrow \text{Objective 2} \rightarrow \text{Activity} \rightarrow \text{Objective} \end{array}$$

Each activity in the series leads to the achievement of an enabling objective. These culminate in the achievement of the terminal objective—the solution of the problem. A teacher education program, for example, is designed by first stipulating for students with the specified entry characteristics, a sequence of enabling objectives that lead to the achievement of the terminal objectives. This can be accomplished through task analysis (see Davies, 1973). Progressive activities are then planned to lead from one enabling objective in the sequence to another and finally to the terminal objective.

Evaluation

Evaluating the program design is accomplished by comparing the actual program design to the preferred program design to see if the former meets the specifications in the latter. Correspondence between the problem and a program should be used as a guide for program selection and development. The program should provide a series of activities that are designed to move subjects with the specific entry characteristics to the terminal objectives.

Decision-making

The fundamental decision to be made during this stage is whether or not the program is designed to solve the problem. If the answer is no, the decision-maker causes the design to be modified until there is an assurance that the program *is* designed to solve the problem. A program development specialist's expertise can contribute to decision-making at this stage.

STAGE 3: TESTING AND ACHIEVING SOLUTIONS

Activities

Activities at this stage involve testing the installation, operation, and effectiveness of the program. If the program is well designed and implemented, a solution will hopefully be achieved.

Evaluation

Evaluation consists of the assessment of the installation, operation, and effectiveness of the program. In evaluating the installation, the actual installation of the program is compared to the preferred installation as specified in the program design. This evaluation includes the acquisition and preparation of facilities, material, and personnel. Personnel must possess or be taught the skills specified in the design. When the program has been properly installed, it is executed and the operation of the program is evaluated by determining the extent to which the program operates according to specifications.

Finally, once a program is operating according to specifications, its effectiveness can be evaluated. The program was designed to bring about a change in characteristics. When it is functioning properly, it can be determined whether or not it does bring about the desired change.

Decision-making

Decision-making proceeds in the same sequence as evaluation. First, decisions relating to installation are made based on the evaluation of the installation. When it is decided that no additional modifications are needed, the program is executed. Its operation can then be evaluated. At this point, decisions are made to modify the operation until the program meets specifications. Finally, the effectiveness of the program is evaluated.

OPTIONAL STAGE: PROGRAM EFFICIENCY

There is a fourth stage that may be added to our three stage model. This stage focuses on the efficiency of the program. It is an optional consideration because there is some doubt about its value in education. Program efficiency is determined as a result of a cost-benefit analysis after an effective program has been installed. When a program has been proven to be effective, it is possible to examine the cost of the program and compare it to other programs considered to have similar benefits or output. This option permits a limited comparison of possible alternatives to the installed program. The qualification "limited" is an acknowledgement of the possibility of incomplete identification of costs and benefits. The purpose of the comparison is to provide the decision-makers with information so that they can decide whether to continue the program or to consider an alternative. It may, therefore, be considered the ultimate step in the process of evaluation (Provus, 1971).

However, there are specific problems associated with cost-benefit analysis of educational or other programs where the benefits include social values. Considerable disagreement has been expressed as to the feasibility of conducting cost-benefit analysis for educational programs. Many maintain that only a relatively small part of the outcome of an educational program is actually quantifiable. The basic step in this process is the careful defining of programs through functional cost accounting as part of the program planning and budgeting process. Detailed identification of program cost increments must be developed for purpose of comparison. However, for the analysis to be meaningful, the program must be compared to alternative programs which have been examined in the same detail and according to the same criteria.

The utilization of cost-benefit analysis in the problem-solving process requires that the following conditions be met (Provus, 1971):

1. The programs that produce measurable results must be sufficiently well defined to be replicated.
2. There must be agreement on both the value and the measure of benefit.

3. Antecedent conditions must be sufficiently well defined and measured to accurately determine their effect on output. (p. 210)

There are numerous situations in education where these conditions are not met. Rather than impose cost-benefit analysis inappropriately with the risk of drawing misleading conclusions, this technique should be reserved for those situations when it is clearly indicated.

KEY ROLES IN THE PROBLEM-SOLVING PROCESS

There are three key interrelated roles that must be performed to execute the problem-solving process successfully: decision-maker, evaluator, and program development specialist.

The role of the decision-maker is to determine the most appropriate course of action or the best alternative in a particular situation. In many cases, different individuals will be authorized to make different decisions. It is essential in defining the context for the problem-solving process that the decisions to be made are sequenced and the particular decision-maker authorized to make each decision is determined. In most cases, the decision-maker will be an administrator.

To be effective in solving problems, the decision-maker must learn to base decisions on data and to simplify the decisions he or she must make whenever possible. The decision-making process can be simplified by realizing that a series of decisions can be broken down into a number of separate decisions which can be dealt with one at a time. Furthermore, many of these decisions may be dealt with on a two-alternative basis. For example, educators decide whether to admit an applicant to school or not, whether to place him in a particular educational program or not, whether to advance him or not, whether to graduate him or not, and so on.

Even decisions that initially involve a number of alternatives can be broken down into a series of two-alternative decisions. Suppose, for example, that an administrator has ten applicants for a teaching position and must decide whom to choose. He might try to determine which applicant most closely meets the job description, the preferred state, by comparing all ten at once. Or he might simplify the process by comparing them two at a time, discarding the one that is least like the job description. After the last comparison, he could decide to hire the one remaining applicant. Or he could go through the same procedure again to check himself before coming to the decision.

A better way of proceeding on a two-alternative basis would be to first compare each applicant's qualifications to the job description in order to decide whether he is qualified for the job or not. All of the unqualified applicants could then be eliminated from further consideration. The remaining applicants would be compared to each other two at a time, eliminating the less preferred of the pair with each comparison. The applicant remaining after all of the comparisons were made would be chosen for the job. In the first instance, there was no provision for screening to decide whether an applicant was qualified or not. If all ten were unqualified, the applicant finally chosen would be best of the bunch, but still not qualified for the job. The second approach is preferred because a mechanism is provided to guard against this possibility.

There are a limited number of comparisons an individual can make simultaneously. Therefore, the fewer comparisons he needs to make, the more accurately he should be able to make them. By comparing two things at a time he should be able to make the most accurate comparisons. Using a computer, on the other hand, it is possible to make a myriad of comparisons. However, no matter how many comparisons a computer can make, if the decision-makers cannot cope with the analysis, it is of no value.

Usually only one or two comparisons between preferred and existing states are necessary in order to make any given decision. For instance, an instructor may wish to decide whether a prospective teacher should be advanced to the next learning unit or not. In order to make this decision, he may need only to compare the student's score on an achievement test to a pre-established criterion (usually a cut-off score) that represents readiness for the next learning unit. If there is no discrepancy between the two or the discrepancy is not serious, the instructor would probably decide to advance the student.

The evaluator is a salaried or contracted employee primarily involved with the collection and analysis of information. This requires technical skills in testing and measurement, statistics, and computer applications. Also, the evaluator often needs to utilize techniques for establishing a consensus of opinions such as in the identification of the preferred state. The Delphi method, which is "a way of replacing the committee with a sequence of individual interrogations interspersed with information feedback," is one such technique (Schmuck, Runkel, Arends and Arends, 1977, p. 174).

Above all, the evaluator must be able to interpret, organize, and communicate information clearly. He or she must be able to organize information to define the context for the problem-solving process and to write specifications and reports. The evaluator must be able to communicate data to decision-makers in a form they can understand. Too often decision-makers are provided with sophisticated statistical results which they do not have the training to decipher and comprehend. An experienced evaluator will convey statistical findings in the form of comparative percentages, using charts, graphs, and diagrams to clarify the meaning of the data.

The third key role is that of the program development specialist. Although program development specialists come in many varieties, developing teacher education curricula requires an instructional design specialist. The primary duty of the instructional design specialist is to develop the instructional program. Skills are needed in task analysis, deriving and sequencing instructional objectives, prescribing instructional methods and the use of instructional aids, and prescribing the content of instruction. The program development specialist should also write specifications describing how the instructional program is to be installed and how it is to operate.

The decision-maker, evaluator, and program development specialist work as a team. The program development specialist provides the expertise needed to design, install, and operate the program. The evaluator collects, analyzes, and interprets evaluation data for the decision-maker as well as for the program development specialist. The decision-maker is responsible for making decisions, coordinating the project, and providing administrative support.

The decision-maker uses the expertise of the evaluator and program development specialist in arriving at a decision. In reality, the decision-maker often delegates the authority to make certain judgments to these experts. The program development specialist should make or substantially influence decisions pertaining to the design, installation, and operation of the program. The evaluator should be heavily involved in decisions concerning problem identification, program effectiveness, and appropriate techniques for observing a variable. Both the evaluator and the program development specialist should be knowledgeable in the area of program evaluation. Their combined skills can be used in deciding on an appropriate method to evaluate the instructional program.

The skills of the decision-maker, evaluator, and program development specialist are a necessary, but not a sufficient condition for problem-solving. Input from consultants may be required for making informed decisions. In developing and evaluating instructional programs, for example, the opinions of subject matter specialists are essential. They represent content area expertise.

Program staff participation is also an important ingredient in the conduct of the problem-solving process. There must be support for change at the staff level since these individuals will be responsible for carrying out the most critical activities. The program staff are also the primary agents providing information needed to identify a discrepancy since they are the persons generally responsible for the routine planning, organization, and implementation of the program. They are also important participants in the establishment of program criteria, the setting of standards, and the interpretation of discrepancy information. For these reasons, lines of communication with the staff must be kept open and viable throughout the process. Feelings of involvement and commitment among the staff members should be fostered.

Communication may be considered one of the keys to the success of problem-solving. Concise and clear communication will ensure that findings will be meaningfully used and that the process receives sufficient staff input to be valid and representative. Positive staff attitudes can be maintained only by regular exchange of information.

THE PROBLEM-SOLVING MODEL
IN TEACHER EDUCATION

Although the problem-solving model can be applied in almost any context, in this book it will be applied to 1) improving teacher education programs, and 2) improving teachers' competencies. To improve teacher education, it is essential to focus on both the process—the program that produces teachers, and the product—the competencies that are learned by those who are to teach. In the book, both pre- and inservice teacher education will be considered.

Applying the procedure to the problem of improving teacher education programs, the problem identification stage identifies discrepancies between the competencies teachers possess and the competencies it is desirable for them to possess. Program design involves the preparation of instructional programs to reduce these discrepancies. During Stage 3, the programs are tested on groups of individuals who exhibit particular discrepancies to determine whether the program is effective in reducing the discrepancies. A program is deemed effective if a predetermined percentage of those in the program reach a preferred level of competency or if other pre-established goals are met. The ultimate decision here is whether or not to adopt a teacher education program for use.

When we apply the procedure to the problem of improving teachers' skills, the focus is on the effectiveness of the individual rather than on the effectiveness of the instructional program. Problem identification concerns diagnosing discrepancies between the existing and preferred competencies of prospective and practicing teachers. Program design involves prescribing instructional programs for those individuals. Testing and achieving solutions is assessed in terms of whether or not the discrepancy was reduced for the particular individual. In effect, this requires the student to achieve a preferred level of competency, for example a score of 90 percent correct on a summative test, before warranting the competency of the individual. If the individual does not attain the desired score, remediation and correctives are prescribed until he or she reaches the predetermined level on the test. The ultimate decision here is whether or not to *certify* the teaching competency of the individual.

Only if we ensure that the instructional programs adopted for teacher training are proven effective in instilling competencies needed for teaching, and only if we ensure that those who are allowed to teach have mastered the competencies taught in these programs, can we be assured of competent classroom teachers.

3

Identifying the "Musts" of Teaching

In many ways, competency-based education reflects the basic pragmatism of American society in its concern for doing, not just knowing how to do, and in continuing to do that which is effective in achieving objectives (Houston & Warner, 1978).

The process we describe for identifying teacher competencies can be used by any group interested in the improvement of teacher education. This includes such organizations as colleges and universities, school districts, professional associations, and task forces representing a wide variety of educational institutions. While the data gathering effort may be directed by one agent, such as a university or a school district, it is imperative that input be obtained from a wide variety of sources. This is necessary to build a broad empirical base and to establish cooperative working relationships for future use of the resulting product, whether it be a curriculum, an evaluation instrument, or a teacher job description. Involvement in the identification of competencies engenders a feeling of ownership in a program, thus increasing the probability of successful installation.

The importance of building a base of support for change is crucial. This support is necessary not only to ensure acceptance of the ultimate program but is also useful in the process of developing the program. Each segment of the educational constituency—practicing teachers, parents, legislators— is a potential contributor to the data base of required and desired competencies. The combination of these perspectives, along with a literature survey and other techniques to be described in this chapter, will maximize the likelihood of developing a realistic, locally applicable program.

PURPOSES FOR IDENTIFYING
TEACHER COMPETENCIES

Before describing the data gathering procedures, a brief discussion of various purposes for identifying teacher competencies is in order. In many instances, a school district or other educational organization will find the competency lists useful for more than one purpose. The lists can be used to provide:

1. A realistic data base for pre- and inservice curriculum development.

2. Criteria for teacher certification.

3. Criteria for hiring teachers.

4. Criteria for supervising and evaluating teachers.

5. Guidelines for self-improvement of skills by prospective and practicing teachers.

6. Public information about the work of the teacher.

The first of these purposes is treated in detail in subsequent chapters. It should be noted here that the fact that our approach begins with the development of a "realistic data base" is more significant than might appear at first glance. The process of validating the data base in the field ensures that the skills identified, when translated into objectives for teacher education, will be clearly relevant to classroom performance.

An empirically derived competency list which clearly delineates the skills teachers are expected to possess will also increase the relevance of inservice training and graduate study to classroom performance. At present the correspondence between need and corrective training is often tenuous and ill-defined. Thus, one often hears the complaint from teachers that inservice programs are a waste of time and that graduate courses do not make them better teachers. In some states, certification renewal and/or salary increments can be obtained by earning a specified number of credits regardless of course content.

The competency lists derived from the data base are also potentially useful for revising certification standards. A major area of concern in recent years has been the lack of correspondence between criteria for certification and the tasks a teacher actually performs. In many states, teacher certification is virtually synonymous with graduation from an accredited program. Thus, in actuality, it is the program which is licensed rather than the individual. The weaknesses of such a system are obvious, particularly since the accreditation status of institutions is routinely renewed and evaluation tends to be based on the institution's appearance on paper rather than on the performance of its product, the teacher. Many commentators have noted that the lack of peer-established criteria for entrance to teaching differentiates it from other professions. We would be surprised and perhaps concerned, for example, if a medical doctor were automatically certified to practice upon graduation from medical school. We expect more direct evidence of individual competency from a doctor. Should we expect less from a teacher?

Determining an individual's readiness to enter the teaching profession is difficult. Some states have required prospective teachers to surpass a cutoff score on the National Teacher Examination (NTE) as a precondition to certification. This particular test, however, has been criticized on various grounds. The argument has been made that the test measures only a candidate's factual knowledge; it does not measure whether the prospective teacher can apply this knowledge by demonstrating appropriate attitudes and performing necessary tasks in the classroom. The relationship between scores on the NTE and teaching effectiveness is largely unsubstantiated. Many consider the test to be culturally biased and claim that it has had the effect, intended or not, of excluding a disproportionate number of minority candidates.

By using the competencies identified in the data base as specifications, a series of instruments can be devised which assess the candidate's skills, knowledge, and attitudes. These specifications, because of procedures used to identify and validate them, are both logically and empirically related to actual teaching requirements. Performance measures and paper-and-pencil tests developed in this way will not be vulnerable to charges of irrelevance and cultural bias. Furthermore, the advance stipulation of characteristics to be measured will enable prospective teachers to know ahead of time what skills they are expected to master.

A systematic method for recording the competencies a prospective teacher has acquired can also assist decision-makers responsible for hiring teachers. The specification of relevant competencies makes it possible to document the knowledge and skills a particular candidate has mastered. In addition to recording course titles, credits, and grades, a transcript could enumerate the proficiencies demonstrated by the candidate. With this information available, prospective employers could more objectively assess the qualifications of candidates for a particular opening.

Another potential use of the competency lists is to provide objective and relevant criteria for teacher supervision and evaluation. Both administrators and teachers alike have cited the need for more specific procedures to guide the supervisory process. In some cases, supervisors have been forced to rely on general "impressions" that yield little in the way of concrete suggestions for improving teacher performance and may be biased by the particular supervisor's preferences. At the other extreme, some attempts to establish objective criteria have resulted in an overemphasis on the easily observed, but sometimes superficial, trappings of classroom procedure to the neglect of more qualitative, instruction-oriented activities.

Teacher evaluation practices are subject to the same weaknesses. However, the legal ramifications of evaluative decisions pose even greater difficulties. Teachers in most states are evaluated on an infrequent basis. Indeed, a common complaint is that a "one-shot" evaluation every few years is hardly an adequate sampling of teaching behavior on which to base the kinds of decisions administrators must make in their role as evaluators. This problem is often compounded by a lack of acceptable evaluation instruments. While the concern about the frequency and duration of evaluation is one which must be addressed by policy-makers, defensible evaluation criteria can be developed from a data base of teacher competencies. Instruments developed according to specifications derived from the data base will increase the applicability of evaluative criteria to classroom performance.

The objectivity of evaluation can be enhanced by the use of an instrument developed in this manner. An additional benefit resides in the specificity with which the characteristics to be assessed can be stipulated. Because each expected competency will be clearly stated deficiencies of a particular teacher can be identified and a plan for corrective action developed. It has often been said that incompetent teachers are rarely dismissed because present instrumentation makes it difficult to document their weaknesses. The subjectivity of many evaluation instruments has contributed to this problem. An instrument based on empirically validated competencies and administered in an objective manner is essential if both the teacher and the evaluator are to be held accountable.

While external evaluation of teaching performance is generally required by state law or district policy, it should be noted that teachers often engage in self-evaluation. Indeed, the argument has been made that self-assessment is more meaningful and more likely to lead to positive change in teaching performance than are the results of *pro forma* visitations which frequently are filed away in a personnel folder, never to be seen again. Checklists can be devised from the data base to assist teachers in identifying possible areas of weakness and determining directions for their own professional growth.

Another important, but often neglected, potential use of such a data base is that of informing the public of the nature and magnitude of the demands on today's teacher. The erosion of confidence in the effectiveness of public schools in recent years has created a chasm between some schools and their constituencies. Certainly the issues mentioned in Chapter 1 have contributed to this situation. It should also be pointed out, however, that many parents and other citizens have inaccurate notions about what the contemporary teacher actually does on the job. They may be misinformed about what the teacher is permitted by law and circumstance to do.

In addition to changes in the teacher's duties due to increasing complexities and expectations, it should be pointed out that much of what the teacher does is not directly observable. The difficulties encountered by trained observers in documenting teaching tasks demonstrate the limitations of this approach. Jackson (1971) comments:

> The ability to plan ahead, to make decisions about the choices of materials and activities, to ponder the consequences of alternative actions, is not usually introduced into the discussion by scholars focusing on the interactional aspects of

TABLE **3.1** Applications of the Data Base.

USE	FORMAT	DECISIONS
Curriculum Development	Competency Statements Objectives	What skills, knowledge, and attitudes must prospective and/or practicing teachers possess? What course and field work will best enable teachers to acquire these competencies?
Certification	Specifications Transcript (with competency documentation)	Is this candidate qualified to enter the teaching profession?
Hiring	Job Description	Does this candidate possess the skills needed to teach in this position? Is this candidate the most qualified applicant for the position?
Supervision	Competency Rating Scale	What are this prospective or practicing teacher's strengths and weaknesses? What skill areas need greater emphasis?
Evaluation	Observation Instrument	Is this teacher performing required duties satisfactorily? Has this teacher made adequate progress in correcting identified weaknesses? Should this teacher be retained?
Teacher Professional Growth	Self-report Rating Scale	Am I performing my teaching duties adequately? In which specific skills could I benefit from additional training?
Public Information	Teacher Job Description	Is the public's perception of the teacher's job realistic and accurate? Are those who make decisions affecting teachers (e.g., legislators, school board members) fully aware of the requirements of teaching?

the teacher's work. A videotaped record of a teacher absorbed in thought after the kids have gone home is hardly the thing on which to try out the latest observational scheme. (p. 25)

The average person, despite ten to sixteen years of school attendance, still has only a limited perception of the range of tasks teachers perform. Thus, beliefs such as "teachers only work part of the day," and "command of subject matter is all that is required to be a good teacher" are common. The dissemination of information about what teachers actually do can help to eradicate misconceptions about the teacher's work.

Detailed competency listings are also potentially useful as a device for informing policy-makers of the teacher's duties. Legislation affecting the teacher's duties, working conditions, salary, and benefits is often passed by statesmen who may have only a very general impression of what the teacher does. Therefore, legislators may not realize the impact particular legislation may have on teachers. Even school board members are often unaware of the range of tasks teachers perform. Enlightening both the public and its representatives about job requirements can help to bring about more realistic policy decisions and to increase productive dialogue about needed improvements in teacher education and in the public schools.

A summary of various uses of the data base is presented in Table 3.1.

DESIGN FOR IDENTIFYING
TEACHER COMPETENCIES

It quickly becomes apparent to anyone attempting to identify teacher competencies that a design is needed to ensure the collection of relevant and comprehensive data. Trying to proceed without a design is like trying to reach a vague destination without a road map: the traveller never really knows whether he has arrived. To avoid this kind of dilemma, it is necessary to know where one is going—the goal, and how to get there—the procedures. It is also important to understand why a particular route was selected— the rationale. The reminder of this chapter and the next will provide the erstwhile nomad with a step-by-step explanation of a design which has been used successfully to identify teacher competencies. As we will emphasize throughout *Improving Teacher Education,* the reader is invited to use this design, to make adaptations as indicated by local circumstances, or to use the Teacher Job Description and Competency List we present.

The goal of the design is to develop an accurate taxonomy of the skills, knowledge, and attitudes teachers need to possess. The procedure for reaching this goal can be divided into five steps:

1. Identifying skills that are required of all teachers

2. Validating these required skills

3. Identifying desired competencies

4. Filtering the competencies

5. Building support for change

Before explaining the "how-to's" of developing the data base, however, clarification of the rationale underlying the design is in order.

The function of Step 1 is to identify those skills which all teachers are required to perform. An analysis of each part of this description will reveal why this is a logical starting point. First, the initial focus is on teaching *skills*. According to *Webster's New Collegiate Dictionary* (1977), a skill is variously defined as "the ability to use one's knowledge effectively and readily in execution or performance; dexterity or coordination in the execution of learned physical tasks; a learned power of doing something competently; a developed aptitude or ability." As this definition indicates, skills reflect underlying knowledge and attitudes. They are learned and, by inference, can be taught. Also, they can be executed with varying degrees of proficiency. All of these characteristics have implications for teacher education efforts. Since skills involve the execution or performance of a task or activity, they can be validated by direct observation. This concreteness is lacking in other attributes, such as knowledge and attitudes.

The first step identifies those teaching skills which are *required*. This emphasis is appropriate because these skills represent the "musts" of teaching which every teacher will find necessary. Obviously, teachers who are unable to demonstrate these required skills at an acceptable level of proficiency will be at a disadvantage in the classroom. Likewise, any teacher education program which does not at the minimum prepare its graduates to execute these skills will be vulnerable to charges of inadequacy.

Another aspect of Step 1 of the design is that the skills required of *all* teachers are identified. Such skills are referred to as "generic" because they compose a core of performance requirements which all teachers, regardless of grade level, subject specialization, or type of learners, must possess. Obviously, appropriate applications of the generic skills will differ depending on the teaching situation. While both a first grade teacher and a secondary vocational teacher must "attend to classroom routine," the particular routines will be quite different—at least we would hope so for the sake of the students! Generic competencies must be supplemented by skills, knowledge, and attitudes specific to the above-mentioned dimensions of specialization (see Chapter 10). Beginning with generic skills, however, allows us to build from a foundation rather than, as has sometimes been the case in teacher education, trying to put the finishing touches on an incomplete structure.

After the initial identification of generic required skills, the design calls for the validation of these skills in the field. This step, one which has generally been neglected in other efforts to develop competency lists, is essential if the resulting product is to be considered job-related with any sense of assurance. What this step does is confirm in the actual classroom setting that the skills specified as required by policy-makers and other experts are indeed required by the exigencies of the teaching situation. This step enables the investigator to separate the wheat from the chaff, thus certifying the accuracy of the data base.

In the final step of the design, the skills, knowledge, and attitudes which are considered *desirable* for the teacher to possess are added to the previously identified required skills. It should be noted that many other competency list projects concentrate solely on this phase of the investigation. This step solicits the opinions of various groups and individuals concerned with the improvement of education as to what competencies the teacher *should* possess. The rationale for identifying desired competencies is that required skills represent only the *status quo* of teacher performance. Of course, teachers should continuously seek to increase their proficiency in executing these essential skills. In addition, however, it is important to augment present requirements with new ideas and techniques. The improvement of teaching preparation and practice necessitates looking not only at what is but also at what should be. By supplementing the "musts" with the "shoulds" of teaching, directions for innovation and improvement of teacher education become evident and can be pursued.

After identifying the "shoulds" and "musts" of teaching it is advisable to filter these derived competencies through the specifications imposed by accreditation agencies. This enables one to reconcile competency statements with established standards that are the basis for accrediting teacher education programs. Finally, the design advocates that a support base be built for change as problems are identified and action is taken to improve teacher education. It is not sufficient to identify problems. An interest in promoting change must be developed among those who can effect change.

We consider the "musts" of teaching in the remainder of this chapter. The steps suggested for establishing the "musts" are listed and discussed in the following section. The "shoulds" of teaching are dealt with in Chapter 4 as well as procedures for filtering the data base through accreditation standards. Building support for change is discussed in Chapter 5.

The following procedures are recommended for developing a list of required teacher competencies. These are discussed in detail in the following sections.

Step 1: Identifying Required Skills

1. Acquire job descriptions to determine what teachers are required to do.

2. Record each competency mentioned.

3. On an index card, record each phrase or statement representing a separate task.

4. Establish major categories of tasks.

5. Subdivide the major categories into topical headings.

6. Obtain teacher evaluation forms.

7. Record skills noted on evaluation forms.

8. Revise topical headings if necessary.

9. Review related literature.

10. Revise skills list and topical headings if necessary.

Step 2: Validating Required Skills

1. Develop checklist of skills.

2. Using the checklist to maintain a record, observe teachers in performance of their jobs.

3. Interview each teacher observed.

    or

1. Develop checklist of skills.

2. Identify master or "exemplary" teachers.

3. Using the checklist, survey master teachers to determine whether they perform the listed skills.

Step 1: Identifying Required Skills

The first step for determining what teachers are actually required to do is to obtain job descriptions. These descriptions define the teacher's duties and thus are the most concrete statement of the teacher's job available. Job descriptions, which are often developed by committees of teachers and principals, generally have the sanction of the school board and thus are official documents. Copies of job descriptions for the position of "teacher" can generally be obtained by writing directly to district superintendents or to personnel directors of large districts. The request should include an explanation of the intended use of the document.

Upon receipt of the job descriptions the investigator should record each competency mentioned. At this point, only those competencies which indicate a skill to be executed should be tabulated. Although job descriptions may also mention knowledge and attitudes considered desirable for the teacher to possess, statements which do not indicate an explicit task or activity should be excluded from this phase of the process. (See Chapter 4.) The excerpt below demonstrates the kinds of tasks which should be extracted from the job descriptions:

> The teacher *meets and instructs assigned classes* . . . *develops and maintains a classroom environment conducive to learning* . . . has a love for children . . . *evaluates student progress* . . . knows stages of child development . . . *supervises assigned extracurricular activities.* . . .

The underlined phrases are tasks the teacher is required to do. These competencies are concrete and assessable, whereas those not underlined do not indicate what the teacher does. Consequently, they do not qualify for inclusion at this point.

As job descriptions are received, each phrase or statement representing a separate task should be recorded on an index card. Because of multiple sources, some statements will duplicate others. When all job descriptions have been reviewed, the cards can be sorted into piles containing variations in wording of the same skill. For example, the statements "the teacher must 'individualize instruction,' 'meet student learning needs,' and 'accommodate varying ability levels' " can all be subsumed under the statement "the teacher must adjust instruction to the level and needs of students."

Once all skills required of the teacher have been collected from the job descriptions, major categories can be established. The purposes of the investigators will, of course, influence the nature of the categories. If the intended use of the data base is to design a teacher education curriculum, for example, useful major categories might be (1) skills directly pertaining to instruction, and (2) skills supportive of instruction. If the purpose of the investigation is to develop an evaluation instrument, major categories might be (1) skills directly observable in the classroom, and (2) skills not amenable to classroom observation.

The next step in the process is to subdivide the major categories into topical categories. Again, this will depend to some extent on the investigator's purpose. It is important, however, to allow categories to emerge from the data rather than to force the statements into pre-established categories. The latter approach compromises and defeats the intent of the inductive method. In the analysis of the data base which led to the model job-related curriculum (see Chapter 9), the following categories were derived from the source job descriptions:

1. Teaching as a Profession

2. Instructional Planning

3. Teaching: Implementing Instructional Plans

4. Interpersonal Skills for Teachers

5. Using Instructional Aids

6. Diagnosing Readiness for Learning

7. Achievement Test Construction and Instructional Evaluation

8. Supportive Services

For the next step in the data collection process, the investigator should obtain a variety of teacher evaluation forms, both those currently in use and "model" or prototypic forms. The rationale for this step is that since evaluation forms are usually rating scales, they are broken down into observable tasks the teacher is required to perform. Thus, they often contain more specific behavioral statements than do corresponding job descriptions.

As with the items obtained from job descriptions, only skills should be recorded. References to knowledge the teacher should have or attitudes the teacher should possess do not meet the test for inclusion in this step. Phrases which describe what the teacher is required to do should be added to the categories already constructed. It is possible that the evaluation forms will yield some competency statements which do not fit into existing categories. If this occurs, categories may be broadened or new categories created to accommodate the additional required behaviors.

At this point, the investigation can be widened to a more formal literature search. Delaying the literature search until after the review of job descriptions and evaluation forms keeps the project on a distinctly job-related course. The rationale for going beyond these two basic sources is that both may be limited by state or regional perceptions and/or legal strictures on the teacher's job. By supplementing these sources with a literature search, the restraints of provincialism can be transcended.

While the extent of the formal literature search will depend upon the investigator's purpose and resources, a few hints may be helpful. Both observational and teacher report literature provide useful information in answer to the question, "What do teachers actually *do* on the job?" The difference between observational and teacher report literature is that in the former a researcher observes and documents teacher performance while in the latter, teachers describe their daily tasks to a researcher or report them in a survey. A general overview of relevant materials can be obtained by consulting the *Education Index.* The year-end indices of publications which specialize in teacher preparation, such as the *Journal of Teacher Education,* can be reviewed directly for pertinent articles. The *Educational Resources Information Center* (ERIC), a computerized network of clearinghouses of educational information, is particularly useful for locating materials such as government publications and reports of federally funded projects. To ensure up-to-date information, leading researchers in the field of teacher behavior and competencies can be contacted directly. This approach circumvents the inevitable lag between research and subsequent publication. (See Appendix A.)

Skills documented in the literature can be added to the preconstructed categories. Again, only tasks actually performed by the teacher are admissible. Although it is unlikely, competencies may emerge which do not fall under existing titles. This may again necessitate broadening or expanding the existing categories.

The foregoing steps will result in a taxonomy of observable skills which the teacher is required to perform. This taxonomy can be labelled a "generic job description" since it encompasses an exhaustive array of tasks all teachers are required to perform, regardless of subject area or grade level. Such a job description has a variety of potential uses, as described at the beginning of this chapter.

Step 2: Validating Required Skills

The investigation thus far has revealed what school systems and research literature say the teacher *must* do. The question may well be asked whether the listed skills are merely superfluous competencies, touted on paper but disregarded in practice. The function of the second stage of the design is to answer this question by subjecting each competency statement to the test of confirmation in the field, the public school classroom. Regardless of its apparent logical relatedness to teaching, any skill which cannot be validated in this way should not be classified as a requirement.

It is crucial that the competencies be validated in the field. Otherwise, the claim that a particular skill is required, generic, and/or job-related is debatable. The most direct and empirically most defensible validation technique is that of observing teachers of the job. To implement this approach, arrangements should be made with school districts to allow researchers to observe teachers in the performance of their everyday classroom duties. Insofar as possible, a stratified sample of classrooms should be selected, including rural and urban settings, a range of grade levels, subject areas, teacher characteristics, and so forth.

Using a checklist of skills compiled in Step 1, the investigators can observe the teachers in the actual performance of their jobs. If the program is conducted under the auspices of a teacher education institution, prospective teachers might be trained as observers, thus providing them with exposure to classroom realities in the process of gathering validation data.

Direct observation is, of course, the purest type of validation. However, it must be noted that certain skills required of the teacher either may not be performed during the necessarily limited observation period or else are qf a nature that they typically take place outside of class time, such as grading papers and attending community functions. To ascertain whether teachers actually perform these functions, the investigator should follow up the observation session with an interview of each teacher.

Another technique which can be used in lieu of or in addition to direct observation is that of sending the list of skills to experts for confirmation. Experts, in this context, should be those who are actually in the field, preferably practicing teachers. In the project which developed the model job-related curriculum, "master" or exemplary teachers were designated by superintendents throughout the state. These teachers were surveyed to determine whether they actually performed each of the listed competencies. Validation percentages for each skill were derived from their responses.

For both observational and expert validations, a solid, conservative confirmation figure was sought. Thus, responses such as "I would like to do this, but can't," or "I sometimes try to do this," were not counted as confirmations. This conservative approach increased the criterion-related validity of the final listing. Any competency statements which did not withstand validation were then removed from the original list.

The result of the Step 1 and 2 procedures is a comprehensive, validated teacher job description. The real world orientation of a job description developed according to these procedures ensures that a teacher education program based on it will be relevant. The Generic Teacher Job Description, Tables 3.2 through 3.9, presents the skills which were identified and subsequently validated as a preliminary phase in the development of the model job-related curriculum.

TABLES **3.2–3.9** The Generic Teacher Job Description.

TABLE **3.2** Teaching as a Profession

THE TEACHER MUST . . .	Job Descriptions	Evaluation Instruments	Observational Literature	Teacher Report Literature	Classroom Observation	Master Teacher Survey (%)
behave ethically.	+	+	–	–	x	98
be punctual and dependable.	+	+	–	–	x	100
display a commitment to student growth.	–	–	–	+	x	98
provide a proper model in appearance.	+	+	–	–	x	98
provide a proper model in verbal usage.	+	+	–	–	x	98
hold classes as scheduled.	+	+	+	+	x	100
enforce rules and regulations.	+	+	+	+	x	98
protect students, materials, and facilities.	+	+	+	+	x	98
report student progress to parents.	–	–	+	+	x	96
be available to students and parents.	+	+	–	+	x	100
supervise extracurricular student activities.	–	–	–	+	x	67
undertake continued professional growth (such as in-service education, visits to other schools).	+	+	–	+	x	100
perform professional services (such as attending faculty meetings).	+	–	+	+	x	98
perform public services (such as participating in school-community activities).	+	+	–	+	x	91

LEGEND (for Tables 3.2 through 3.9)
Columns 1 – 4:
   +   support found for item in respective data source
   –   no support found for item in respective data source
Column 5:
   x   positive confirmation of item by direct classroom
        observation or follow-up interview
Column 6:
        percentage of master teachers confirming item

TABLE 3.3 Instructional Planning

THE TEACHER MUST . . .	Data Sources				Validation	
	Job Descriptions	Evaluation Instruments	Observational Literature	Teacher Report Literature	Classroom Observation	Master Teacher Survey (%)
become familiar with curricular objectives.	−	+	−	−	x	98
fit plans to school goals.	−	+	−	−	x	85
state specific long- and short-term goals clearly.	+	+	+	+	x	83
write lesson plans.	+	+	−	−	x	89
prepare for class.	−	−	−	+	x	100
make thorough plans.	+	+	+	+	x	89
involve students in organization and planning.	−	−	+	−	x	80
individualize plans when necessary.	+	+	+	+	x	91
organize classwork and homework so that they support each other.	−	−	−	+	x	96
use student feedback—verbal and nonverbal—to modify teaching practices.	−	+	−	+	x	96
keep reasonably to a schedule.	−	−	+	−	x	98

TABLE 3.4 Teaching: Implementing Instructional Plans

THE TEACHER MUST . . .	Job Descriptions	Evaluation Instruments	Observational Literature	Teacher Report Literature	Classroom Observation	Master Teacher Survey (%)
use innovative teaching techniques.	–	+	–	–	x	87
make content relevant to current and future needs of students.	–	+	–	–	x	96
use a variety of instructional techniques.	+	+	+	+	x	96
be able to supervise more than one instructional activity simultaneously.	–	–	+	–	x	91
attend efficiently to classroom routine.	–	+	–	–	x	94
organize the classroom.	+	+	–	–	x	94
develop and maintain a classroom atmosphere conducive to effective learning.	+	+	+	–	x	96
focus the attention of the class.	–	–	+	–	x	93
give directions clearly.	–	–	+	+	x	96
explain information in a logical, orderly way.	–	–	–	+	x	98
acknowledge student statements and paraphrases.	–	–	+	–	x	89
provide feedback to the student.	–	–	+	+	x	98
demonstrate flexibility.	–	–	+	–	x	98
encourage student participation.	+	+	+	+	x	100
be open to student input and class discussion.	–	+	+	+	x	100
correct student errors.	–	–	+	–	x	98
motivate learning and personal improvement.	+	+	–	+	x	93
provide for orderly transition between lessons.	–	–	+	+	x	96
close lessons in a logical way.	–	–	+	–	x	83
provide opportunities for students to learn material.	–	–	–	+	x	98
provide remedial help.	–	–	–	+	x	91
use community resources in providing instruction.	–	–	–	+	x	76

TABLE 3.5 Interpersonal Skills for Teachers

THE TEACHER MUST . . .	Data Sources				Validation	
	Job Descriptions	Evaluation Instruments	Observational Literature	Teacher Report Literature	Classroom Observation	Master Teacher Survey (%)
exhibit stable emotional and social adjustment.	+	+	+	−	x	100
tolerate ideas differing from own.	−	−	−	+	x	98
accept criticism constructively.	−	+	−	−	x	96
use nonverbal communication skills.	−	−	+	−	x	96
demonstrate proper listening skills.	−	−	+	−	x	98
show enthusiasm.	+	+	−	+	x	100
display consistency and enforce limits.	+	+	−	−	x	96
display genuine interest in and respect for students.	−	+	+	+	x	100
be considerate and fair with students.	−	+	−	+	x	100
help students develop a desirable set of values.	−	+	−	−	x	100
encourage students to set and keep standards of classroom behavior.	+	+	−	−	x	100
promote positive self-image in students.	−	+	+	−	x	98
show an awareness of the students with whom he is not working at the moment.	−	−	+	+	x	98
be accepting of students, even when not accepting their behavior.	−	−	+	−	x	98
provide feedback to students regarding misbehavior.	−	−	+	−	x	96
use positive reinforcement techniques.	−	+	−	+	x	94
enforce discipline.	+	+	−	+	x	96
maintain effective control—without allowing the control to become more important than the instruction.	+	+	+	−	x	98
maintain open lines of communication with parents and students.	+	+	+	+	x	98
counsel students, parents, and confer with colleagues.	+	−	+	+	x	94
establish a cooperative relationship with other professionals.	+	+	−	+	x	100

TABLE **3.6** Using Instructional Aids

THE TEACHER MUST . . .	Data Sources				Validation	
	Job Descriptions	Evaluation Instruments	Observational Literature	Teacher Report Literature	Classroom Observation	Master Teacher Survey (%)
use instructional materials, such as workbooks, texts, and audiovisual aids.	+	+	+	+	x	96
use chalkboards.	−	−	+	+	x	94
help to evaluate and select texts and other materials.	+	−	−	−	x	85
gather multi-level materials.	−	−	+	−	x	91
secure logistical support.	−	−	+	+	x	76
prepare, organize, and use materials wisely.	+	+	+	+	x	94
supervise teachers' aides and assistants.	+	−	+	−	x	52

TABLE **3.7** Diagnosing Readiness for Learning

THE TEACHER MUST . . .	Data Sources				Validation	
	Job Descriptions	Evaluation Instruments	Observational Literature	Teacher Report Literature	Classroom Observation	Master Teacher Survey (%)
become familiar with students' backgrounds.	+	−	−	−	x	94
utilize diagnostic and standardized instruments and specialized personnel.	+	+	−	−	x	85
make referrals to specialized personnel.	+	+	−	−	x	85
diagnose student characteristics, both cognitive and affective.	+	+	−	−	x	80
form groups for effective teaching.	+	+	+	−	x	78
help students set appropriate goals for themselves.	+	+	−	−	x	80
use evaluation diagnostically.	−	+	−	−	x	80
recognize and treat individual student behaviors.	−	−	+	−	x	96
provide for individual differences.	+	+	+	−	x	91

TABLE 3.8 Achievement Test Construction and Instructional Evaluation

THE TEACHER MUST . . .	Data Sources				Validation	
	Job Descriptions	Evaluation Instruments	Observational Literature	Teacher Report Literature	Classroom Observation	Master Teacher Survey (%)
assess the readiness level of students.	-	-	+	+	x	76
assess or evaluate student progress.	+	+	-	+	x	100
use adequate samples of work in evaluation.	+	-	-	-	x	87
use informal evaluation techniques.	-	+	-	+	x	96
provide follow-up for students.	-	-	+	-	x	87
construct cognitive tests of adequate validity and reliability.	-	+	-	-	x	76
correct papers.	-	-	+	-	x	98
certify student accomplishment.	-	-	-	+	x	83
analyze student progress on a regular basis.	-	x	-	-	x	98
use evaluation to improve teaching.	-	+	+	+	x	91
use evaluation to determine whether objectives have been met.	-	+	+	+	x	91

TABLE 3.9 Supportive Services

THE TEACHER MUST . . .	Data Sources				Validation	
	Job Descriptions	Evaluation Instruments	Observational Literature	Teacher Report Literature	Classroom Observation	Master Teacher Survey (%)
maintain records required by law.	+	+	+	+	x	96
prepare accurate and punctual reports.	+	+	+	+	x	94
supervise students.	-	-	+	+	x	87
collect funds.	-	-	+	+	x	78
attend to "housekeeping."	-	-	+	+	x	87
monitor activities (study hall, playground, etc.).	-	-	+	+	x	59

4

Identifying the "Shoulds" of Teaching

The Generic Teacher Job Description presented in Chapter 3 is intentionally limited to those tasks which are currently performed. Thus, it represents the *status quo* of teacher practice. In order to innovate and improve teacher education, however, it is necessary to go beyond the "musts" and looks at the "shoulds." Those skills which are mandated by policy as well as those which are essential to the teaching act should be the first order of business for any teacher training program. However, if teachers are to be truly competent in the classroom, they must surpass required standards.

We recommend a five-step design for determining these required and desired competencies. Steps 1 and 2 identify and validate the required skills (see Chapter 3). The third step, which we describe in this chapter, identifies the skills, knowledge, and attitudes considered desirable for the teacher to possess. The subsequent steps filter the data base through constraints imposed by accrediting bodies and develop a strategy for building support for change.

In the first two steps, emphasis was placed on the empirical soundness of the data: facts were sought rather than opinions. One reason for making this distinction between the "musts" and the "shoulds" is that many other studies of teacher effectiveness and teacher competencies have failed to separate the two; thus, the resulting products have mingled fact with fantasy about teaching and have confused rather than clarified the issue. The recommended steps for the identification of desired teacher competencies are listed below and discussed in the following sections.

Step 3: Identifying Desired Competencies

1. Determine whose opinions should be solicited.

2. Determine the most appropriate techniques for soliciting the opinions of the selected sources.

3. Obtain the statements of desired competencies from the opinion sources.

4. Add the statements to the categories established in Steps 1 and 2.

5. When (if) the existing categories have been exhausted, analyze the remaining statements for commonalities.

6. Create new categories.

7. Combine the product of Steps 1 and 2 with that of Step 3 to produce the Generic List of Teacher Competencies.

Optional

8. Establish priorities for competencies.

Step 4: Filtering the Data Base

1. Determine the sources of standards for the teacher education program.

2. Determine the interrelationships among the standards to be met.

3. Identify the requirements established by the sources and determine their implications for the curriculum.

Step 3: Identifying Desired Competencies

Steps 1 and 2 concentrated only on skills because of their concrete, verifiable nature. Step 3 focuses on opinions, that is, generally held views and the judgments of experts. Opinions are sought not only about what teachers should do—skills, but also what they should know and believe—knowledge and attitudes.

In the identification of the "musts" of teaching, some items in job descriptions and other sources were excluded either because they were not required skills or because they were not validated. For example, there were two such items in the job description cited in Chapter 3: 1) the teacher must have a love for children, and 2) the teacher knows stages of child development. These items would qualify for inclusion in Step 3 because they are opinions about nonskill attributes that are desired of the teacher.

The first step in compiling additional skills, knowledge, and attitudes desired of the teacher is to determine whose opinions should be solicited. A variety of sources suggest themselves, as indicated in Table 4.1. Again, a real world orientation is preferred to reliance on secondary sources. Each source of opinion has particular strengths and possible limitations. The investi-

TABLE 4.1 Data Sources for Identifying Desired Teacher Competencies.

OPINION SOURCE	CONTRIBUTION	LIMITATIONS	ACCESS TECHNIQUES
Teachers	Actual classroom experience First hand knowledge of realities, needs	Possible status quo orientation May lack overall perspective	Interview Survey
Principals and other supervisory personnel	Responsible for hiring, evaluating teachers Overall perspective of schools	Removed from day to day classroom experiences Possible role conflict	Interview Survey
Parent and community groups	Reflect community concerns and expectations	Groups may not be representative May lack knowledge of teachers' duties	Survey Request official statements
School board members	Responsible for establishing policy Oversee teacher employment	May lack knowledge of teachers' duties	Interview Survey Request policy statements
Legislators	Pass legislation affecting teachers	May lack knowledge of teachers' duties	Interview Survey

State Departments of Education	Administer certification statutes	Possible status quo orientation	Interview Request official guide-lines
Teacher Educators	Experience in teacher training Expertise in various fields	May be compromised by existing program Removed from daily classroom realities	Interview Survey
Teachers Organizations	Represent collective teacher opinion	Groups may not be representative May have political biases	Interview Request official guide-lines
Administrators organizations	Represent collective administrator opinion	Groups may not be representative	Survey Request official guide-lines
Competency list compilers	Represent previous research in field	Questionable generalizability to local situation	Survey Review publications

gators should seek as wide a range of opinion as possible to ensure a compre-hensive and balanced compilation.

The next step is to determine the most appropriate techniques for soliciting the opinions of the various sources selected. In some instances, it may be possible to obtain the views of an entire population, such as all the members of a state legislature. Surveying the entire population of teachers in a state, on the other hand, would be a massive undertaking. To reduce the data gathering to manageable proportions, scientific sampling must be done. To ensure representative samples, however, the technical assistance of a sampling expert may be needed.

Questionnaires can be used to obtain the views of many of the groups. A structured questionnaire may be used; however, such an instrument may be inappropriate for two reasons. First, the items must be carefully developed, which often requires the assistance of a specialist. A poorly constructed survey instrument can exclude choices and/or prejudice the responses. For example, a television preference poll may contain the item, "Circle the channel you are watching: 4, 8, 12." The respondent may be watching Channel 2 or may be watching a cable channel. Hence, he will be unable to respond because of the arbitrary nature of the choices. A more appropriate item would be, "Which channel are you watching?" A second drawback of the structured format is that in order to make sure the instrument is getting the desired information and is appropriate to the intended audience, it will be necessary to pilot test it, a procedure which is often time-consuming and cumbersome.

To avoid these and other difficulties associated with a structured question-naire, we recommend using an open-ended format. The model project simply asked the respondents to list the skills they felt teachers-in-training should acquire, the knowledge they need to master, and the attitudes they should develop. (See Appendix B.) A cover letter explaining the intended use of the information should accompany the survey. Provisions for follow-up should be arranged so that maximum return can be obtained.

Opinions can also be solicited through interviews, if this is feasible. In the model project, for example, a group of seventy teacher educators were individually interviewed in sessions ranging from thirty minutes to several hours. A standard interview format was followed (see Appendix C). In addi-tion, the professors were encouraged to expand upon areas of individual expertise.

A number of organizations concerned with improving teacher education can be contacted by phone or mail. Many of these groups have policy state-ments or guidelines indicating the position of their membership on various aspects of the teacher's training or on-the-job performance. Statements about the skills, knowledge, and attitudes desired of the teacher can be gathered from such guidelines. Competency lists developed by other individuals or projects may also be useful opinion sources. The model project, for example, reviewed thirteen such lists and abstracted from them competency statements not previously identified (see Appendix D).

Because the competency list is opinion-based and derived from multiple sources, some recommended qualities may contradict others, either in appearance or in substance. In some cases this simply reflects the fact that different behaviors are desirable in different situations. For example, "displaying a sense of humor" (Table 4.5) would not be appropriate when the teacher has to "deal with violent students" (Table 4.5). Other discrepancies are legitimate differences of opinion which demonstrate the diversity of expectations held about teachers and their desired behavior. The recommendations that the teacher should "operate a democratic classroom" (Table 4.5), and "believe that the teacher should be 'boss' " (Table 4.4) provide an illustration of such differences of opinion.

Another clarification should be made regarding the listings in the "desired attitudes" subdivisions. According to Fishbein and Ajzen (1975) attitude can be defined as a "learned predisposition to respond in a consistently favorable or unfavorable manner with respect to a given object" (p. 6). In a strict sense, attitudes are distinct from beliefs, preferences, interests, values, and intentions. Recommendations of attitudes teachers should possess, however, are frequently cast in terms of behaviors, values, or other affective traits. In order to preserve the authenticity of the data base, these suggestions were reproduced intact, despite the fact that many of them are manifestations of attitudes rather than attitudes *per se.*

After statements of desired competencies have been obtained from the opinion sources, the next step is to add them to the categories already established in Steps 1 and 2. Each of these categories will now have four subdivisions:

1. Required skills identified and validated as part of the Generic Teacher Job Description

2. Desired skills and activities identified by opinion sources

3. Desired knowledge identified by opinion sources

4. Desired attitudes identified by opinion sources

The recommendations made by sources surveyed in Step 3 represent the skills, knowledge, and attitudes which underlie or are supportive of the required skills. To illustrate, one of the required skills in the category of Instructional Planning (Table 4.3) is "the teacher *must* 'write lesson plans.' " Examples of desired competencies which are supportive of or prerequisite to this skill include:

Desired skills/activities:
The teacher *should*

- set instructional priorities
- develop a sequence of objectives and activities to provide continuity in learning
- use tables of specifications for planning
- use teachers' editions in planning

- write behavioral objectives in measurable terms
- determine and select appropriate instructional strategies and activities
- select activities that will motivate for learning
- plan a variety of activities
- plan follow-up activities to reinforce learning

Desired knowledge:
The teacher *should* have a knowledge of

- the relationship between instructional strategies and learning styles
- behavioral objectives: their formation and use
- sequencing skills
- individual needs
- games and activities for fighting boredom

Desired attitudes:
The teacher *should*

- believe that good planning is prerequisite to good teaching
- believe in flexible planning
- believe that learning should be made relevant
- be sensitive to the needs of different cultural groups

When all items which apply to existing categories have been exhausted, the next step is to analyze the remaining statements for commonalities. This step will create new categories. Typically, these additional categories will be composed of items of knowledge which, according to opinion sources, are desirable background information for the teacher. For example, the category "History of Education" was added because opinion sources recommended that teachers should have a knowledge of "the history of educational practice," "the history of public education," and so forth. Since no required skills were found to be associated with this topic in Steps 1 and 2, a new category was created in Step 3 to accommodate it.

A comprehensive Generic List of Teacher Competencies is the result of combining the product of Steps 1 and 2 with that of Step 3. This list is presented in Tables 4.2 through 4.12. The first eight tables, Tables 4.2 through 4.9, are expanded versions of the categories presented in Chapter 3, incorporating the data derived from opinion sources. Tables 4.10 through 4.12 present the additional categories constructed solely from opinion sources:

Table 4.10   Educational Theories
Educational Research
Human Growth and Development
History of Education

Table 4.11   Philosophy of Education
Human Culture and Values
Communication Skills
Teaching Thinking Skills

Table 4.12   Teaching of Reading
Community Resources and Services for Youth
Personal and Community Health

In the model project, no attempt was made to prioritize the competencies. Establishing the relative importance of the statements is necessary when sufficient resources are not available to pursue the development of all the desired competencies. To provide curriculum developers with comprehensive data, however, the competencies were left unranked. This provides a picture of the widest possible range of opinion regarding teacher performance and allows the curriculum developers to use their professional judgment about what should be taught, how it should be sequenced, and how it should be taught.

For some purposes, it may be necessary to establish priorities for these competencies. One standard procedure is to poll a group of experts as to the relative importance of each item. For example, if a school district wished to use the data base to develop an evaluation instrument, the list of items could be given to a group of principals, supervisors, and teachers. They would be asked to rate each competency on a continuum such as the following:

IMPORTANT   1   2   3   4   5   NOT IMPORTANT

The mean rating for each item can then be computed and the competencies listed in rank order. This will provide the instrument developers with a listing of the competencies in the order of their perceived relative importance.

As mentioned previously, the competencies identified as desired are useful as indicators of the supportive skills, knowledge, and attitudes which undergird required skills. They also suggest needed improvements and directions for innovation in teacher education. The information contained in the Generic List of Teacher Competencies is a starting point for making the "musts" and "shoulds" of teaching a reality.

Step 4: Filtering the Data Base

The identification of required and desired competencies, or the "musts" and the "shoulds" of teaching, results in a comprehensive data base. As pointed out in the discussion of Step 3, the competencies thus derived were not prioritized in order to preserve intact a record of *all* skills, knowledge, and

TABLE 4.2 Teaching as a Profession.

Category: TEACHING AS A PROFESSION

Required Skills/Activities: (from Job Description) THE TEACHER MUST . . .	Desired Skills/Activities: (from opinion sources) THE TEACHER SHOULD . . .	Desired Knowledge: (from opinion sources) THE TEACHER SHOULD HAVE A KNOWLEDGE OF . . .	Desired Attitudes: (from opinion sources) THE TEACHER SHOULD . . .
behave ethically.	Provide a model of integrity.	professional organizations.	possess moral integrity.
be punctual and dependable.	Project a proper, professional	professional ethics.	be intellectually honest.
display a commitment to student	image.	certification and recertifica-	have a love for learning.
growth.	exhibit pride in the profession.	tion requirements.	be humble about his/her knowl-
provide a proper model in appear-	strive for professional improve-	teacher contracts and benefits.	edge.
ance.	ment.	teacher retirement systems.	respect authority.
provide a proper model in verbal	provide a proper model for	professional negotiation prac-	be dedicated to work and stu-
usage.	written and verbal communica-	tices.	dents.
hold classes as scheduled.	tion.	the changing role of profession-	believe that students and
enforce rules and regulations.	take initiative.	al organizations.	teachers are equal before the
protect students, materials, and	go through prescribed channels	policy-making.	law.
facilities.	of command.	fiscal realities in education;	be prudent and uphold confiden-
report student progress to par-	avoid criticism of other	school finance.	tiality.
ents.	teachers or administrators.	the school's function in	respect the rights of others.
interpret school rules for par-	share materials and ideas with	society.	be concerned about all students,
ents.	co-workers.	school organization.	even those with whom he/she
be available to students and	accept extra duties when neces-	goals of the State Department of	has no contact.
parents.	sary.	Education.	take pride in his/her profes-
supervise extracurricular stu-	demonstrate knowledge of sub-	district and school rules and	sion.
dent activities.	ject matter.	regulations.	have a liking for the teaching
distribute materials (such as		the "chain of command."	profession.
Parent-Teacher Organization		community expectations.	see his/her job as important.
notices).		teacher evaluation procedures.	demonstrate a commitment to the
perform professional services		accountability.	purpose of public education.
(such as attending faculty		legal liability of the teacher.	possess a feeling of profession-
meetings).		laws affecting education.	alism.
		student rights and responsibili-	believe that a vocation can be
		ties.	an organizing thread for one's
		due process.	life.

undertake continued professional growth (such as in-service education, visits to other schools). perform public services (such as participating in school-community activities).	liability coverage. federal programs and how to take advantage of them. supplemental educational programs (such as Title I). trends and issues in education.	be open-minded toward continued professional education (such as in-service). believe that asking for help is often the correct response. believe that one can--and must--stand alone for one's beliefs. be receptive to constructive criticism. have determination to be thorough and accomplish all tasks. be demanding of the best in other professionals, teachers and administrators. Identify him/herself with the school and its purposes. support school policies. be willing to work on committees. take interest in school-related activities. be willing to put in more time and effort than the "bare minimum." be willing to undertake public projects. be loyal to the community.

TABLE 4.3 Instructional Planning.

Category: INSTRUCTIONAL PLANNING

Required Skills/Activities: (from Job Description) THE TEACHER MUST . . .	Desired Skills/Activities: (from opinion sources) THE TEACHER SHOULD . . .	Desired Knowledge: (from opinion sources) THE TEACHER SHOULD HAVE A KNOWLEDGE OF . . .	Desired Attitudes: (from opinion sources) THE TEACHER SHOULD . . .
familiarize him/herself with curricular objectives. fit plans to school goals. state specific long- and short-term goals clearly. write lesson plans. prepare him/herself for class. make thorough plans. involve students in organization and planning. individualize plans when necessary. organize classwork and homework so that they support each other. use student feedback--verbal and nonverbal--to modify teaching practices. keep reasonably to a schedule.	conduct a needs assessment to determine the needs of community, school, and student in order to design a curriculum to meet these needs. plan curricula. engage in cooperative planning with other teachers. set instructional priorities. schedule days so that all subjects get maximum coverage. base goals and objectives on a theory of learning and on a theory of development. develop a sequence of objectives and activities to provide continuity in learning. use Tables of Specifications for planning. use teachers' editions in planning. write behavioral objectives in measurable terms. determine and select appropriate instructional strategies and activities. write study guides for chapters in texts.	levels of thinking. the relationship between instructional strategies and learning styles. curriculum structure: the requirements and development. behavioral objectives: their formation and use. sequencing skills. programmed instruction. design of learning modules. individual needs. games and activities for fighting boredom. activities of interest to students. the Defined Minimum Program (state curriculum). mainstreaming. the affective domain. alternative methods for designing a curriculum. career opportunities. community resources for teachers.	believe that good planning is prerequisite to good teaching. believe in flexible planning. believe that some subjects are more important than others. believe that learning should be made relevant. have a realistic view of goals. believe that students should have input into some decisions affecting them. be sensitive to the needs of students of different cultural backgrounds. desire to individualize instruction.

formulate units on materials not
in texts.

synthesize methodology and content.

select activities that will motivate for learning.

plan a variety of activities.

select appropriate reinforcement
activities.

plan follow-up activities to
reinforce learning.

modify plans on the basis of
results.

be flexible in changing lesson
plans.

design activities for different
"levels of learning" (Bloom,
Gagné, Taba).

use mastery learning models.

prepare alternative plans.

adapt plans to match varying
student backgrounds.

adapt plans for different learning styles.

plan for the non-college-bound
student.

plan for extremely heterogeneous
classes.

plan for the non-reader.

prepare plans for substitutes.

prepare students for career
choices.

plan for metric conversion.

TABLE 4.4 Implementing Instructional Plans.

Category: TEACHING: IMPLEMENTING INSTRUCTIONAL PLANS

Required Skills/Activities: (from Job Description) THE TEACHER MUST . . .	Desired Skills/Activities: (from opinion sources) THE TEACHER SHOULD . . .	Desired Knowledge: (from opinion sources) THE TEACHER SHOULD HAVE A KNOWLEDGE OF . . .	Desired Attitudes: (from opinion sources) THE TEACHER SHOULD . . .
use innovative teaching techniques. make content relevant to current and future needs of students. adjust instruction to the level and needs of students. use a variety of instructional techniques, such as tutoring, lecturing, group discussion, learning centers, field trips, interest centers, experience charts, question-and-answer format, drill, audio-visual materials, small group sessions, team teaching, probing questions, inquiry method, resource centers, programmed materials, instructional games, peer teaching and role playing. be able to use more than one instructional activity simultaneously. attend efficiently to classroom routine. develop and maintain a classroom environment conducive to effective learning. organize the classroom.	guide students to speak proper English without criticism. manage time and schedules. implement lessons. be actively involved in classroom activities. give directions. use questions at a variety of cognitive levels. write cursive letters correctly. be able to adapt teaching to sudden changes. stress creativity among students. use creative activities. teach for concept attainment. make students responsible for their own learning. use dramatic skills to create and hold interest in lessons. resist premature closure. provide experiences in which the learners apply what they have learned. maintain a balance between freedom and security in the classroom. involve parents in remediation. teach library skills.	instructional techniques and materials. a variety of teaching methods. the strengths and weaknesses of methodologies. study skills. inquiry teaching models. the decision-making process. the open classroom concept. values clarification. team teaching. departmentalized teaching. methods and detection of cheating.	believe that teaching is an important job. believe that one can make a difference in another's life. believe that one learns as one teaches. believe that one's values are reflected by one's approach to teaching. believe that students should be exposed to the consequences of their decisions. be willing to admit when he/she doesn't know something. be willing to apologize when he/she has made a mistake. be resilient in the face of frustration. accept the inevitability of some failure. be willing to act as a model for students in terms of proper dress, speech, and habits. believe that the teacher should be "boss." be friendly to other teachers. be willing to undertake clerical duties as a "necessary evil."

focus the attention of the
class.
give directions clearly.
explain things in a logical,
orderly way.
acknowledge student statements
and paraphrases.
demonstrate proper listening
skills and provide feedback to
the student.
demonstrate flexibility.
encourage student participation.
be open to student input and
class discussion.
correct student errors.
use motivational techniques and
encouragement strategies, such
as praise, encouragement, incentives for learning, competition, the students' own
interests and the best possible environmental conditions
(seating, lighting, etc.).
contact students when they are
off-task.
provide for orderly transition
between lessons.
group students for effective
instruction.
close lessons in a logical way.
work with individual students.
provide opportunities for students to learn materials.
provide remedial help.
use community resources in providing instruction.

teach language and communication
skills.
work with learning disabled or
exceptional children.
work with emotionally disturbed
children.
provide multi-cultural activities in the classroom.
use programmed materials.

have a love for students.
be trusting toward students.
always expect the best from
students.
have faith that every student
can succeed in life.
believe in the importance of
students.
believe that students are inherently good.
desire to help students learn.
have confidence in students.
believe in the ability of all
to learn.
empathize with the slow or
deprived student.
In general, the teacher is
expected to be:
pleasant, cheerful, unselfish,
impartial, humanistic, truth-
ful, emotionally mature,
sensitive, straightforward,
affectionate, unflappable
(poised), self-confident, independent, persistent, independent, courageous, optimis-
tic, loyal, generous with
time, tactful, dedicated,
conscientious, responsible,
dependable, cooperative,
wholesome, forgiving, caring,
compassionate, sympathetic,
genuine, tolerant, sincere,
understanding, patient,
polite, patriotic, possessed
of goodwill, possessed of
endurance, possessed of ini-
tiative.

TABLE **4.5** Interpersonal Skills.

Category: *INTERPERSONAL SKILLS*

Required Skills/Activities: (from Job Description) THE TEACHER MUST . . .	*Desired* Skills/Activities: (from opinion sources) THE TEACHER SHOULD . . .	*Desired* Knowledge: (from opinion sources) THE TEACHER SHOULD HAVE A KNOWLEDGE OF . . .	*Desired* Attitudes: (from opinion sources) THE TEACHER SHOULD . . .
exhibit stable emotional and social adjustment (poise, patience, and tact). be tolerant of ideas differing from his/her own. accept criticism constructively. utilize nonverbal communication skills. show enthusiasm. display consistency (enforce limits). display genuine interest in and respect for students. be considerate and fair with students. help students develop a desirable set of values. encourage students to set and keep standards of classroom behavior. promote positive self-image in students. show an awareness of the students with whom he/she is not working at the present moment. be accepting of students, even when not accepting their behavior.	provide leadership. assert him/herself with peers and superiors without alienating them. display emotions in a healthy, constructive manner. display a sense of humor. use voice modulation for controlling purposes. accept emotional expression from students. deal with underlying reasons behind students' actions. make students feel wanted. operate a democratic classroom. confront and deal with interpersonal problems and conflicts directly and constructively. listen carefully to and facilitate responses from others. use questioning without causing defensiveness. use class discussion as a disciplinary technique. ignore some irrelevant student behaviors.	interpersonal needs (Glasser and Adler). human relationship concepts. principles of communication. dynamics of peer relationships. group processes (group dynamics). motivational techniques. guidance techniques. values clarification. sociology. public relations. multicultural values. drug abuse prevention. the philosophy of encouragement. the Kohlberg model. the principles of a variety of psychologically-based classroom management models such as Adlerian, transactional analysis, behavior modification, and reality therapy. referral services which may be needed to supplement classroom management skills.	believe in the "golden rule." be committed to the betterment of mankind. believe in firmness and consistency. be willing to touch all students. be willing to share with others. be accepting. have self-control. be supportive. be encouraging. have a sense of humor. be tolerant of ambiguity. be socially sensitive. be considerate of others. be highly motivated toward helping people. be willing to share ideas with others. be non-discriminatory. be receptive to all students. feel positively toward the handicapped. be assertive in controlling the class and in working with others. mind his/her own business and not gossip.

provide feedback to students regarding misbehavior.
use positive reinforcement techniques.
enforce discipline (possibly by using a classroom management model).
maintain effective control-- without allowing the control to become more important than the instruction.
help students to improve manners.
teach students to work together.
work with small groups.
maintain open lines of communication (rapport) with parents and students.
counsel (consult with) students, parents and colleagues.
establish a cooperative relationship with other professionals.

get help before a class gets "out of hand."
maintain a correct classroom noise level.
promote socialization among students.
be able to deal with large groups.
teach students how to work together.
use sign language and other communication skills for the handicapped.
deal with violent students.
deal with controversial topics in class.
deal effectively with emergency situations.
conduct student elections.
help students from a variety of cultures function in a pluralistic society.
provide all students with some opportunity for success.
be skillful with parent-teacher conferences.
make effective home visits.
be able to function in an organization.
use proper interview techniques.
conduct him/herself properly at job interviews.
deal with "problem" (hostile) parents.

be willing to compromise with students and other professionals.
respect the talents of other teachers.
be non-competitive toward other faculty members.
respect the values and the rights of parents.
believe that parents are important influences on learning.

TABLE 4.6 Using Instructional Aids.

Category: USING INSTRUCTIONAL AIDS

Required Skills/Activities: (from Job Description) THE TEACHER MUST . . .	Desired Skills/Activities: (from opinion sources) THE TEACHER SHOULD . . .	Desired Knowledge: (from opinion sources) THE TEACHER SHOULD HAVE A KNOWLEDGE OF . . .	Desired Attitudes: (from opinion sources) THE TEACHER SHOULD . . .
use instructional aids, such as workbooks, texts and audio-visual aids. use chalkboards effectively. help to evaluate and select texts and materials. secure logistical support. construct materials. prepare, organize and use materials wisely. supervise teachers' aides and assistants.	organize materials and facilities for optimal learning. use a variety of media techniques. use materials compatible with learner abilities. use games in teaching. assemble and operate lab apparatus. make charts. prepare bulletin boards. use simple office machines. use logistical support (such as ditto) machines. use computers. use the library. use community resources. make the classroom as attractive as possible.	resources available for the classroom. criteria for selecting resources. instructional materials. audiovisual aids and equipment. uses of the library. information sources in education. materials and aids used in the subject area.	believe that the teacher is only part of the delivery system. be willing to use materials and aids.

TABLE 4.7 Diagnosing Readiness for Learning.

Category: DIAGNOSING READINESS FOR LEARNING

Required Skills/Activities: (from Job Description) THE TEACHER MUST . . .	Desired Skills/Activities: (from opinion sources) THE TEACHER SHOULD . . .	Desired Knowledge: (from opinion sources) THE TEACHER SHOULD HAVE A KNOWLEDGE OF . . .	Desired Attitudes: (from opinion sources) THE TEACHER SHOULD . . .
observe student behavior. familiarize him/herself with students' backgrounds. utilize diagnostic and standardized instruments and specialized personnel. diagnose student characteristics, both cognitive and affective. form groups for effective teaching. help students set appropriate goals for themselves. use evaluation diagnostically. recognize and treat individual student behaviors. provide for individual differences.	describe the physical, intellectual, social, and emotional characteristics of the student. gather data from cumulative records. develop observational skills. write anecdotal reports of observed behavior. select appropriate diagnostic tools. gather information systematically. use data for making appropriate educational decisions. be systematic in comparing observed behavior with norms. make valid inferences from data collected regarding student conceptual and language development. diagnose student difficulties. diagnose different learning styles. write descriptive analyses and summaries of diagnoses. interpret diagnoses into appropriate objectives. recognize characteristics of learning handicaps. identify students in need of special services. be able to conduct referral.	the methods of studying students. tests and measurement. diagnosis and testing. student characteristics. individual differences. behavior norms. learning styles. learning disabilities. sociological differences. cultural and ethnic differences. rural lifestyles. exceptionality and its needs. emotionally disturbed students and their problems. visual motor difficulties and remediation techniques. "mainstreaming." child abuse and its prevention.	be realistic. be objective in viewing facts. be tentative in reaching conclusions before all the facts are in. be sensitive to cultural differences. be willing to recognize individual differences. accept students today as different than they once were.

TABLE 4.8 Achievement Test Construction and Instructional Evaluation.

Category: ACHIEVEMENT TEST CONSTRUCTION AND INSTRUCTIONAL EVALUATION

Required Skills/Activities: (from Job Description) THE TEACHER MUST . . .	*Desired* Skills/Activities: (from opinion sources) THE TEACHER SHOULD . . .	*Desired* Knowledge: (from opinion sources) THE TEACHER SHOULD HAVE A KNOWLEDGE OF . . .	*Desired* Attitudes: (from opinion sources) THE TEACHER SHOULD . . .
assess the readiness level of students. assess or evaluate student progress. use adequate samples of work in evaluation. use informal evaluation techniques. provide follow-up for students. administer and/or grade standardized tests. construct cognitive tests of adequate validity and reliability. correct papers. certify student accomplishment. analyze student progress on a regular basis. use evaluation to improve his/ her teaching and to determine whether objectives have been met.	design or interpret an evaluation policy. plan and implement evaluation strategies. design or select activities to measure the attainment of objectives and criteria. develop tests and feedback mechanisms. grade creatively. record and report grades. construct effective evaluation instruments. report evaluation conclusions. employ formative and summative evaluation. assist the learner in interpreting evaluation results. interpret data from a variety of evaluation strategies.	the philosophy and theory of measurement. the measurement process and its limitations. test construction. objectivity. validity. reliability. interpretation of test results. grading systems.	believe that the teacher is responsible for learning, no matter what the entry conditions of the student. believe in evaluation.

TABLE 4.9 Supportive Services.

Category: SUPPORTIVE SERVICES

Required Skills/Activities: (from Job Description) THE TEACHER MUST . . .	Desired Skills/Activities: (from opinion sources) THE TEACHER SHOULD . . .	Desired Knowledge: (from opinion sources) THE TEACHER SHOULD HAVE A KNOWLEDGE OF . . .	Desired Attitudes: (from opinion sources) THE TEACHER SHOULD . . .
maintain records required by law (such as South Carolina attendance register). prepare accurate and punctual reports. supervise. collect funds. attend to "housekeeping." monitor (study hall, playground, etc.).	work on committees. use a management system to control record keeping. have a systematic approach to records. have filing skills. monitor student health. be able to administer first aid. lock and unlock doors and windows. operate combination locks. assist during fire drills. conduct field trips.		

TABLE **4.10** Additional Categories.

ADDITIONAL CATEGORIES

EDUCATIONAL THEORIES THE TEACHER SHOULD HAVE A KNOWLEDGE OF . . .	EDUCATIONAL RESEARCH THE TEACHER SHOULD HAVE A KNOWLEDGE OF . . .	HUMAN GROWTH AND DEVELOPMENT THE TEACHER SHOULD HAVE A KNOWLEDGE OF . . .	HISTORY OF EDUCATION THE TEACHER SHOULD HAVE A KNOWLEDGE OF . . .
the application of theory to educational practice. developmental theory. explanations of human behavior. theories of intelligence. Bruner's models of representation. Guilford's model. theories of transfer of knowledge and information. psycholinguistic theory. learning theory. models of how and why people learn. taxonomic organizations proposed for learning and instruction. curriculum theory. theories of instruction. Gagné's theory of instruction. theories of counseling. personality theory. attitude theory. self-concept theory. Maslow's theory. Kohlberg's model. motivation models. theories of classroom management. decision-making models for students.	research methods. objective observation and reporting. quantitative methods. elementary statistics. research techniques. educational research and innovation. data management skills. empirical research into learning. research in teaching. classroom data-analysis techniques.	physical development. mental development. social development. physical norms for different age groups. characteristics of different age groups. mental norms for different age groups. social norms for different age groups. life-stage psychology.	the history of educational practices. the history of education. the history of public education. modern trends in education.

TABLE 4.11 Additional Categories.

ADDITIONAL CATEGORIES

PHILOSOPHY OF EDUCATION THE TEACHER SHOULD HAVE A KNOWLEDGE OF . . .	HUMAN CULTURE AND VALUES THE TEACHER SHOULD HAVE A KNOWLEDGE OF . . .	COMMUNICATION SKILLS THE TEACHER SHOULD HAVE A KNOWLEDGE OF . . .	TEACHING THINKING SKILLS THE TEACHER SHOULD . . .
ethical and moral notions about the way we live. alternative philosophical views of man. epistemology. the philosophy of learning. the philosophy of education.	anthropology. cultural anthropology. cultural rituals and arts. multicultural values. the culture of students. dealing with students of various backgrounds. sociology. value systems. moral development (Kohlberg's model). human values. family and community relations.	principles of communication. language acquisition. the structure of the English language. speaking. spelling. grammar. composition. pronunciation and vocabulary. language skills. written and oral communication skills. penmanship skills. phonetic spelling.	teach thinking skills. teach how to follow directions. teach students how to learn. teach methods of promoting language and conceptual development. teach the scientific method. stimulate inquiry techniques. teach analytical skills. teach problem-solving techniques. teach logic. teach decision-making. present decision-making models to students. help students extract meaning. teach study skills. teach reading comprehension. tie together all activities to develop cognitive skills.

TABLE **4.12** Additional Categories.

ADDITIONAL CATEGORIES

TEACHING OF READING	COMMUNITY RESOURCES AND SERVICES FOR YOUTH	PERSONAL AND COMMUNITY HEALTH
THE TEACHER SHOULD HAVE A KNOWLEDGE OF . . .	THE TEACHER SHOULD . . .	THE TEACHER SHOULD HAVE — A KNOWLEDGE OF . . .
how to build reading into the planning of all instruction. techniques in reading (overview). how reading skills progress through the grades. the development of reading materials at various grade levels. reading readiness. structural analysis in reading. the use of basic techniques of reading instruction such as the whole word, phonics, alphabet-spelling techniques, or the SQ3R method. the use of diagnostic-prescriptive techniques, including the reading-phonics approach. syntax and decoding. the teaching of comprehension skills. the teaching of reading skills (sequencing of skills). library science. children's literature.	be familiar with community functions. understand how various professionals function. understand the various agencies that provide community resources for students. use community services and personnel. know when and how to make referrals. know about community resources for teachers.	personal hygiene. first aid. the detection of childhood diseases. the detection of drug and alcohol use. health education.

attitudes deemed important by constituent groups. As depicted in Table 3.1, this data base can be used for a variety of purposes. The next phase of the process is to filter the data base through various standards and specifications.

The purpose of this step is to reconcile the competency statements with established standards for teacher education programs. This step corresponds logically to the process described in Chapter 3 for identifying the skills required of all teachers. Instead of the individual teacher, however, we now focus on the teacher education program as the unit of analysis. Just as the *required* skills represented what the "real world" demanded from the teacher, we now look at what the "real world" demands from the teacher education program. What specifications *must* the teacher education program meet in order to stay in (or go into) business?

The first step in answering this question is to determine the sources of standards for the teacher education program. Local, state, regional, and national institutions and agencies are involved in establishing such standards. These standards represent the opinions of experts regarding essential characteristics of a teacher education program, and by inference, of the teacher trainee. It should be pointed out that we are not discussing teacher certification or program accreditation *per se*. The procedures for attaining accreditation are complex and beyond the scope of this book. Rather, we are using the specifications developed by these groups as guidelines for making decisions about the makeup of various components of the curriculum. It should also be noted that, at this stage of the process, we are focusing on requirements for preservice teacher education. Certainly, implications for inservice teacher training are also present in the data base. These will be discussed in Chapter 6.

Before reviewing various sources of standards, the interrelationships among them should be clarified (Student NEA, 1975):

> The state agencies and the regional and national accrediting associations all attest to being independent. Their activities, however, are significantly interwoven through joint evaluation efforts, through accrediting prerequisites, through reciprocity agreements, through the professional associations and learned societies, and through the actions of the federal government. NCATE, for example, relies on regional accreditation as evidence of the overall general quality of an institution. NASDTEC, in turn, relies on NCATE accreditation as the standard of quality for an institution. (pp. 16–17)

As this passage points out, there is significant overlap among the various sources of standards. The state, regional, and institutional standards, however, vary from place to place. Thus, they are not as generalizable as those established by NASDTEC and NCATE. For this reason, we will briefly discuss the kinds of parameters established by state and other agencies. Our fundamental emphasis, however, will be on filtering the data base to meet the NASDTEC and NCATE standards which are applicable to all teacher education programs.

Both NASDTEC and NCATE are national accrediting agencies. NASDTEC, the National Association of State Directors of Teacher Education and Certification, is made up of the officials responsible for teacher certification in each state. This body issues the Standards for State Approval of Teacher Education which represents the "consensus" of these state directors of teacher education as to what constitutes an acceptable program of teacher education. NCATE, the National Council for Accreditation of Teacher Education, is composed of five organizations: the National Education Association (NEA), the American Association of Colleges for Teacher Education (AACTE), the Council of Chief State School Officers (CCSSO), the National School Boards Association (NSBA), and the National Association of State Directors of Teacher Education and Certification (NASDTEC). (Student NEA, 1975, p. 12.) NCATE evaluates and accredits separately each teacher education program offered by an institution (for example, elementary education, secondary English, and so forth).

Six regional accrediting agencies are concerned with the standards met by the institution as a whole. The requirements of the appropriate regional accrediting agency must be met as a prerequisite to NASDTEC or NCATE approval of teacher education programs. The articulation of the teacher education program with other programs, along with organizational, financial, and physical support, are reviewed periodically through self-studies and on-site visitations. For the purpose of teacher education curriculum development, regional accreditation standards can be consulted to be sure there is no conflict in course hour balance among components.

Each state also establishes standards for teacher education programs. While it is true that "each state has the exclusive legal responsibility for the quality and content of professional preparation/certification programs within its boundaries," (Standards, 1976, p. 109) such responsibility is in effect usually delegated to national accrediting associations. Forty-five states use the approved-program approach (Hodenfield & Stinnett, 1961, p. 5). That is, "certification is based upon the recommendations of the institution that the student has completed a program of teacher education according to the minimum standards of the state" (Student NEA, 1975, p. 4). These minimum standards of the state are generally based on NASDTEC Standards for State Approval of Teacher Education.

The common types of requirements established by states in addition to those used by NASDTEC and NCATE are as follows (Study Commission, 1976):

The present general or qualitative requirements for licensure as a teacher (elementary or secondary) appear to be simple enough. They are threefold: (1) typically, the states have citizenship, health, age, and moral requirements; (2) all states minimally require a bachelor's degree for certification; (3) about eight states also require specialized courses in state history, state and federal governments, agriculture and conservation (however, several of these states allow substitution of acceptable scores on proficiency exams in lieu of courses). (pp. 102–103)

Credit hour requirements in general education and in professional courses are also stipulated by many states (Study Commission, 1976, p. 103).

Standards developed by various professional associations and learned societies are applicable to particular areas of specialization. These recommendations, such as those established by the National Council of Teachers of English for the preparation of English teachers, will be discussed in Chapter 10, Teaching Specializations. The specifications of many of these groups are incorporated in the NASDTEC standards. Rather than specify particular requirements as NASDTEC does, NCATE's Standard 2.4 refers program developers to these associations directly (*Standards,* 1977):

> In planning and developing curricula for teacher education, the institution studies the recommendations of national professional associations and learned societies and adopts a rationale for the selection and implementation of pertinent sets of recommendations for each teacher education program. (p. 7)

Each teacher training institution may have particular specifications which must be taken into account in designing curricula. Many institutions, for example, have general education requirements which are common to all students regardless of major. Credit hour requirements for graduation must also be taken into account. These constraints must be considered in developing various courses of study. The program development specialist, however, should not be dissuaded from trying to change institutional requirements if they seriously compromise the quality of the program. For example, the professional core courses derived from the required competencies may require a reduction in the number of general education units to accommodate them. If certain general education courses are institutional requirements but have little else to recommend them, the program development specialist should use whatever channels are available to alleviate the constraint.

The types of standards and specifications discussed above must be considered by curriculum developers. In practice, however, these standards are generally relatively easy to accommodate; many, in fact, are derived from the NASDTEC/NCATE specifications. Because the NASDTEC/NCATE standards must be met by all teacher education programs seeking accreditation, and because they are the basis for interstate reciprocity, we will consider them to be *generic* standards.

As implied by the term "filter," the purpose of this step is to identify the requirements established by NASDTEC and NCATE to determine their implications for the curriculum. At this point, we are looking at the broad, general outline of the components and courses rather than at specific competencies. Also, our primary focus is on the professional core courses, those to be derived from the data base. NASDTEC and NCATE standards apply to the other components as well and will be discussed in the appropriate chapters. Because the data base concentrated on generic competencies, these skills will predominate in the professional core.

It should be kept in mind that NASDTEC and NCATE standards represent minimum requirements. Thus, exceeding them is a step toward improving teacher education. Also, the standards do not specify particular courses or credits. Rather, they mention topics, understandings, and skills to be addressed in the teacher education programs. Thus, considerable latitude is provided for program design.

The method of determining teacher competencies described in this and the previous chapter resulted in *required* and *desired* competencies. As stressed in Chapter 3, the categories identified as "musts" are essential; thus, unless they *conflict* with NASDTEC or NCATE standards, they will be retained and will constitute required courses in the professional core. Those categories which emerged as "shoulds," however, are desired but do not have the empirical support of the required categories. Naturally, as many categories as possible should be incorporated in the curriculum. However, time limitations and the need to provide adequate balance with other components must also be taken into account. Therefore, the NASDTEC and NCATE standards can be examined for criteria which will help program developers decide on the viability of each "unvalidated" category. Possible decisions to be made about these remaining categories include:

1. Develop as a professional core course.

2. Combine with related competencies in a validated category.

3. Combine with related competencies in another unvalidated category (that is, collapse two or more categories to form one course).

4. Incorporate category in the general education component.

5. Cover competencies in category in a number of other courses or field experiences.

6. Omit the category.

These particular categories are presented as examples. Users of this process would, of course, apply the filtering process to their particular data base. (See Table 4.13.)

In addition to the desired competencies identified in the preceding section of this chapter, there are other attitudes and skills needed by the effective educational practitioner if she wishes to move beyond the *status quo* of teaching practice. A review of the accepted laws of learning and the more recent research in education will augment the list of "musts" and "shoulds" that was developed during the needs assessment stage of the job-related curriculum.

A related research review is an essential aspect of any problem-solving effort. The development of a curriculum for the improvement of teacher education is not an exception to this principle. At this point we will look at some of the characteristics of the competent teacher which have been supported by research in education. In identifying the skills, knowledge, and attitudes considered desirable for a teacher to possess, it is recommended that the literature in the discipline be reviewed. The tempo of education today, both in terms of practice and research, has resulted in unprecedented change. This is reflected in the rapid growth of what we know about effective teaching. Consequently, a teacher competencies list needs to be periodically updated. The design of a new program or the modification of an existing program should have the benefit of the most current knowledge in the field of education. A few of the more relevant findings in educational research and their significance for teacher competencies are discussed in the following paragraphs.

Recent research indicates that the teacher should have a knowledge of the relationship between time on task and student achievement. This knowledge must be a factor in the design of the classroom learning experience both in terms of long-range instructional activities as well as the daily lesson plan. Bloom (1976) advocates a mastery learning model which in essence recommends that the student "master" the material covered in the course before proceding to more advanced material. The conceptual model developed by Carroll in 1963 posits that given the appropriate conditions for learning, virtually all students can master what they are taught. Two of the five factors which influence learning can be manipulated by the teacher. These are the opportunity to learn and quality of instruction. Unfortunately, the opportunity to learn is frequently ended before the student has, in fact, learned. While the subject of mastery learning is examined in some detail in Chapters 19 and 20, Designing Programs for Professional Growth, and Testing and Achieving Solutions in Professional Growth, it should be noted at this point that time on task is one aspect of mastery learning. The effective teacher will not only allot sufficient time on task to assure mastery for different types of students but also for different areas of study or competencies. Anderson (1975) found a positive relationship between time on task and achievement. That is, in fact, a principle that most teachers readily recognize from their own classroom experiences. However, it was also found that there exists a positive relationship between selected student and environmental characteristics and percent of time on task. As a result, the following model was developed to illustrate the relationship between time on task and achievement.

CEB   cognitive entry behaviors
AEC   affective entry characteristics
QI   learning environment including the quality of instruction
TOT   time on task
ACH   achievement

The implications of research on time on task for instructional design are obvious. The effective teacher must be cognizant of this aspect of education.

TABLE 4.13 Filtering the Data Base.

CATEGORY*	NASDTEC
HISTORY OF EDUCATION	Professional Education 3.3 II D "understanding of the foundations underlying the development and organization of education in the United States"
PHILOSOPHY OF EDUCATION	Professional Education 3.3 II D "understanding of the foundations underlying the development and organization of education in the United States"
HUMAN CULTURE AND VALUES	Professional Education 3.3 III "knowledge, humaneness, and sensitivity which reduce conflict and tension and promote constructive interactions among people of differing economic, social, racial, ethnic, and religious grounds or sex, language, cultural, and other differences." General Education 3.2III I "America's pluralistic culture and heritage"
COMMUNICATIONS SKILLS	General Education 3.2III A "language skills as essential tools in communication."
EDUCATIONAL THEORIES	

TABLE **4.13** (continued)

NCATE	DECISION
2.3.2 Humanistic and Behavioral Studies "problems concerning the nature and aims of education, the curriculum, the organization and administration of a school system, and the process of teaching and learning can be studied with respect to their historical development and the related philosophical issues."	These standards are met satisfactorily by other required courses. Retain in professional core as "recommended" course.
2.3.2 Humanistic and Behavioral Studies "problems concerning the nature and aims of education, the curriculum, the organization and administration of a school system, and .the process of teaching and learning can be studied with respect to their historical development and the related philosophical issues."	Combine with category Theories of Education to form new required professional core course.
2.1.1 Multicultural Education "The institution gives evidence of planning for multicultural education in its teacher education curricula including both the general and professional studies components."	Incorporate multicultural objectives wherever applicable in each professional core course,
	Covered in general education requirements, Implications for selection criteria for entrance to program.
2.3.3 "The professional studies component of each curriculum includes the systematic study of teaching and learning theory with appropriate laboratory and clinical experience."	Combine with category Philosophies of Education to form new required professional core course.

TABLE **4.13** (continued)

CATEGORY*	NASDTEC
EDUCATIONAL RESEARCH	Professional Education 3.3. II B "knowledge of research, methods, materials, and media appropriate to teaching. Emphasis shall be in the student's field(s) of specialization." 3.3.II F "Willingness to analyze teaching as a means of continually improving teaching skills."
HUMAN GROWTH AND DEVELOPMENT	Professional Education 3.3. II A "knowledge of the processes of human growth, development, and learning, and the practical application of this knowledge to teaching."
TEACHING THINKING SKILLS	Professional Education 3.3. II A "knowledge of the processes of human growth, development, and learning, and the practical application of this knowledge to teaching."
TEACHING OF READING	Professional Education 3.3. II G "ability to teach reading skills appropriate to the level of the student and to the subject content."
COMMUNITY RESOURCES AND SERVICE FOR YOUTH	
PERSONAL AND COMMUNITY HEALTH	General Education 3.2 III H "the principles of physical and mental health as they apply to the individual and the community."

TABLE **4.13** (continued)

NCATE	DECISION
	Develop as new professional core course. Emphasis on research and innovation in various subject areas.
	Develop as new professional core course.
	Develop as new professional core course.
	Develop as new professional core course.
	Incorporate major concepts in professional core courses such as Teaching as a Profession.
	Covered by general education course.

*See Tables 4.2 - 4.12 for detailed listings of competencies in each category.

The model developed by Anderson introduces three other factors which contribute to achievement. These are cognitive entry behaviors, affective entry characteristics, and quality of instruction. In developing a data base of needed and desired teacher competencies, we have largely placed emphasis on those teacher behaviors which essentially contribute to the third factor—quality of instruction. However, it is the interaction among these three factors that determines whether instruction will be effective. In essence, this research indicates that the effective teacher can successfully match the student to the instructional method (treatment) that works best for that student. It is common for both school personnel and educational psychologists to explain school failure as a result of social class, personality problems, or some other (usually considered unchangeable) trait of the student, rather than to focus attention on the individual student's present status, his pattern of strengths and weaknesses, his methods of approaching problems, and his interests, in order to prescribe an educational experience which is likely to succeed for him where others have failed (Brophy & Good, 1974, p. 197). It is no longer a matter of identifying the most effective instructional mode, but rather of identifying the most effective mode for the particular student. The research area of interaction includes not only aptitude-treatment interactions but also student-teacher interactions and other forms of classroom dynamics. While much of the work in this area has been inconclusive, there are still some findings which should influence classroom management practices.

Specifically, the educational practitioner should be familiar with recent research pertaining to teacher directiveness and warmth. Directiveness is used as an umbrella heading to cover such characteristics as indirectness, acceptance of students' ideas, use of directions, teacher talk and questions versus student talk and questions, and classroom management and control. Generally, it has been found that teacher indirectness (use of questioning, acceptance of students' feelings and ideas, and so on) has a curvilinear relationship with student achievement, but the *optimum* degree of teacher directiveness is lower for concrete learning tasks than for more abstract learning tasks (Soar, 1968). Much of the research indicates that greater acceptance of students' ideas is associated with higher levels of students' initiations of interactions with the teacher (Emmer, 1967), with higher student creativity and with lower student anxiety (Soar, 1966).

Warmth in terms of teacher behavior in the classroom covers such areas as praise, criticism, acceptance, or indifference. While much of the research on the effect of teacher warmth on student achievement is inconclusive, there are some consistent patterns in the findings. Higher teacher praise is usually associated with more positive student attitudes toward school and learning and more positive student self-concepts (Spaulding, 1963). Greater teacher criticism has been found consistently to be associated with lower student achievement motivation and higher fear of failure (Campbell, 1970), lower student self-concept (Spaulding, 1963), and higher student dependency (Soar, 1966).

A factor commonly found to correlate with praise and criticism is teacher expectations. Early in the school year, using the school records and observations of students during classroom interaction, all teachers form differential expectations regarding the achievement potential and personal characteristics of their students. Teachers begin to treat students differently in accordance with their differential expectations of them. Students tend to respond differentially to the teacher because the teacher treats them differentially. In general, each student will respond to the teacher with behavior that complements and reinforces the teacher's particular expectations of him. If continued indefinitely, this process will cause the students toward whom teachers hold inappropriate and rigid expectations gradually to approximate those expectations more and more. Where expectations are inappropriate and rigidly high, the student will probably have more than his share of interactions with the teacher during the year. He will receive a great deal of encouragement and cajoling from the teacher. If the teacher's expectations are inappropriately and rigidly low, the student will have fewer interactions with the teacher. He will get less praise and more criticism than his classmates receive in comparable situations. Perhaps most importantly, he will be subjected to half-hearted teaching in which the teacher attempts to teach him less material and is less persistent in teaching him the material that she does cover.

While it would be unreasonable to expect a teacher to form no premature expectations of her students, the competent teacher is aware of her expectations of her students both in terms of their origin and their limitations. She is also aware of the potential impact of her expectations upon student performance over the period during which she has regular contact with the student and structures her interactions with the student accordingly.

In summary, the competent teacher should be knowledgeable of the most recent developments in the field of education as well as the earlier accepted laws of learning. In addition, she should be capable of critically examining educational research, noting consistent patterns in findings and their relevance to her instructional responsibilities.

The professional core course Understanding Educational Research and Innovation is designed to develop in the prospective teacher an understanding and appreciation of the role of research in educational practice.

New developments in educational research must be considered by any program to improve teacher education. Both required and desired teacher competency lists should be updated periodically through examination of current educational research.

5

Building Support
for Change

At this point in the problem-solving process, the emphasis shifts to the pragmatic task of building support for the planned change. Steps 1, 2, and 3 bring into perspective the discrepancies between present and preferred teacher competencies. The fourth step is filtering the data base through the various standards and specifications of accrediting agencies and/or professional licensing bodies. Anticipating potential sources and strategies of resistance should also be a part of the initial problem identification stage. The interpersonal, organizational, and environmental dynamics which impact on the planned change should be assessed with similar intensity as that devoted to the identification of teacher education problems *per se*. The fifth step of the initial discrepancy analysis focuses on the gap between the present degree of support for and involvement in the change effort and the optimal level of commitment.

Many ambitious and seemingly well-designed programs have aborted because of a failure to secure meaningful commitment to change. Innovators frequently assume that their programs will succeed simply on the basis of merit. The obvious superiority of a new program over an established program seems virtually to guarantee that an innovation will be welcomed by all and installed with fanfare. Unfortunately, this rarely proves to be the case. Anticipated physical and financial constraints are often much easier to overcome than is unanticipated resistance to change from within the organization or from the external environment. In many case histories of change efforts, no sooner is consensus reached on the shape and direction of the innovation than countertactics begin to develop.

While it may appear defeatist to anticipate resistance, it is much more realistic to be aware of potential barriers to change and to develop contingencies to deal with them than to adopt a Pollyanna posture. Glidewell (1961), suggests that the innovator "must become a 'probability expert.' He should be a gambling man, who eschews 'sure bets' and 'long shots' simultaneously. But, like a professional gambler, he should seek the bets that give him a probability edge over chance" (p. 657). If one is seriously committed to seeing the innovation adopted, its success should not be left to chance.

Because of the wide variations in organizational contexts, Step 5 is less prescriptive than the previous steps. A discussion of possible sources of resistance is provided along with suggestions for gaining support for the proposed change, both from within the organization and from without.

SECURING INTERNAL COMMITMENT TO CHANGE

Development of innovative teacher education programs necessarily takes place within the context of at least one organization. This may be a university, a school district, a teachers' organization, or even a combination of these. Securing commitment to change within the organization is a fundamental goal. In the event that such commitment cannot be secured voluntarily, however, the innovator should develop mechanisms to move the organization toward acceptance of the change effort. This may be accomplished through manipulating organizational incentives or through manipulating the external environment to bring pro-change pressure to bear. In some situations, both of these approaches can be used simultaneously.

The concept of readiness is a useful way of looking at an organization's potential for effectively implementing a new program. Using this approach, the evaluator formulates indicators of readiness and assesses the organization's status with respect to these indicators. Two dimensions of readiness should be examined: the organization's capacity to change and its motivation to change. Parenthetically, it should be noted that these dimensions roughly correspond to categories of readiness characteristics which are considered in determining a learner's readiness for a particular instructional sequence. As in the case of the individual learner, organizational readiness must be assessed in terms of the characteristics which must be present or attainable in order for the preferred state to be achieved. That is, a given organization may be ready for one kind of change but not ready for a different kind of change. The trick is to determine whether or not the organization is or can be made ready to adopt the particular program desired.

A number of factors influence an organization's capacity to change. Organizational norms and roles, for example, should be examined. Schmuck et al. (1977) offer the following definitions: "By norm, we mean the shared expectation of a certain range of behavior within a specific context will either be approved or disapproved; by roles, we mean the set of norms that specifies how a person in a particular position should behave" (p. 17). If, for example, a proposed new preservice teacher education program will require a substantial increase in the amount of time university faculty spend in the public school classroom, existing expectations of what it means to be a professor may be violated. (Although it might be an unfair generalization, it should be noted that many professors have spent long, arduous years in doctoral programs expressly to *escape* the public school classroom.) In many cases, individuals within an organization may agree that a particular change is desirable and even necessary. However, if it conflicts dramatically with existing roles and norms, resistance can be anticipated.

The history of an organization's response to previous change efforts can also be reviewed. Some organizations have developed a pattern of enthusiastic support for a proposed change during its developmental stages. Rhetoric and dedication abound. Yet the program is allowed to fizzle before implementation. Other organizations seem to accept only incremental change. Still other organizations seem impervious to change; like Melville's Bartleby the Scrivener they "prefer not to."

Capacity to change is also dependent on the resources available to bring about the change. This includes physical resources, such as facilities, materials, and equipment. It also includes financial or in-kind support. Human resources must also be assessed. What talents, energies, and skills can be marshalled to bring about the proposed change? Too often, change efforts are stymied by constraints which could be resolved. Constraints such as limitations in physical, financial, and human resources should be seen as detour signs rather than as roadblocks. Alternative providers of needed resources, perhaps in the external environment, should be sought.

Motivation to change is the second major dimension of an organization's readiness level. One might envision a kind of organizational Maslow's hierarchy to determine which needs of the organization will be met by the change. Motivation can also be seen as the organization's willingness to change and its perserverance in adopting the particular program proposed.

An organization's motivation to change, however, is frequently dependent on the advantages its members see in changing and the disadvantages they see in maintaining the present state. If these two are reversed, that is, if there seem to be stronger inducements to retain the *status quo* than to adopt the change, resistance can be expected.

Increasing the organization's willingness to change can be accomplished by stacking the cards in favor of the proposed change. In practice this means revising the reward structure of the organization so that the incentives for changing are greater than those for not changing. The inducements must be meaningful, which is generally translated in terms of dollars and cents, but can also include other incentives such as those which improve an individual's status, security, or schedule.

Existing reward structures are often rigid and frequently have legal as well as historical bases. Therefore, planners should attempt to modify those structures which have flexibility, such as those governing the number of teaching hours required for full-time status. Some universities have devised methods of including hours spent in field supervision in the formula for determining salary and rank. A number of school districts have rewarded inservice participants with release time, salary credit, and so forth. Titles can also be useful incentives, as long as they represent real distinctions and are not just token recognition. In some cases, it may be possible to influence legislation to revise the existing reward structure so as to favor the change effort. This approach will be considered in more detail later in this chapter.

It should also be recognized that, although the preceding discussion speaks of the organization as an entity, it is, after all, made up of individuals. Within the organizational context, individual members each exhibit different levels of readiness for change. Often, it is the individual anxieties and resistance tactics which impede the adoption of a new program. The organization's structures are frequently used by individuals as a barrier against change.

RECOGNIZING RESISTANCE TO CHANGE

Despite strategies to increase motivation and to present the intended change as nonthreatening, a variety of "reasons" for resistance can be expected. Such resistance will most likely arise from those directly affected by each particular phase of the project and will be proportional to the degree of adjustment or personal change the organizational change is perceived to require. For example, during the developmental phases of a preservice project, teacher educators will be most likely of the involved groups to demonstrate resistance because the proposed changes will have a dramatic impact on their current equilibrium and incentive system. On the other hand, once the program has been installed, cooperating teachers and other public school personnel may resist the new and more challenging supervisory demands the program places on them. This might be termed the "when the shoe is on the other foot" phenomenon.

Resistance takes many forms. The following statements, for example, represent some of the common individual reactions which may be expected during the developmental phase, that phase when the shoe is on the foot of the teacher educator:

1. "Why reinvent the wheel? We already have similar courses. Why change for the sake of change?"

The first argument is perhaps the most commonly encountered in efforts to implement change. Satisfaction with the *status quo* is generally at the root of this position. Individuals who espouse the "why reinvent the wheel" argument are generally willing to accept only minor incremental changes in the existing program. Their view is that a tune-up of the current courses will suffice rather than a major overhaul or a new model. This is often a defensive position, akin to saying, "Don't rock the boat when I'm teetering on the edge." Resistance of this type is a norm in many organizations.

2. "Look at what happened over at Mediocre University. They tried a
    new program and ended up in worse shape than when they started."

A second common response is that of the alarmist. Innovation is seen
as not just a threat to the *status quo* but as an invitation to chaos. Any
new approach is *a priori* doomed to failure. Proponents of this view are
fond of "look at what happened's" and "what if's." Reactionaries can surface
at any stage of the project life and can overtly or covertly sabotage the
potential effectiveness of the program.

3. "Let's not be hasty. With ten more years of development, we can
    work all the kinks out of the program before field-testing it. We don't
    want to buy a pig in a poke!"

A third response, which may seem reasonable but is in fact often defeating
to the change, is that of the delayer. According to this view, an innovation
must be preplanned, planned, replanned, then go back to the drawing board.
This is not to say that revisions and modifications are unnecessary; indeed,
they are essential. There is, however, a limit to the productivity of paper
planning prior to implementation. Havelock (1973) relates this stance to a
kind of passive resistance: "The most primitive, but sometimes the most
effective, strategy for coping with change is to do *nothing:* 'It will pass';
'These things come and go in cycles'; 'If we ignore them, they will go away' "
(p. 6). At some point, one must see if the program will fly. The delayer
would postpone the flight indefinitely.

4. "It's a great idea, but it just won't work. Why aim for utopia when
    the program we have is barely functional."

The next tactic, that of the so-called realist or pragmatist, is to acknowledge
the potential value of the innovation but to dismiss it as not feasible. Innovations are called "pipe dreams," "pie in the sky notions," and "utopian
schemes" by these resisters. Their comments about the project will take
the form of exaggerated projections of the cost, effort, and resources required.

5. "Change is definitely needed. But not this kind of change. What we
    need is Psychologically-Based Incidental Learning Encounter (Psy-
    BILE)."

Another source of resistance comes from those who have "a better idea."
Regardless of the validity of the proposed change, these individuals are certain
there is a superior approach but are generally unable to articulate or develop
it. This kind of resistance can usually be distinguished from legitimate differences of opinion as the most effective approach.

6. "Let's not kid ourselves. We can't do much to improve teacher per-
    formance anyway. All we can do is give them some background infor-
    mation and then it's up to them."

A fatalistic posture will be assumed by others. This view sees even the
current program as almost useless. The assumption that education can have
little impact on one's behavior and skills would seem to be incongruous in
an institution whose *raison d'etre* is to educate. This view is, unfortunately,

all too prevalent. Sometimes this position is disguised in the form of "research tells us nothing about" whatever innovation is proposed.

7. "Who does he think he is, anyway—coming up with all these crackpot schemes? I know just as much about teacher education as he does. He probably beats his wife, too."

Following close on the heels of the fatalist is the *ad hominem* artist. Unable or unwilling to find fault with the proposed innovation, this individual finds fault, and usually plenty of it, with the innovator. In extreme cases, nothing is beyond the criticism of this resister. The credentials, salary, personal life, and motives of the project staff are scrutinized. The vulnerability of the innovator to such an approach is well documented, as Guskin (1979) notes: "Traditionally, the innovator is not popular; he is an annoying minority, a gadfly, an irritant who nevertheless likes to think he will stimulate a pearl within the establishment's hard shell" (p. 10). Awareness of the possibility of personal invective and a thick skin are essential attributes of the innovator.

8. "How will this affect me? I don't have time to teach new courses, serve on the Faculty Senate, publish, and consult, too!"

The last kind of resistance listed above is probably the hidden agenda of a number of the other postures of resistance: "What's in it (or not in it) for me?" The individual may recognize the need for change and the appropriateness of the recommended innovation on one level. On another level, closer to the heart and wallet, he may see the innovation as a threat to his job, his role, and/or his security. Any major innovation will have an impact on the reward structure, organizational dynamics, and other characteristics of an organization. It will also change and probably increase demands on the individual's time and energy. It may also, as in the case of team teaching or increased classroom participation by college faculty, increase vulnerability to criticism and threaten one's role image. Concerns such as these are often the bottom line of other kinds of resistance.

OVERCOMING RESISTANCE TO CHANGE—THE INTERNAL APPROACH

An awareness of the causes and symptoms of resistance is important. The innovator, however, must also devise ways of eliminating or neutralizing such resistance. Techniques for overcoming resistance by manipulating the organization's external environment will be dealt with later in this chapter. Another approach is to deal with resistance through manipulation of the organization itself.

In discussing the organization, it should be noted that a distinction can generally be made between the formal and informal power structure. The former is basically the visible structure of decision-makers and those responsible for executing decisions and policy. In some situations this power may be more apparent than real. The informal power structure is composed of influential members of the organization who through their prestige, the power of their personalities, or some less evident form of power exercise varying degrees of control over the decision-making process. In some organizations this distinction is artificial. However, in anticipating support or opposition it may be wise to assume the existence of a "dual" power structure and plan accordingly.

The first step in the process of overcoming resistence to change is to identify the possible sources of resistance at each phase of the project's life. This is relatively easy to accomplish. One can ask "which individuals and/ or groups will have to make actual changes in their activities during this phase?" While it is possible that resistance may occur from other quarters during a given phase, it is unlikely. This approach also allows the decision-maker to identify phases which are potentially more hazardous than others. For example, the initial phase of program installation can be predicted to be quite difficult, because of the many task groups which will be required to change current practices simultaneously.

Once the potentially resisting groups have been identified, provisions should be developed for alleviating authentic concerns and neutralizing disruptive tactics. Perhaps the most potent, yet seemingly simple, way of accomplishing both ends is that of adequate mechanisms for information flow and feedback. A certain degree of legitimacy will accrue the proposed innovation through continuous exposure to it. That is, as individuals in the organization receive more information (in the form of memoranda, progress reports, shared related information, and so forth) about a program, it seems less alien to them. Certainly, these documents should contain meaningful information. But the tendency to "keep the program under wraps" to avoid criticism is more likely to backfire. The cry of "we weren't informed" is a serious blow to the integrity of a program, one which should not be allowed to develop.

"We weren't involved," a similar lamentation, can also be avoided by providing highly visible feedback mechanisms. Involvement is not synonymous with support. It is, however, essential for credibility. In some situations, it may be possible to co-opt the most vocal resisters by giving them an active role in program development. This, however, is clearly a risky venture and one which should be attempted only if a clear picture of the organizational dynamics is available. If provisions for feedback are conspicuously available, and feedback received is documented and handled responsibly, the complaint "we weren't involved" can only reflect on the complainer.

Potentially resisting individuals and groups should be treated with caution regardless of the degree of involvement in the program they exhibit. Innovators are frequently startled by a kind of "sleeping dog" reaction. The organization may give tacit or active approval to development efforts: individuals seem to be involved in program planning. However, as the program nears the installation phase, the sleeping dog awakens and snaps ferociously. The mistaken assumption of the innovator in this situation is that involvement is synonymous with support. Indeed, if a proposed change is threatening to the status or security of individuals, they may become involved just to keep tabs on the program. Sometimes this is not a consciously chosen course of action but rather a self-protective response. The assumption that those who show interest are supportive can lead to an overassessment of the degree of program advocacy present in the organization. Such an assumption, while attractive, is naive and ignores the very real threat any change poses to many individuals and also underestimates the potential difficulties inherent in change efforts. Thomas and Bennis (1972) point this out.

> If meaningful change is to occur it may, in fact, mean that a particular group or faction will "lose" and another "win" in terms of their respective images of what the future should be. Strategies which speak of . . . consensus, and attempt to deny the reality of "win-lose" conditions with respect to change, are somewhat limited in this sense. (p. 17)

The support of key decision-makers within the organization should also be sought. Individuals such as university presidents, deans, and department heads, or district superintendents and principals, have formal and informal powers which often can make or break a program. Their support can make the transition to the new program much easier. Gaining and publicizing the support of key decision-makers within the organization is also a useful way of neutralizing resistance. Many will resist change until it becomes clear that people in positions of authority within the organization are for it— then they vie for head drummer on the bandwagon.

Whatever sanctions can be devised to give the change effort an aura of inevitability will also help to overcome resistance. Sanctions include changes in the reward system which favor the innovation as well as actions such as creating a new office to administer the new program.

OVERCOMING RESISTANCE TO CHANGE— THE EXTERNAL APPROACH

As the preceding discussion indicates, it is unwise to assume that the merits of the proposed change alone will guarantee its installation. Provisions must be made for soliciting internal support. They must also be made for bringing influence (or more bluntly, pressure) to bear on the organization to lead (or more bluntly, force) it to accept the innovation. The degree and potency of resistance will vary depending on the organizational climate and other factors. There are, however, various approaches which can be used to minimize the momentum of resistance.

While predicting and developing strategies to cope with internal organizational dynamics is important, it is also essential to understand and manipulate the external environment as well. As the above discussion indicates, relying on the good faith of the group to accept change is often dysfunctional. Many individuals will pay lip service to the need for improvement while others will serve as active or passive blockers in the change process. If the organization feels pressure from outside to change, however, the innovation stands a much greater likelihood of being implemented.

In higher education, particularly in teacher education, the mystique of "responsiveness to the clientele" is currently in vogue. Colleges of education claim to be responsive to public schools and to other constituencies. This responsiveness is often more rhetorical than real, however. One reason for this is that the external environment—the public schools, educational policy-makers, and the community—has traditionally not perceived itself as capable of making demands on the dispensers of higher education. The idea that "they know what is best" or "they'll do what they want regardless of our needs" has prevailed. The era of accountability combined with the increasingly obvious discrepancies between teacher preparation and classroom performance requirements has reduced this deference to the ivory tower. Similarly, classroom teachers are becoming more directly involved in determining their own inservice training needs. No longer are central office or administrative planners able to convince teachers "this is what you need."

To bring about needed change, then, one important step is to identify those individuals and groups outside the institution who can influence it. By mobilizing support from outside the organization, the innovator can influence the organization to accept and accommodate the change. Bringing the external demand for change into visibility is often a much more productive enterprise than is tilting at windmills within the organization.

Not only is outside support important as a way of influencing the organization's acceptance of the new program, it is also critical as a way of verifying that the new program, once implemented, will be accepted by the environment. Up-front support commits the groups in the environment—such as school district personnel, state department officials, and so on—to smoothing the way for the innovation and its product—teacher educators trained in the new program. Without some assurance from the environment that the product will be welcomed, the change effort is an academic exercise.

The organization can be visualized as surrounded by its environment. The two are separated by a semipermeable membrane which permits information and influence to flow between the two. Figure 5.1 depicts this relationship between a college of education involved in preservice training and its environment.

Individuals and groups in the external environment who can influence the organization generally fall into one of three categories:

1. Educational policy-makers (legislators, regulatory agencies, school boards, and so forth)

2. Potential employers and colleagues of the teacher in training (public school administrators and teachers)

3. Groups concerned with educational improvement (community groups, educational interest groups, and so forth)

FIGURE **5.1** **Organization: Readiness to change.**

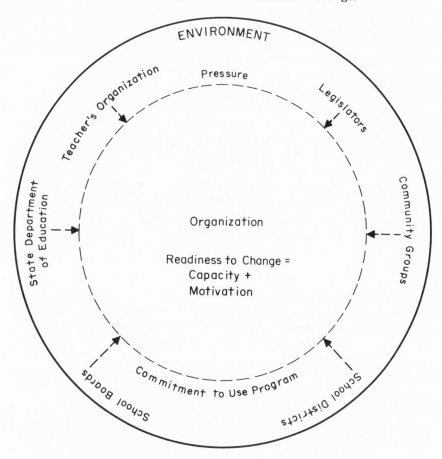

Involving key representatives of these groups in the change effort from its inception is critical. Meaningful support for the innovation is much more likely to develop if a feeling of ownership is promoted both in the organization itself and in the environment.

The innovator should determine the widest possible realistic target population and geographical area for soliciting external pressure. In some instances it is feasible to get statewide involvement in the change effort. In other locales, a county or district-wide base of support is appropriate. In general, the area from which support is drawn should include the service area of the organization as well as the surrounding areas likely to be impacted by the change. Support for the conceptual base of the innovation can also be solicited from experts in the field. An innovative inservice program, for instance, will be perceived as more respectable if nationally recognized staff development leaders herald it than if its only apparent support comes from those who developed it.

The groups thus identified should not be considered solely as agents of persuasion. While they can influence the organization, to perceive them solely in this way can create a feeling of alienation. More importantly, it overlooks their most significant role, that of contributing ideas. Chapters 2 and 3 presented procedures for obtaining the input of these groups in identifying the "musts" and "shoulds" of teaching. We are not suggesting that outside groups be "conned" into approving the program just to put pressure on the organization. Rather, we are saying that the external environment often has a clear and unbiased view of the changes needed to bring teacher education programs up to standards required by the "real world."

Involvement in the program can also be fostered by soliciting written endorsements. Key officials in the groups listed above can be contacted and asked to write letters to indicate their perceptions of the need for change in teacher education and the potential benefit of the innovative approach in bringing about this change. In the model project, for example, legislators, superintendents, and association leaders from around the state wrote letters indicating their support for the concept as well as their endorsement of the work that had already been done to move toward the needed change.

Commitment to the change effort can also take other forms, such as the donation of time, resources, and/or influence. A demonstration that there is a demand for the eventual product of the program—the teacher trained in a job-related curriculum—will do more to dissolve resistance than even the most polished persuasion. Making the support broad based, concrete, and visible will transform the need for the program from a vague prospect to an accessible goal.

In general, the approach advocated in this chapter is that the innovator should be proactive. Resistance to change at the individual and organizational levels can and must be anticipated and handled effectively if the change effort is to have a reasonable probability of success.

6

Identifying Inservice
Training Problems

Although a wide variety of professional growth opportunities are available
to the practicing teacher, the term "inservice" calls to mind the typical brief
workshop dealing with a particular topic or skill. Generally, such sessions
are sponsored by the local school or district and teachers are expected or
required to attend. Little information is available regarding teachers' perceptions of this limited but ubiquitous kind of session. Most studies which have
attempted to assess these factors have concentrated on intensive programs
with quite specific objectives and target populations, such as a summer training
program in the inquiry approach for elementary social studies teachers or
a short course in behavior modification techniques. Despite a lack of focused
research about inservice and its impact on teaching effectiveness, publications
are replete with criticisms, calling inservice sessions a "waste of time," an
"insult to teachers' intelligence," and so forth. Inservice has been called the
"neglected stepchild of teacher training" (Edelfelt, 1974). Lortie (1975), in
his investigations of the sociological aspect of teaching, comments:

> "In-service training" in American public schools rarely rises above a superficial
> level; it seems to consist primarily of short "workshops", faculty meetings, and
> infrequent visits to the classroom by central office supervisors. School systems
> generally have not assumed responsibility for systematically improving staff per-
> formance through serious training programs. (p. 234)

One explanation for the relatively low priority inservice training has conventionally held is that such training was perceived by school boards and

administrators not so much as an investment but as a formality. Typically, only 2 percent of a district's operating budget is allocated to inservice teacher training (Wilen & Kindsvatter, 1978, p. 394). Rarely, until recent years, were graduate courses taken by individual teachers toward certification renewal coordinated in any systematic way with staff development needs.

A number of factors have recently converged, however, to make strong inservice programs not just a nicety but a necessity. Edelfelt (1974) cites the decline in student population as contributing to this necessity in at least two ways. First, as elementary and secondary enrollments decline, faculty retrenchment is required. The ramifications of this phenomenon for preservice training have been discussed previously. A slowdown in teacher turnover is another effect, one which has implications for inservice efforts. As the job market tightens, teacher mobility decreases.

The investment of substantial resources in inservice training is much more defensible when the likelihood of return can be demonstrated. Thus, efforts toward staff development make much more sense when staff continuity can be assured. Staff continuity increases both the justification for and the need for improved inservice programs. A stable core of teachers can sometimes become a stagnant core of teachers. As Calhoun (1975) points out, "Even if summarily replacing unsatisfactory incumbents with eager candidates were feasible, the simple truth is that the surplus of teacher applicants is a quantitative, not a qualitative, oversupply" (p. 311).

Another force contributing to the recent concern for improving inservice programs is the increased emphasis on accountability in all school-related undertakings. As teachers are held more accountable for the performance of their students, so are teachers holding principals, district officials, and outside consultants accountable for delivering relevant inservice. The question of who should control inservice has also become a political issue. Teachers' organizations in particular have made demands for parity in the control of inservice.

The most common frustrations engendered by inservice programs are a result of inadequate planning, follow-through, and follow-up. The one-shot workshop on individualizing instruction or classroom management is unfortunately as common as it is futile. In addition, constraints often prevent the inservice participant from carrying out the procedures suggested during an inservice program. Harris, Bessent, & McIntyre (1969) provide some illustrations of this phenomenon:

Teachers may be exhorted to try new methods, but unless all system modifications which are necessary to put the methods into practice are made, the new practice is impeded. For example, grading, marking, and reporting practices may underlie resistance to modifications in instruction, and unless organizational rules are relaxed, teachers may be reluctant to change. In other instances teachers may find it impossible to accept the organizational consequences of adopting the new instructional practice. This may be illustrated by the demand of team teaching on planning time and the differentiation of teaching responsibilities. Similarly, staffing patterns may not be flexible enough to permit the introduction of the program that is being promoted by an in-service effort. (p. 41)

The Catch-22 dilemmas created by such discrepancies lead to a general discounting of the efficacy of any inservice effort. The "ho-hum, another inservice day" syndrome can frequently be traced to the feeling that regardless of the overt objectives of the inservice program, there is an unstated understanding that change is neither desired nor expected. It is little wonder, then, that teachers find inservice to be a "waste of time."

Harris, Bessent, and McIntyre (1969) cite three major reasons for the inadequacies of many inservice programs:

1. Inappropriate activities—selected without regard for the purposes to be achieved.

2. Inappropriate purposes—a failure to relate in-service programs to genuine needs of staff participants.

3. Lack of skills among program planners and directors who design and conduct instructional improvement efforts. (p. 15)

A look at these deficiencies reveals that they are strikingly similar to the weaknesses commonly found in preservice programs. Inservice as well as preservice is afflicted by a lack of precision about content and delivery. The identification of training needs of practicing teachers is critical to the development and execution of appropriate inservice programs. Yet, as implied by the third factor cited above, those responsible for inservice programs have not been effective in identifying and responding to these needs.

A review of the literature will reveal that the three concerns cited above are echoed by other observers. A procedure for identifying inservice needs and planning appropriate activities to meet these needs is a necessary prerequisite to the development of any effective program. One of the central aims of *Improving Teacher Education* is to offer such procedures in a simple, usable form. The identification of the problem or the assessment of inservice needs must be accomplished first. Only then can programs be designed to meet these needs.

Accommodating both the professional development needs of individual teachers and the staff development needs of various organizational units has been one of the most persistent dilemmas in designing effective inservice programs. Frequently, administrators and others responsible for inservice planning focus on the latter need without making an adequate assessment of the former. This often occurs not because planners deliberately wish to ignore the training needs of individual teachers but because this has traditionally been considered the "business" of the particular teacher. Inservice planners have had little access to information about the specific strengths and weaknesses exhibited by particular teachers. Moreover, questions of confidentiality and privacy of information arise when planners attempt to use evaluation results or other information in personnel files as a data base for identifying inservice priorities.

Thus, information about a particular teacher's competencies or lack thereof is frequently available only via the teacher's lounge grapevine, inferences made on the basis of indirect factors as the number of office referrals, and so on. The objectivity and accuracy of these sources is, obviously, suspect. The insular nature of most conventional teaching situations makes the conventional classroom teacher a hostage of his or her own inadequacies. To admit shortcomings seems tantamount to risking professional and personal rejection.

Traditional teacher evaluation practices also contribute to some extent to this situation. The periodic visitation by a principal or other administrator is seen not as a vehicle for improving instruction but as a trial by fire. Too frequently, the mere presence of this evaluator produces grossly atypical "performances" on the part of both teacher and students. Even the conference generally held as an evaluation follow-up too frequently focuses on superficialities. Because the administrator conducting the evaluation is in a position to "hire and fire," a teacher is understandably reluctant to admit deficiencies or to discuss areas of needed improvement.

Teachers' inservice training needs can be identified in a number or ways. A combination of these approaches is desirable since the inservice planners can obtain a more accurate and comprehensive picture of training needs via a multipronged assessment than they can using any single inventory. Above all, it must be emphasized that some kind of formal needs assessment with feedback to the participants is essential if there is to be any degree of confidence on the part of teachers that the inservice program is designed to meet their needs. The assessment techniques used, furthermore, *must* be appropriate to the organizational unit to be trained as well as to the intended scope and intensity of the training.

Accordingly, it would be a waste of time and effort to use the results of a very general district-wide survey of staff training needs to plan a series of inservice sessions for teachers in the business education department of a particular high school. The training needs of a group must be determined at an appropriate level of specificity. While the general district-wide needs can serve as a context for the more specific departmental needs, the assumption should not be made that they are coterminous. Thus, if training is to be organized at a job-alike or departmental level, planning should be done specific to the needs and characteristics of that unit. This can help avoid the all-too-common frustration which occurs, for example, when secondary teachers are given training in how to construct attractive bulletin boards when they may feel a much more fundamental need for training in behavior management, teaching thinking skills, or in managing their own planning time. The failure to address root or causal needs can lead to the view that inservice sessions are irrelevant or even frivolous. Some districts offer a smorgasbord of educational fads as the yearly inservice fare. "Everything they show us how to do in inservice is either inappropriate or too time-consuming," is the frequent expression of this sentiment.

One of the difficulties inherent in conventional inservice programs which thorough needs assessment and planning can prevent is that of the conflict between individual professional growth and staff development needs. Because of the wide diversity of specializations, experience, and backgrounds of teachers, inservice sessions planned for the average teacher or geared toward the lowest common denominator of training need are of limited value. Rather than targeting specific competencies in which teachers need additional training, the hit or miss philosophy has prevailed. Obviously, those teachers for whom inservice more often misses than hits the target cannot be expected to be other than frustrated.

STAGE 1: PROBLEM IDENTIFICATION

A problem identification procedure which considers training needs at the individual teacher level as well as at the district, building, and job-alike levels can lead to the design of effective inservice programs. After data about training needs is gathered, it must be filtered at each level in order to identify commonalities in training needs. (See Figure 6.1.) Once problem areas are identified and their interrelationships at the various organizational levels analyzed, inservice programs to solve the problems can be devised. Such programs can ensure that individual and staff level inservice activities will be synergistic rather than counterproductive. Chapter 12 offers considerations for designing the inservice program as well as examples of such solutions.

Step 1: Assess Practicing Teachers' Mastery of Generic Competencies

A starting point for identifying inservice needs is to assess practicing teachers' mastery of the "musts" and "shoulds" or generic competencies. As explained in Chapters 3 and 4, these skills, knowledge, and attitudes represent what is required and desired of the teacher. The job-related approach uses these competencies to structure the preservice curriculum. They also represent a minimal level of competency for the practicing teacher. A realistic look at today's educational problems, however, suggests that many practicing teachers do *not* possess these skills. This statement is not meant in a pejorative sense. A variety of reasons, such as inadequate preservice training, outdated approaches, and changes in the demands on teachers, explain this discrepancy. Whatever the reasons, all teachers must possess the fundamental competencies if today's difficulties are to be solved.

By using the process described in Chapters 3 and 4, generic teacher competencies can be identified. Based on this information, a test bank can be developed to measure these competencies. (It should be noted here that assessment of actual performance of these competencies may be preferable but is generally not feasible.) An examination which is carefully designed to sample from each of the domains of teacher competencies considered to be important

FIGURE 6.1 Problem Identification: Inservice Training Needs.

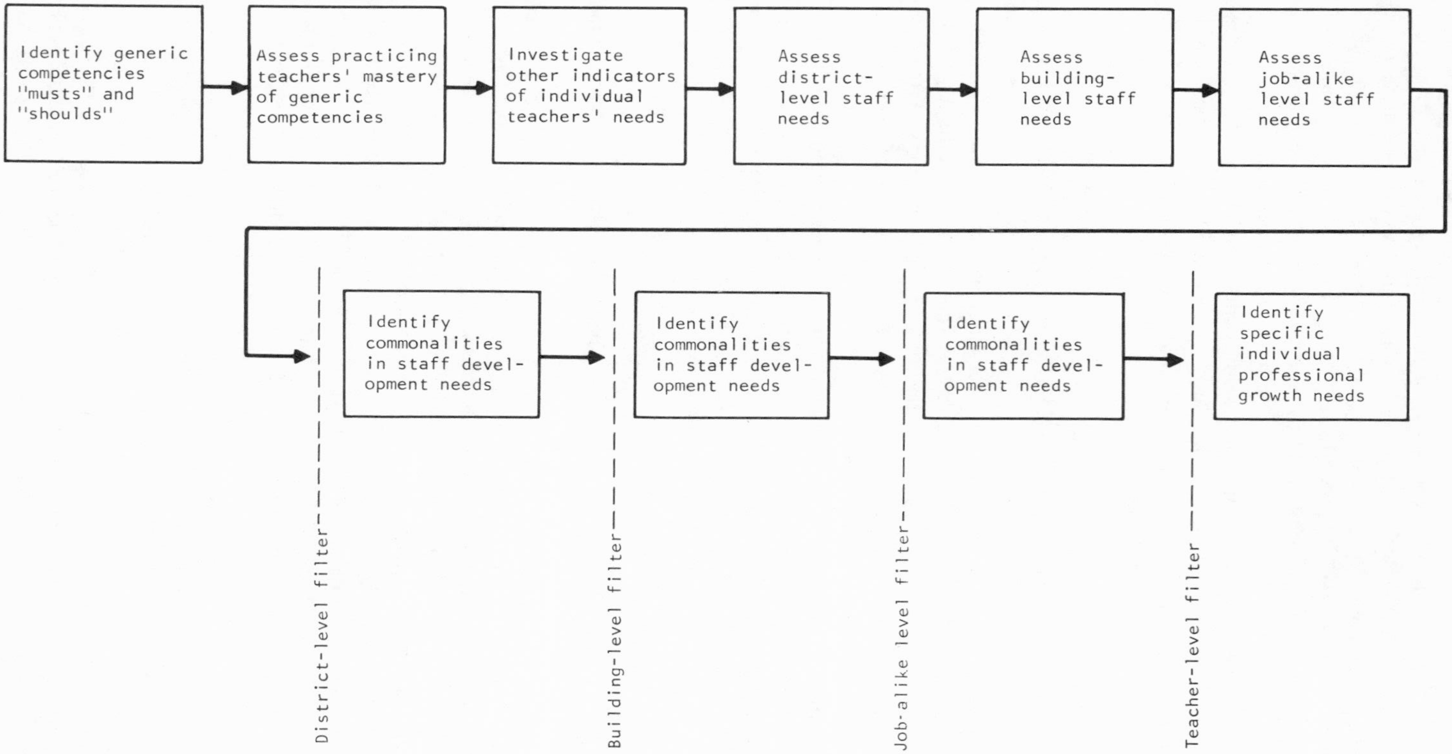

Identify generic competencies "musts" and "shoulds"

Assess practicing teachers' mastery of generic competencies

Investigate other indicators of individual teachers' needs

Assess district-level staff needs

Assess building-level staff needs

Assess job-alike level staff needs

Identify commonalities in staff development needs

Identify commonalities in staff development needs

Identify commonalities in staff development needs

Identify specific individual professional growth needs

District-level filter

Building-level filter

Job-alike level filter

Teacher-level filter

can be administered to all of the teachers in a particular school, district, or even state. Results can be used to plan inservice programs which will focus on the major areas of weakness identified by the examination.

The anonymity of individual teachers should be scrupulously maintained. A coding system, however, might be used to provide feedback to individual teachers as to their particular profile of generic competency attainment. This information can be quite useful to the teacher for planning his or her own program of professional growth. Results can also be reported at the job-alike, school, and district levels. This information can serve as one important source of input for staff developmental planning.

Step 2: Investigate Other Indicators
of Individual Teacher's Training Needs

Another technique for soliciting information about inservice training needs is the teacher self-report instrument. A fundamental assumption underlying such an approach is that teachers are aware of and willing to admit their weaknesses. It seems clear that most teachers do have knowledge of which aspects of teaching cause them difficulties. Even if their self-assessments are somewhat distorted, perceived needs are often a useful starting point for getting to underlying needs. To reduce the probability that teachers will give socially desirable rather than accurate responses, the intended purpose of the inventory should be made clear and anonymity guaranteed. It may also help to have the instrument developed and administered by personnel who do not have "hiring and firing" power, such as a committee of teachers, central office personnel, and other individuals. The generic competencies identified by using the process described in Chapters 3 and 4 can also be used as a basis for developing a self-report inventory.

An additional potential source of information about inservice training needs is teacher evaluation results. Such evaluations, generally conducted by principals or their designated representatives, vary from district to district in their scope and specificity. By looking at the evaluations of all teachers or a randomly selected sample of teachers in a particular school or district, planners can see commonalities in teacher strengths and weaknesses. Two caveats bear emphasis here. First, the confidentiality of personnel records must be maintained. One way of ensuring this would be to cover or remove all identifying information from the evaluation form before copying it for the purpose of inservice planning. A second factor to keep in mind is that evaluative judgments frequently reflect the personal biases of the evaluator. This is a particularly critical pitfall to avoid when no objective source of cross-validation is available. Thus, if all the teachers in a particular school are rated low on a characteristic such as "maintains adequate school records," this may reflect an administrator's overemphasis on functions which affect him in the performance of his job or inadequacies in the record-keeping procedures rather than a wholesale weakness on the part of the faculty.

Step 3: Assess District Level Staff Training Needs

It may appear contradictory that the problem identification procedure jumps from the individual, or micro level to the district, or macro level. The intervening levels are then considered in descending order of size, by building and department (job-alike) respectively. The rationale for this approach is that policy is generally made at the district level. The input provided by the assessment of individual teacher competencies can be reviewed in terms of its implications for reaching established district goals. If it becomes apparent that serious discrepancies exist between the direction the district is pursuing and the competencies its teachers possess to move in this direction, district level inservice priorities to remedy this gap will need to be established. On the other hand, an analysis of individual teacher competencies may reveal strengths that were previously overlooked at the district level. That is, individual teachers are often hired and then become merely "personnel file folders" to central office and other planning personnel. A close look at their aggregate skills may indicate that the district is capable of achieving far different and sometimes far superior goals if teacher strengths can be capitalized on.

The district level problem identification step must take into account not only policy established by the local school board but also other influences in the environment. This corresponds to the process carried out in the identification of the "musts" and "shoulds" at the preservice level. State mandates (such as the required allotment of time to inservice), legislation which affects teaching (such as implications of Public Law 94-142), and community concerns can best be appraised at the district level.

Depending on the size and organization of the district, articulation concerns may also be used in decision-making about inservice priorities. In some districts, each school "does its own thing," which frequently leads to wide disparities in the quality and content of instruction across schools. A district level assessment of articulation problems can help to provide a framework within which effective inservice programs can be developed.

An additional advantage of initially looking at individual teacher characteristics at the district level is that it helps to avoid putting particular teachers on the spot. If information about teacher competencies were analyzed at the school level, the possibility exists that principals or other officials could identify individual teacher's profiles of competencies and attitudes based on their knowledge of the individuals. Thus, the district should report the information as a school profile so as to maintain teachers' confidence in the confidentiality of the process.

Teachers' attitudes toward current inservice offerings can also be assessed. The information derived from such planners determine the present state in terms of teachers' views of the relevance of inservice. If teachers in a given district exhibit a strongly negative affect toward the relevance (or other measured characteristic) of inservice, this serves as an indication that a drastically different approach may be needed to overcome negative attitudes. On the other hand, if teachers' attitudes toward current inservice practices are positive, the discrepancy between the present and preferred state may not be as difficult to achieve. It should be noted, however, that positive attitude toward inservice may not necessarily mean that all is well. Teachers may express satisfaction simply because they expect little from inservice. Inservice planners will need to evaluate the results of attitudinal surveys cautiously and view them as only one of many indications of the current level of inservice effectiveness. An example of a Likert-type instrument which can be used to measure teachers' attitudes toward the relevance of current inservice sessions is provided in Appendix E.

Step 4: Assess Building Level Staff Needs

The information obtained from individual and district level assessments can be used as a framework for identifying building level professional growth needs. The school inservice program should identify commonalities in the individual training needs of staff members as well as district and school-specific needs.

An important cautionary note is that inservice planners at the building level should carefully distinguish between administrative matters and inservice matters. The former, such as attendance policies, should be handled in faculty meetings or through other administrative channels. If the two are confounded, teachers' perceptions of inservice as a professional growth opportunity will be diminished. A clear distinction between these two functions should be scrupulously maintained both in form and content.

The articulation needs within a school must also be considered. Thus, one aspect of the building-level inservice program can be a kind of cross-pollination process among the various job-alike units. For example, the reading teachers can present information regarding students' reading achievement levels and implications for instruction in other content areas to the entire staff. Changes in the science curriculum which may have implications for the math program can also be considered in formulating the building level program.

The results of curriculum evaluation can also be used as a source of information for inservice planning. Review of the educational goals and their relative attainment by a school can bring into focus students' instructional needs, and by extension, teachers' inservice training needs. If curriculum evaluation reveals that students in a particular school are weak in study skills, inservice sessions might be geared toward helping teachers plan and deliver appropriate learning experiences to improve these skills. Teachers should, of course, be informed of the process used to identify the inservice emphasis. Otherwise, they are likely to assume that study skills are simply the newest inservice fad rather than a real need as evidenced by students' performance on standardized tests and other indicators. Many excellent sources of curriculum evaluation criteria and procedures are available.

Step 5: Assess Job-alike Staff Training Needs

At the job-alike or departmental level, training needs shift from the generic to the specific. That is, it is at this point that content and level specialization concerns should be addressed. The particular skills needed by English teachers to improve students' composition skills, for example, should be addressed at this level. The rationale for organizing the majority of inservice sessions at the job-alike level is that the more similar the level of teachers attending an inservice program, the more likely it is that the session will be specific enough to be relevant to all participants. While there is much exhortation in the literature that inservice should be totally individualized, there does not seem to be much evidence to support the effectiveness of this extreme. Individual peculiarities of teacher competencies are best handled in other ways (such as, through close supervisory practices, graduate coursework, and so forth).

On the other hand, there is evidence available that teachers prefer "meetings organized and arranged for teachers of similar grades, disciplines, or programs, to those arranged for all teachers, without regard to their grades or disciplines." The investigators who drew the above conclusion surveyed a random sample of 228 Chicago public school teachers in 1977, asking them to describe an ideal inservice session. In response to the open-ended question, "How was the meeting organized?", 71 percent stated they preferred inservice sessions designed for teachers with "similar assignments and responsibilities" over other patterns (Ngaiyaye & Hanley, 1978, p. 305). In other studies as well, teachers exhibit a more positive attitude toward the usefulness of inservice sessions when they are organized on a job-alike rather than *en masse* (school or district level) basis.

Staff development priorities can best be ranked through group diagnosis techniques. A preliminary step in accomplishing this diagnosis is to determine the specific organizational entities to be considered "working units." As explained earlier, most inservice efforts are more likely to have positive affective and performance consequences if they are delivered on a departmental or job-alike basis. This implies that identification of needs be conducted at the corresponding organizational level. It is also important that the findings of other phases of inservice needs assessment be provided to the individual units so that they will be aware of the larger context. A group of secondary science teachers engaged in the identification of their inservice priorities, for example, should be informed of the fact that a need identified for the entire school is that of providing a greater variety of instructional activities to accommodate individual differences. Without an overall framework of inservice need at the macro level, various working units may plan and participate in inservice activities which are divisive rather than complementary.

Information gleaned from the needs assessment procedures can be provided to the particular working unit as it begins the task of focusing on inservice priorities. This groundwork is essential if the identified needs are to be useful, both in terms of their relevance and in terms of the degree of commitment they are likely to engender. While many of the preliminary needs assessment procedures cited synthesize individual concerns to come up with systemic concerns, actual group participation in the final determination of priorities is essential. A group can be expected to have quite different attitudes toward a list of needs presented to them as "this is what the evidence says you need" and a list of needs that they themselves formulate when they are given an opportunity to discuss and evaluate the evidence.

7

Evaluating at the Problem Identification Stage

Stage 1 of the problem-solving process is the identification of a problem. The decision must be made whether a need actually exists for a new program or for modifications to the existing program. If no problem can be identified, there is no reason to continue with the procedure.

During problem identification two important issues must be addressed. First, a need for a new program or for modifications to the existing program must be identified. This involves careful examination of present needs and whether or not they are being met within the existing system. Second, a determination must be made as to whether there is actually adequate support for change. Support for change must be evident at several levels. It is most desirable that the need for change be recognized and supported by practitioners in the field of education as well as by institution or program administrators and staff. However, if there exists sufficient demand by educational practitioners, a mechanism by which the program can be administered will be found. Thus, as Chapter 5 pointed out, it is possible to overcome obstacles such as insufficient support for innovations in teacher education in existing institutions.

Evaluating at the problem identification stage essentially follows a context evaluation format (Stufflebeam, Foley, Gephart, Guba, Hammond, Merriam, & Provus, 1971, p. 218). It establishes the parameters of the program to be evaluated and then describes and analyzes it. It requires that certain philosophical questions be answered. Among these are the establishment of values and goals for the program. It looks for new or emerging value orientations outside of the program-sponsoring agency to change the value orientation within the agency. The focus is on the variables considered important for achieving implicit goals. Greater emphasis is placed on the theoretical and empirical knowledge in the field of education. It is at this point that consideration is given to the question of whether practice is consistent with accepted theory.

At the problem identification stage, a baseline of data on the operations and accomplishments of the system must be developed. In order to accomplish this, a comprehensive communications network must be established. This will later serve as a mechanism for disseminating public information.

At this stage, the evaluation model proposed for the job-related curriculum searches for opportunities and pressure outside of the immediate system to promote change and improvement within the system. Change is based largely on assessment of the needs, values, attitudes, and priorities of educational practitioners. It also looks to research and development literature, practice within other systems, and community values and attitudes. Immediate concerns are emphasized, but the future is also considered. Effort is made to project educational values and needs.

Adequate evaluation at the problem identification stage is basic to the success of the program. It is at this stage that the rationale is developed for criteria and objectives. The relevant environment is defined and the actual and desired conditions pertaining to that environment are described. This basically involves the recognition of existing levels and establishment of preferred levels of educational characteristics. Unmet needs and unused opportunities are described as well as the problems that prevent needs from being met or opportunities from being used. The identification of problems provides a starting point for the development of the ultimate objectives and indirectly contributes to the development of terminal and enabling objectives. Inadequate problem identification virtually assures serious problems in the design, installation, and operations of the program. It is the function of evaluation at this stage to identify inadequacies in the problem identification so that correctives can be effected before the process continues.

Step 1: Determining the Context

The context indicates what is relevant to the evaluation and what is not. Therefore, the first step in the evaluation is to circumscribe the context. This is accomplished by identifying the services and/or products provided by the organization. In the case of the teacher education program, the practicing teacher may be considered the product. The service is teacher education. The mission of the organization is to provide quality services and products. All information that pertains to the improvement of the services and/or products provided by the organization is relevant to the evaluation. Other information is not.

The evaluator must determine the scope of the evaluation. This includes determining the types of decisions that will be made. The recommended evaluation procedures for the job-related curriculum include four decision points—problem identification, design, installation and operations, and program effectiveness. At the first three decision points, the decision-maker is faced with three options—continue as is, terminate, or modify. In assessing program effectiveness, the options are to continue as is or to terminate. However, these procedures may be modified for the specific program being evaluated. For example, in some instances it may be desirable to limit the decisions to continue or modify.

The evaluator must identify the individuals in the organization who are authorized to make the decisions. The appropriate decision-maker will determine the particular decisions that are to be based on the evaluation as well as how these decisions are to be made. At this point the evaluator reconciles differences with the decision-maker and makes certain the general approach to the evaluation will provide an appropriate basis for making the decisions.

Finally, the evaluator must determine the resources to be committed to the evaluation (money, personnel, facilities) and determine whether or not the evaluation can proceed.

Step 2: Identifying a Need

The initial step in identifying a need for change is to determine which characteristics must be observed as a basis for making the predetermined decisions pertaining to the program. The specific characteristics to be observed should have been determined or, at least, implied in discussions with the decision-makers about the specific decisions to be made. Generally, in the instance of the teacher education program, the characteristics to be observed are those associated with teacher performance in the classroom. These should be related to identified teacher competencies. The specific characteristics will be dependent upon the type or nature of the teacher education program under evaluation. However, those competencies associated with basic professional performance would provide a sound basis for the evaluation of any professional program.

The evaluator must plan a method of observing each relevant characteristic. Detailed specifications must be formulated for observing each relevant characteristic as well as determining the extent to which it actually exists. The specifications should include a description of the instruments to be used in making the observations and the sequence of activities to be followed. If a characteristic cannot be observed, given present knowledge and/or resources, it should be eliminated from further consideration. Emphasis in the job-related curriculum is on skills rather than attitudes eliminating much of the concern with unobservable characteristics. The elimination of characteristics upon which a decision must be based may be taken as an indication that the decision cannot be based on empirical evidence.

The decision-maker may indicate the method he prefers for observing particular characteristics. For example, he may not only have decided that he will base his decisions on the examination of particular characteristics; he may have decided that particular measurement instruments will be used to observe the characteristics. Often, however, these basic evaluation decisions will be made by the evaluator or largely with his input.

At this point, it becomes necessary to identify existing and preferred levels of each characteristic that is retained. This involves collecting accurate information on the existing level of each characteristic and establishing a preferred level of each characteristic. The order in which these activities are undertaken is interchangeable. The decision-maker may have already established the preferred level of a characteristic that will be used as a criterion for decision-making. In this case the preferred level has been predetermined before the existing level is established. On the other hand, the decision-maker may have specified that the existing level of a characteristic is to be identified first. Then, based on a knowledge of the realities of an existing state of affairs, an appropriate preferred level is projected.

When the preferred level is established before the existing level is determined, the focus of the evaluation is on the attainment or lack of attainment of preferred characteristics. In this case, we are evaluating an organization only with respect to the attainment of predetermined preferred characteristics.

When the existing levels of the characteristics are determined first, the purpose of the evaluation is to evaluate all of the characteristics of the organization. In this case, all of the relevant existing characteristics are observed first. Then it is determined whether or not what is existing is preferred. The success of the organization is judged in terms of whether or not existing characteristics reflect that which is preferred.

Sometimes the evaluator is involved in establishing the preferred level of a characteristic. In this case, the evaluator employs a method of establishing the preferred level from sources such as surveys of opinions, civil laws, and writings by members of professional organizations, researchers, and subject matter experts. This is essentially the procedure that was followed in the job-related curriculum.

The next step is to compare the existing level of each characteristic with the preferred level and describe any discrepancy. Since the two states are rarely, if ever, equivalent, some discrepancy will exist. The size of the discrepancy is recorded.

It is now necessary to decide whether or not action should be taken to reduce the size of the discrepancy between the existing and the preferred level of the characteristic. The decision-makers with the technical assistance of the evaluator must now interpret the seriousness of each discrepancy and decide which of the discrepancies are to be reduced, if any. The judgment actually focuses on a "how large is too large" problem. The decision-makers must answer the question, "How large must a discrepancy be before something needs to be done about it?" This essentially becomes a value judgment. Discrepancies that are not large enough are eliminated from further consideration. The remaining discrepancies are ranked in order of their importance to the decision-makers and retained for possible future reference in program design.

In translating this procedure into use with the job-related curriculum, concern (characteristics to be observed) is with the competencies, both those necessary and those desirable, for educational practitioners. The identified competencies are based primarily on an observation of what teachers actually do on the job. Hence, the name "job-related curriculum" was derived. From the step of identifying competencies, it is simply another step to determine whether these competencies are being developed as desired. This obviously involves identifying the existing level of competencies of the practitioners in the field as well as establishing the preferred level of these competencies. Again, practitioners and experts in the field of education are best able to determine whether there exists a serious discrepancy between the preferred level of necessary and/or desired competencies and the existing level of these competencies. Two basic questions may be raised:

1. In the preservice program: What skills or competencies does the student lack upon entering the teacher education program that you wish for him to acquire before he leaves the program? What characteristics does the student have upon entering the program that you want to change before he leaves the program? Does the existing program effect these changes?

2. In the inservice program: What new skills or competencies does the teacher need to develop? What old skills or competencies does he need to improve? Does an existing program bring about these changes?

The decision to proceed with program design will be based partly on the response to these questions. Ideally, educational practitioners will have already determined, through formal and informal communications, that needs exist. Approaches will have already been made to the system responsible for teacher education to establish new programs or modify existing programs to meet these needs. Under these circumstances it is only necessary for the program staff to systematize and formalize the needs assessment. Having determined that a need exists, the second aspect of evaluation at this stage is determining whether or not there is sufficient support for change.

Step 3: Evaluating Support

It is certainly desirable that support for change in an existing program or for a new program be manifested within an agency or institution which is already responsible for teacher education. However, support by practitioners and experts in the field is absolutely critical. If enough demand exists by the "consumer" of teacher education—the teacher and the school administrator—a mechanism will be found to provide the service or program which they desire.

The two concepts, field-based identification of needs and field-based support for change, are basically opposite sides of the same coin. A fundamental assumption is that support for change cannot exist unless the need for change has been acknowledged. Similarly, a sincere realization that there exists a need for change must be accompanied by adequate support. It should be noted that a handshake and a verbal expression of "best wishes with the new program" is not what one considers adequate support. Adequate support should take two forms. It should be manifested by adequate financial support for the changes. This may involve the commitment of funds to cover total program development and implementation cost or, if grant-in-aid assistance is obtained, necessary matching funds or in-kind contributions. Financial support also includes the provision of staff time and services and physical resources. The specific source of the financial support is irrelevant, however, it is important that the financial support reflect field-based demand. In other words, if the funds do not come directly from those requesting service, it should be made available at their request so that the commitment to program change or a new program is made by those who will benefit from its provision.

This brings us to the second manifestation of support—that is commitment to use the "product" of the desired program or program change. In the case of preservice programs, this means that graduates of a new or modified teacher education program will be employed by the school districts who have expressed support for change. In the case of inservice training, this would be manifested by the participation of educational practitioners in the program and by their employment of new skills and competencies in the classroom. However, these manifestations for support are not actually available at the initiation of a program. It is during this stage that a decision to proceed with the program development process is dependent upon these assurances of product use. Unfortunately, this manifestation of support is not existent at this point. In order to determine whether adequate support for the program exists, it is necessary to rely on verbal report from practitioners and experts in the field. This can take the form of letters of endorsement and support from superintendents, members of boards of trustees, principals, master teachers, and other educators who are in decision-making roles throughout the area to be served by the proposed program. Endorsements are necessary at the Stage 1 decision point in the evaluation process. However, they may also be functional at later stages when the initial enthusiasm among program administrators and staff may flag under the difficulties and tedium sometimes encountered in the program development and implementation process. Expressed field demand sometimes provides needed impetus. The letters of endorsement represent a mandate to educational administrators and decision-makers from those whom they are supposed to serve.

On the basis of these considerations, a major decision point is reached. Financial support for the program must be assessed. Does it represent a measure of serious interest and effort? Verbal endorsement for the program and assurances of need and future use of the program output must be examined. A fine judgment must be made as to whether these verbal assurances can be projected into employment practices at a later date—sometimes as distant as four years. On the basis of these determinations, a decision is reached. The decision is one of three options: the project will be terminated, it will be continued, or it will be modified. If the feedback option of modification is selected at this stage, a renewed effort will be made to establish that there exists sufficient demand and support for change. It should be noted at this point, that establishing the demand for change is not synonymous with creating the demand for change. It is not the responsibility of the program staff to create or increase demand. It has been recognized that this endeavor would ultimately be self-defeating. It is, however, perfectly legitimate for the program decision-makers to require a reassessment of field demand. This may involve an additional survey of support for the program including more contact with practitioners, administrators, and potential employers in the field. The purpose would be to determine whether expressed support does in fact represent the extent of field demand or whether additional public information and contact with educators will uncover additional support for change. It is understandable that program decision-makers will not wish to make decisions given partial information. However, it should be reiterated that it is not the role of the staff to sell the program in the field, only to accurately assess existing support.

PART III: Designing Teacher Education Programs

8

Determining the "Whats" and "Hows" of the Teacher Education Program

A knowledge of what needs to be improved in teacher education is only a starting point. The problem-solving model, as outlined in Chapter 2, moves from identifying problems to designing programs to solve them. During Stage 2, the data base of teacher competencies is translated into pre- and inservice programs.

A common criticism of conventional teacher education programs has been that the "what" or content of courses, and the "how" or the instructional delivery system do not complement one another. While one may not totally agree with McLuhan's edict that "the medium is the message," the need for compatibility between what is taught and how it is taught is crucial in teacher preparation. This concern might be less significant in another professional training or liberal arts field; however, prospective teachers need to analyze consciously the relationship between content and method as part of their transition from student to teacher. In this chapter, procedures are given for building the discrete competencies listed in the data base into preservice teacher education curriculum as well as for determining how the content is to be taught.

As mentioned in Chapter 3, the skills identified as required are to be considered the skeleton of the teacher education program. If prospective teachers are to function effectively in today's classroom, they must demonstrate mastery of at least these skills. Thus, the basic content of the program is derived directly from the Generic Teacher Job Description. Some of the skills, knowledge, and attitudes necessary to master the required competencies are identified as "shoulds" or desired competencies. Other prerequisite content and activities must be inferred from the competency statements.

Each category of competencies identified as required or desired represents a potential course in the new curriculum. The filtering process described in Chapter 4 provides a means of assessing the "desired" categories, those without field validation. These categories were reconciled with NASDTEC and NCATE standards, providing the program development specialist with information on which to base a decision as to the most appropriate placement and organization of these competencies in the curriculum.

At this point, it is necessary to reassess the original categorization scheme used to classify required competencies. The logical relatedness of competencies was used as the basic criteria used to sort competency statements. This may or may not, however, result in groupings which will coalesce as courses. The second screening of categories should look for answers to questions such as the following:

1. Is there a more logical or practical way of arranging the competencies?

2. Are the competencies in a given category cohesive and mutually supportive?

3. Should a given category be subdivided to create more than one course?

4. Can the competencies in more than one category be combined to form a new course?

Before actual course development begins, of course, judgments such as these are somewhat arbitrary. Clusters of related competencies within categories should also be identified.

After tentative decisions have been made regarding general course divisions, course descriptions can be written for the new courses. In the model project, most of these courses were a part of the professional core component, although a few were general education and/or cognate courses. It is conceivable that new courses could also emerge in the teaching specializations.

A clarification should be made here as to what is meant by new courses. Any course which is suggested by the data base should be regarded as new in the sense of being "model" or "prototypic." At this point in the curriculum development process, it is dysfunctional to look at existing courses to see if they appropriate the new courses. Additional feedback about the correspondence of the new courses to real world requirements is needed before any decision can be made as to whether existing courses can be adopted as is or revised to meet the design specifications.

Preliminary course descriptions are essentially narrative summaries of the competencies listed in each category. To emphasize the job-related approach, descriptions should be phrased in terms of what the student will learn, or what skills he will acquire, rather than simply a listing of content elements. A rationale relating the course to the demands of the classroom teacher's job can also be included. In addition, the sources of the data base suggesting the need for the particular skills can be cited. An example of a course description of this type is as follows:

Diagnosing Readiness for Learning
Students learn to identify typical and atypical physical, intellectual, emotional, and social characteristics of children and youths as these characteristics pertain to learning. Direct and indirect observational techniques are learned as well as the selection, administration, and interpretation of diagnostic instruments. Students also learn to design appropriate diagnostic instruments. Emphasis is on diagnosis for the purpose of prescribing appropriate instruction and making referrals.

Laboratories are offered at the early childhood, elementary, middle school, and secondary levels. The student selects one of the four labs according to his interest. In the lab the student is shown how to diagnose for learning readiness in the classroom. *Rationale:* A central task of the teacher is to diagnose student readiness for the purpose of prescribing instruction and referring students to other professionals for assistance. It is necessary for the teacher to develop observational and diagnostic skills. *Data base:* Job description, questionnaire, faculty interview, and competency list data stress the importance of teachers developing observational and diagnostic skills. References to the diagnostic responsibilities of teachers include detecting exceptionality, learning styles, learning readiness, and individual differences in the classroom. The data also strongly indicates the teacher's need to select, administer, and interpret testing instruments.

When the first draft of the curriculum has been completed, feedback from individuals and groups should be solicited. This serves as a checkpoint to see if the product derived from the data base is actually representative of the intent of those individuals who provided the impetus for the project. This reduces the possibility that extrapolating from the data base might distort the job-related emphasis. This checkpoint provides a concrete document for soliciting the constituency's reactions. Additional areas of improvement may become apparent, such as needed revisions in current instructional procedures, area of specialization coursework, and so forth.

Feedback can be obtained in a number of ways. Reactions to mailed copies of the descriptions is one possibility. More productive responses, however, can probably be obtained through group reaction to the individual course descriptions as well as to the framework of the entire curriculum. Group response at this point is indicated because it provides a context in which the teacher can look at the proposed curriculum from a broader perspective than the confines of one classroom, school, and district. In the model project, for example, the master teachers from around the state and other persons who participated in earlier phases of the design were convened in a central location to react to the proposed curriculum. In this way, individual responses as well as group synergy were tapped.

Participants in the review sessions were asked to assess the overall curriculum as well as each component. Open-ended questionnaires were used to focus group discussion. (See Appendix F.) A separate reaction sheet was provided for each aspect of the program (such as, each area of specialization, each cognate sequence, and so forth). Participants were asked to respond to the proposed course offerings as either "acceptable as is" or "needs revisions." Recommendations for revising each phase of the curriculum were compiled. In addition to the group meetings, the questionnaire cited above was mailed to those organizations and individuals who had also contributed to earlier phases of the design but were unable to attend the session.

Reactions to the curriculum content were analyzed and appropriate adjustments made. It is interesting to note that very few revisions were suggested for professional core courses, the component derived most directly from the data base. The revisions which were suggested generally were related to whether a particular course should be "required" or "recommended." Recommendations for other components basically concerned providing maximum flexibility in the preparation of the teacher (See Chapter 10 for a more detailed discussion).

COURSE DEVELOPMENT PROCEDURES

The transition from data base to course outline is one which requires careful structuring. Without such planning, deviations from the data base can occur quite easily. The following phases are suggested to keep course development on target:

1. Write

2. React

3. Rewrite

4. Review

5. Reconcile

6. Refine

It might be necessary to repeat the cycle of feedback and refinement several times before a given course is satisfactorily outlined. Because the courses are to be made available for different instructors and/or teams of instructors, they must be detailed enough so that the possibility of misinterpretation is negligible. At the same time, sufficient flexibility must be provided so that variations in instructor style and student needs can be accommodated.

The first step recommended for course development is to identify persons with expertise in each skill or subject to be covered in a given course. This helps to ensure that each content element will be developed adequately. If a faculty is involved in course development, the major topics of each course can be listed and faculty members given an opportunity to select areas of interest or expertise. Figure 8.1 gives an example of a checklist that can be circulated. It was taken from the course Teaching as a Profession.

Please indicate in the columns to the left whether you are interested in participating in the development of and/or teaching of the following topics:

FIGURE **8.1** **Teaching as a Profession.**

Developing	Teaching	Teaching as a Profession Topics:
		evolution of the teaching profession
		school organization and administration
		school finance
		school curriculum
		community-school relations
		school law and regulations
		teacher evaluation
		teacher certification and certification renewal
		teacher benefits
		career opportunities
		federal programs
		professional organizations
		professional publications
		attitudes and behaviors expected of the teacher
		social and philosophical foundations of the teaching profession
		the work of the teacher

It is also useful to select a coordinator for each course. This person assumes responsibility for getting input from the various individuals who volunteered to assist in course development. The coordinator is also responsible for drafting a preliminary version of the course outline. The coordinator may be a subject matter expert or a program design specialist skilled at synthesizing information.

While the specifications for course outlines may vary from institution to institution, a number of items should be covered. First, descriptive information about the course is needed, including the course number, title, catalog description, intended audience, credit hours, statement of prerequisites and instructor(s). Some of this information, however, such as the course number, may not be available until the entire curriculum has been completed. All instructors qualified to teach the course can be tentatively identified at this point.

The goals or terminal objectives of the course should be specified in terms of what the student will be able to *do* as a result of the course. Enabling objectives, those which facilitate the attainment of the terminal objectives, are also necessary. Each enabling objective should specify the content element as well as the mental or physical process to be performed by the student.

Instructional procedures and field experiences should also be included in the course outline. In accordance with the assumptions made by the model project, instructors should be granted rather wide latitude in making decisions as to the appropriate instructional activities. Thus, instructional procedures should be indicated in general terms unless particular activities are essential to the achievement of course objectives. Field experiences can also be suggested, with the proviso that varying conditions may require modifications.

Course outlines should also include listings of required texts, supplementary readings, materials, films, and other appropriate instructional aids. Most of the courses can be designed so that they are not textbook-bound. Instructors can then select from a variety of resources. This helps to ensure that the skills taught will be generic rather than situation specific.

Course requirements should also be specified. These include the specific assignments to be used to evaluate each objective. Assignments should be keyed to the objectives to make this relationship obvious. The relative weight of each assignment and criteria for scoring it should also be indicated. (See Chapter 20 for further information on student evaluation.)

A suggested course schedule is also a useful part of the course outline. Broad topic headings can be blocked out so that the instructor will have an indication of the suggested order of presentation and the relative length of time to be spent on each segment of the course. Here again this schedule should be thought of as a guideline; the actual schedule will be determined at the instructor's discretion.

After preliminary course outlines containing these elements have been written, the reactions of other faculty members should be solicited. In particular, those persons who volunteered to participate in the course design should have an opportunity to react to the outline before further development. Course outlines can be circulated for feedback or the coordinator can arrange a group meeting to assess the initial product. It is also advisable to obtain feedback from some of the practitioners who contributed to the data base.

Once reactions to the draft have been obtained, it will be necessary to revise the outline. While the coordinator for each course may handle this, it is probably more efficient to have all courses revised by one program design specialist. This will help to ensure that all courses follow a consistent pattern and that the data base is adhered to. A designer with an overall perspective of the curriculum will be able to spot gaps in content coverage, overlapping objectives, and other inconsistencies both within and across courses.

This second draft of each course should also be circulated for feedback. This is not only useful for pinpointing any weaknesses in the course but is also politically wise. The opportunity for input must be available if cooperation is to be obtained during program implementation. As Silberman points out, teachers are in an excellent position to sabotage any curriculum they do not wish to follow. Participation in course development is not a guarantee that this will not occur, but it at least "covers" the program staff in the event that accusations of "we weren't involved" arise.

After the reactions to the second draft have been obtained, revisions may again be necessary. It is unlikely that major modifications will be required. If significant changes are needed, another feedback cycle is indicated.

The next phase involves reconciling across courses so that all elements of the data base are covered. At this point, it will be possible to determine an initial sequencing of the courses. This can be done by analyzing the entire spectrum of objectives to see which are prerequisite to others. During this process, certain objectives which may inadvertly have been omitted may become apparent as needed prerequisites to other objectives.

An additional refinement phase may be needed before the course outlines can be considered final. In a sense, the outlines will never be "final" because the process of refinement will continue each time the course is taught. The courses will also need to be revised periodically as changes occur in the requirements of the teacher's job.

Once course outlines have been developed, attention should focus on how the courses are to be taught. In this phase of curriculum development, as in previous phases, the recommendations of practicing teachers and other individuals and groups associated with education should be sought. As part of the problem identification phase for the job-related curriculum, for example, an open-ended survey was administered to such a group. One item solicited their suggestions for "methods of teaching the content" of a teacher education program. The following recommendations for instruction were cited most frequently:

1. Teachers in training should have early, frequent contact with students in actual classroom settings.

2. Instructors should have recent public school teaching experience at the appropriate grade level and subject area.

3. Appropriate teaching practices should be modeled by the instructor or by actual classroom teachers.

4. Teachers in training should be exposed to a wide variety of public school settings (such as, large/small school, urban/rural schools, all grade levels, all ability levels, individualized/traditional classes, and so forth).

5. Emphasis in coursework should be on practical application rather than on theory.

6. Instructional techniques should be reality-oriented (such as, actual classroom problem situations, simulations, videotaped sessions, and so forth).

7. Team teaching, "exchange" teaching, and other shared-teaching arrangements should be used by preservice teacher education instructors.

It is interesting to note that the suggestions made by practicing teachers correspond quite closely to recommendations made in the literature promoting more job-related preparatory programs.

As this list reveals, practicing teachers in the sample expressed relatively little concern about the particular method of instructional delivery. On the other hand, they placed great emphasis on the relevancy of the content, the instructional setting, and the background of the instructor. Taken as a whole, their recommendations suggest that a pragmatic, field-oriented preservice teacher education program is needed.

The recommendation that prospective teachers have contact with public school students beginning immediately and continuing throughout their preservice training was strongly indicated in the data base. According to these teachers, this contact should take place as much as possible in a naturalistic setting (that is, the classroom) rather than in a contrived situation such as a one-to-one tutoring or small group lab arrangement. Many conventional programs do require the preservice teacher to engage in tutoring or small group instructional activities. However, the learners with whom prospective teachers work in these programs are either self-selected (that is, they volunteer to be tutored) or else they are chosen by a public school contact person. Moreover, the tutoring frequently takes place outside school hours and often somewhere other than in the public school classroom. From these experiences, prospective teachers may develop unrealistic notions about what behaviors can be expected of the learner in the classroom environment. This is not to say that such activities are totally useless; indeed, they may be quite helpful as precursors to actual classroom practice. However, they should not be overused, extended too long into the prospective teacher's program, or misrepresented as the "real thing." Opportunities to do intensive tutoring are all too infrequent in the day-to-day classroom routine. Hence, prospective teachers who have worked only with individuals or small select groups will have a distorted view of what is in store for them in the classroom. Many master teachers traced the common disillusionment and occasional failure of student teachers to unrealistic preparation—lectures, readings, and practice in how to teach the model student in the model classroom with model materials.

Yet, as was mentioned in Chapter 1, exposure to classroom experiences is a means to an end, not an end in itself. Increasing the duration and scope of field experiences *may* result in better prepared entry level teachers; however, there is little evidence to support the assumption that this in and of itself will accomplish very much. Sending prospective teachers into the field to "observe" or "assist" teachers without adequately preparing them beforehand is a disservice to both the prospective and the practicing teacher. Often, teacher education students are not given any concrete criteria or task for classroom observation and participation. Sometimes, the opposite is true. The assigned task is inflexible and does not fit meaningfully into the ongoing flow of classroom activities. The assignment, for example, might be to develop and teach a learning game on syllabication rules. It apparently does not occur to the instructor that not all teachers cover syllabication rules at the same time. Thus, when the prospective teacher's field assignments are inadequately or inappropriately structured, he may be an intrusion in the classroom, distracting the students and making the teacher feel even more overburdened than usual.

The recommendation that preservice teacher education be more field-oriented requires a greater degree of coordination between the training institution and the public school than is presently the norm. One mechanism which would facilitate this coordination is that of using university instructors and public school teachers as an advisory team to the prospective teacher. With this approach, the school-based advisor can identify experiences in the schools from which the trainee is most likely to benefit. The advisor, for example, might suggest a number of classrooms for observation, perhaps to compare and contrast different classroom management styles.

With a public school teacher and a training institution representative as coadvisors, the prospective teacher should have the best of both worlds. Obviously, however, the advisor teams need to be carefully selected and screened for compatibility. Procedures must be established for maintaining communication between the two as well as with the teacher in training. Because of the typical limitations on the time available for advisement, a particular institution-based/school-based advisor team may counsel a number of prospective teachers, with release time or remuneration as an incentive.

The second recommendation, that instructors have recent public school teaching experience can be seen as an indictment of the "ivory tower" syndrome which has pervaded many teacher education programs. Practicing teachers often perceive professors of education as being out of touch with the current realities of the public school. Phrases such as "idealistic," "obsolete," "too theoretical," "impractical," and "impossible" are frequently used by teachers to describe the instructional procedures recommended by teacher educators for use in the classroom.

The recommendation that appropriate teaching practices be modeled by the instructor or by a classroom teacher is another reaction against conventional approaches. The picture of a professor lecturing on the shortcomings of the lecture method comes to mind. Teachers want to see how various teaching methods are actually applied in the classroom. Reading or hearing about appropriate questioning strategies, for example, is quite different from actually seeing a teacher use these strategies or from using them oneself. Many prospective teachers express frustration because they know what to do, but not how to do it.

It should be pointed out, however, that suggestions such as these and the criticisms they imply are almost inevitable and have much to do with role perceptions. The popularity of the old adage, "Those who can, do; those who can't, teach; those who can't teach, teach teachers," attests to the pervasiveness of this view. Seeing the teacher educator through stereotypic lenses, however, leads to a discounting of the strengths he may offer the prospective and the practicing teacher. The teacher educator is in a position to be an advocate for the "should be's" of instruction. He is in a position where familiarity with the state of the art is maximized. Practicing teachers, on the other hand, are frequently too caught up in the day-to-day problems of the classroom to maintain an overall perspective. The teacher educator frequently recommends instructional techniques that are indeed superior to *status quo* teaching practices. It is not so much the viability of a given theory or instructional approach that is questioned, but rather the inability of the instructor to demonstrate its applicability and feasibility in the public school setting.

The concern about teacher educators' lack of recent classroom experience can be seen as a question of credibility rather than of competence. Teachers want some assurance that those who tell them "how to teach" understand the context in which this advice is to be applied. Evidence of good faith seems to be what teachers are asking for. That is, they want to see teacher educators in the public schools. They want to see their instructors demonstrate recommended techniques in an actual classroom setting with "real" students. Maintaining an overall perspective while involved in the realities of the classroom will require a tightrope performance by teacher educators. It is clear, however, from mounting teacher sentiment and sanctions such as those in the latest NCATE standards, that teacher educators had better start practicing on the balance beam.

The next recommendation, that teachers in training be exposed to a wide variety of public school settings, is practical for a number of reasons. First, this exposure will increase the likelihood that prospective teachers make well-informed decisions about their intended grade level and subject area specializations. Another advantage is that of increasing the teacher's awareness of what goes on in classrooms other than his own. All too frequently, a teacher is isolated from colleagues even in the same corridor. Many teachers never develop an overall perspective of what goes on in the various organizational levels. This contributes to articulation gaps, unrealistic expectations, and scapegoating about what "those teachers over at X School do." Also, today's society is much more mobile than ever before. Exposure to a wide variety of settings during the preparatory period will make career adaptations easier should, for example, a move from a rural to an urban setting be required. This overview will also help teachers understand the characteristics and needs of students with different backgrounds from their own.

The fifth and sixth recommendations are similar in nature: (5) emphasis in coursework should be on practical application rather than on theory; and (6) instructional techniques should be reality-oriented. Both suggestions involve getting down to earth in teacher education. Again, the teacher educator is faced with the problem of balance. On the one hand, he must make an attempt to show how things should be, and on the other hand, he cannot afford to ignore how things actually are. Given this situation, it might be advisable for the instructor to let the prospective teacher in on this dilemma, since it is one he too will eventually face. Aware of the dialectic between what is and what should be, the prospective teacher will be more likely to have a realistic view of what can be achieved through successive approximation.

It should be recognized that the degree of practicality and realism in activities to be expected in professional education coursework is limited by the situation itself. That is, verisimilitude is difficult to achieve when removed from the actual classroom situation. Attempts to ignore this basic reality have led to contrived and often ludicrous activities, such as having a class of prospective teachers pose as elementary students while demonstration lessons are taught by classmates. Certainly, examples drawn from classroom situations should be used. Insofar as possible, theory should be translated into practical applications.

Beyond this admonition, however, one risks encroaching on the instructor's prerogative. Telling the instructor "how" particular content should be taught is extremely risky. Not only does it ignore variations in teaching style, which are likely to remain regardless of directives to perform in another manner, but it also ignores the particular needs and characteristics of the individual student and the group. Given content can be taught and learned in a variety of ways. To say that only one approach is suitable for a given objective violates the prerogative of the instructor and may lead to the very kind of inapplicability the program is supposedly designed to avoid.

Thus, the oft-heralded position that "prospective teachers should be taught by the same method that they are expected to use in their own teaching" is frequently unsound. One need not learn about learning centers, for example, through the medium of a learning center. In planning appropriate activities for teacher education coursework, form should not be overemphasized at the expense of content. The preestablished course objectives and evaluation criteria provide a framework for instruction.

The laboratory experiences which accompany coursework can be specified in more detail. They should be designed to provide the link between the college classroom and the public school classroom. A gradual progression in the degree of public school involvement can be built into the laboratory component of the curriculum. The laboratory or field activities can be conceptualized as a hierarchy which moves the individual from the student role to the teacher role. The prospective teacher, through a structured sequence of field activities, moves from observer to participant. It should be noted that while the hierarchy forms a logical sequence of activities, it is not a rigid prescription.

The bottom rung of this hierarchy is the visitation. Visitations provide an opportunity for the prospective teacher to see first hand a variety of educational programs, facilities, and supporting services. Teachers in training, for example, should be exposed to as many different school and school-related settings as possible. For this kind of overview function, the principle of "more is better" applies. Visitations should be frequent during the early portion of the student's course of study and will diminish as more structured activities are appropriate.

Observations, the second level of the hierarchy, are more focused than visitations. Prospective teachers should have a purpose for each observation session. They may, for instance, be asked to observe and develop a sociogram to depict the group dynamics in a classroom. They may be asked to perform a kind of shadow study by observing and recording the tasks performed by one teacher during a typical day.

Analyzing and critiquing teaching practices, instructional materials, student behavior, and the like are appropriate activities at the third level of the field experience hierarchy. Without the classroom context provided by prior visitations and observations, these activities might be virtually meaningless. It is only within a particular context that the utility of a textbook, a test, or a teaching method can be critiqued. At this level, the prospective teacher begins to see how the puzzle fits together or, in some cases, why it doesn't.

Demonstrations serve as an intermediate step between passive and active participation. As used in this typology, demonstrations are "model" presentations. It is suggested that these be delivered by practicing teachers. Prospective teachers should be provided, or should develop criteria for evaluating the demonstration. If a reading teacher presents a Directed Reading Lesson (DRL), for example, students should be aware of its components.

The next step of the ladder is that of simulation. At this stage, prospective teachers practice teaching behaviors through role playing, microteaching, and other simulated situations. Again, performances can be checked against criteria and feedback provided so that the teacher in training can build on strengths and correct deficiencies.

At the next level of the hierarchy, the student prepares materials for use in the classroom. Such material may include lesson plans, learning centers, tests, audio-visual aids, and so forth. These materials should be developed to meet a particular need in a particular classroom, rather than merely to meet a course requirement. Evaluation of the products should include not only the generic criteria for judging a product of the particular type but also the practical criteria of suitability for the classroom situation.

At the next level of the hierarchy, prospective teachers begin to implement their skills. Early practice may take place in contrived situations, such as tutoring or working with a small group. Such activities should take place in the public school, if at all possible. The student should eventually practice working with the entire class, although the duration of such practice may be limited. Frequent practice in applying skills in the actual classroom setting should precede the formal student teaching period.

As a final step in the progression from student to intern or student teacher, the prospective teacher learns to perform a variety of instructional support tasks such as record-keeping, classroom maintenance, and so forth. He learns the day-to-day routines which accompany the instructional duties of the teacher. Many of these tasks cannot be learned apart from the context in which they occur. That is, it makes little sense to teach one procedure for collecting lunch money or for recording attendance when each school may have a different routine. The performance of tasks such as these are best accommodated in an actual classroom setting. In the model curriculum, the bulk of these activities takes place during the apprenticeship phase of student teaching. The integration and performance of both instructional and support skills is concentrated in the internship phase.

The final major suggestion, that team teaching and other shared-teaching approaches be used, is also related to the trend toward field-based, practical teacher education. Successful implementation of the job-related curriculum requires flexibility in staffing patterns. The practical emphasis of the program and the need for wide exposure to various teaching contexts make it necessary to suspend the "one course—one instructor" dictum. However, staffing flexibility does not necessarily lead to a formalized team-teaching structure. Nor does it mean that every course will require multiple instructors. What it does mean is that the best possible instructor(s) for each course segment should be obtained. For example, one instructor, a school district curriculum coordinator, may be an expert in the design and construction of learning centers. Another instructor, perhaps an elementary reading teacher, may be more skilled in the day-to-day management of learning centers. The strengths of both of these instructors can be tapped through the shared-teaching approach.

In keeping with the overall goals of the teacher education program, instructors involved in shared teaching should represent a variety of personal characteristics, backgrounds, and perspectives. The following list of variables indicates some of the factors which should be considered in determining combinations of instructors: teaching level, employer (university, school district, and so forth), years of experience, variety of experiences, race, national origin, sex, age, and so forth.

A number of assumptions underlie the shared teaching approach. First, the criterion of excellence demands that the best qualified instructors be recruited. The assumption that a professor with expertise in one aspect of course content will automatically be well versed in all other aspects is no longer acceptable. For example, the course Philosophies and Theories Applied to Education investigates a variety of theories and their practical classroom applications. We cannot assume that an instructor who is an expert in Piaget's stages of development is also likely to be an expert in Rogerian counseling techniques. Rather than giving the student a course strong on Piaget but weak in Rogers, the shared-teaching approach will enable the program to provide the best possible instruction in each theory. In some cases, one lecturer might present the theoretical background and then another instructor could cover the practical applications of these concepts. Some coursework lends itself to multidisciplinary examination by a group of instructors.

Because the objectives, content, and evaluation procedures for each course can be specified in advance, it is possible to identify those objectives which are written at the knowledge level. Self-paced instructional modules or programmed materials can be developed to present these content elements. This provides an effective, efficient way of conveying information, thus freeing the instructor's time and energy for higher level objectives such as those at the application level.

Teachers in training will benefit from the shared-teaching approach in many ways. First, this system will introduce them to a greater variety of teaching styles than they would ordinarily encounter. Such exposure is valuable particularly if students are encouraged to analyze the teaching styles of their various instructors. Second, the shared-teaching approach provides an opportunity for students to observe collegial interactions, an important aspect of professional behavior. Team teaching and other cooperative arrangements in the public schools makes it imperative that prospective teachers in training be aware of practices other than the conventional self-contained classroom. Shared teaching can, in a sense, model these alternatives. Another advantage of the shared-teaching approach is that students are likely to benefit from hearing varying perspectives about educational issues and instructional techniques.

As noted at the beginning of this chapter, the "hows" of instruction can be inferred from the "whats." That is, objectives which require only that the student be able to recall information can be accommodated through packaging the content in the form of modules. Objectives which call for application of a principle or skill will often require that the student demonstrate mastery in a lab or actual classroom setting. In addition to the instructional approach inherent in the objective, the instructors are seen as the ultimate decision-makers with regard to selecting appropriate instructional techniques to teach the content. The preplanning completed during the course development phase reduces the amount of team coordination necessary for effective instruction. In effect, the pre-established objectives and content specifications provide the "what" for the instructor or instructors. The "how" should remain, as discussed above, basically their prerogative.

Throughout *Improving Teacher Education,* we have emphasized the importance of working from a data base to design teacher education programs. The data base established for the model job-related curriculum led to the design of a comprehensive professional core of courses to be taken by all prospective teachers. Chapter 9 describes the professional core component. In addition, implications derived from the data base for teaching specializations are considered in Chapter 10. General education requirements are impacted by the data base as well and are examined in Chapter 11. At the inservice level, the job-related competencies can serve as a baseline for designing programs which go beyond entry level requirements. Chapter 12 deals with designing inservice programs and Chapter 13 provides guidelines for evaluating both pre- and inservice program design.

9

The Professional Core Component

Throughout *Improving Teacher Education,* the problem-solving model has been used as a procedural guide. Thus far, our recommendations have included steps for identifying problems in teacher education and some basic procedures for designing appropriate programs to solve these problems. As part of the problem identification stage, a specific listing of required and desired competencies, the "musts" and the "shoulds" of teaching, was provided as an example or prototype of a data base for decision-making.

In this chapter, we present a model professional core which was designed to reduce discrepancies between present and preferred teacher education programs. This model program serves two functions in the book. First, it is a prototype of the job-related curriculum. Some institutions or organizations seeking to change their teacher education programs will find that it meets their needs and will want to implement it as is. Other groups will want to modify or use portions of it to fit specific contexts. For these purposes, the Teacher Resource Guides which have been developed for each of the professional core courses will prove invaluable. The second function of the model curriculum is to serve as a case study of how implications of the data base can be operationalized. The user who opts to use the process to develop an indigenous data base will find the model curriculum useful as an example.

Because of the job-related emphasis of the data base of generic competencies, the professional core is the heart of the recommended teacher education curriculum. As the discussion in Chapters 10 and 11 pertaining to teaching specializations and general education will elaborate, these components are designed to support the professional core. In many conventional programs, the opposite case prevails. That is, courses concentrating on professional skills take a back seat to general education and discipline-centered coursework. Our approach focuses on professional competencies as an integrated body of skills, knowledge, and attitudes rather than as a collection of discrete, unrelated objectives.

The professional core is designed to provide all prospective teachers with the generic competencies they will need as entry level teachers. The assumptions underlying the core components are that the skills prospective teachers need are 1) identifiable, 2) teachable, and 3) assessable. These assumptions may appear so obvious as to be trivial. Many teacher education programs, however, are not derived from identified skills but rather the result of haphazard proliferation. The second assumption, that the competencies teachers need to develop are teachable, is contradictory to the widely accepted notions that 1) teachers are born not made, or that 2) teachers can learn needed skills only through trial and error on the job. Through the job-related approach, identified skills are taught in terms of their classroom applications and prospective teachers are given ample opportunity to practice and refine them. The third basic assumption, that attainment of these skills is assessable, is another distinctive feature of the job-related approach. Evaluation, both of program and student, is integral, rather than incidental, and continuous, rather than casual.

CURRICULUM STRUCTURE: OBJECTIVES

The ultimate objectives are the end goals of the teacher education program. They specify the skills and characteristics the program graduate is expected to demonstrate. On the conceptual level, ultimate objectives indicate the kind of teacher to be produced by the program. Ultimate objectives are also valuable as evaluative criteria against which the actual characteristics of program graduates can be compared.

Contributing to the attainment of ultimate objectives is a series of terminal objectives. Objectives at this level of specificity provide checkpoints in the student's transition from entry level characteristics to exit level characteristics (that is, attainment of ultimate objectives). Most often, terminal objectives are synonymous with course goals; that is, they specify the skills the student will master as a result of the instructional activities in a given course.

In addition, some of the terminal objectives are built into various courses as unifying threads; that is, wherever appropriate they are spiralled through the curriculum. Knowledge and skills pertaining to multicultural education, for example, are developed in the context of various courses such as Human Development and Teaching, Interpersonal Skills for Teachers, Diagnosing Readiness for Learning, Fundamentals of Teaching Reading, and so on. Skills for working with exceptional children in the classroom are also developed in a number of courses.

The most specific type of outcome in the professional core are labelled enabling objectives. A number of related objectives derived from the data base comprise the enabling objectives for each course. Mastery of each enabling objective contributes to the student's attainment of the terminal and ultimate objectives of the program.

Attainment of the ultimate objectives, however, is more than a function of mastering a specified list of enabling objectives. In the job-related approach, the whole is greater than its parts. For example, the ability to integrate various skills as well as the ability to apply them in classroom settings are essential outcomes. These objectives, however, are developed gradually through participation in activities spanning a number of courses.

It is useful, therefore, to make a distinction between the horizontal and the vertical dimensions of the curriculum. The horizontal dimension can be visualized as a linear progression of enabling objectives which lead to the attainment of terminal objectives or course goals. Each of these enabling objectives is taught in sufficient depth for the prospective teacher to achieve mastery. The terminal objectives are generally subtasks of the ultimate objectives. While this explanation is obviously an oversimplification of the relationship among objectives and courses, it does focus on the sequential arrangement of competencies on the horizontal dimension.

The vertical dimension of the curriculum, on the other hand, is concerned with integrating the competencies taught in separate courses. The purpose of this dimension is to ensure that the student will be able to understand the relationships among separate objectives both within and across courses. The vertical dimension focuses on factors such as growth into the role of a teacher, the ability to integrate various competencies, and the ability to apply skills in the classroom. The vertical dimension can be conceptualized as four skill strands which are interwoven throughout the various courses. As the student progresses through the program, his skills in these four areas of functioning are reinforced and broadened. The four skill strands which comprise the vertical dimension are (1) planning skills, (2) implementation skills, (3) assessment skills, and (4) interaction skills. Each course, depending on its content, is made up of objectives which contribute to one or more of these functional skills. Planning skills are called for in a variety of contexts: the teacher plans instructional activities, plans for strengthening student morale, and plans classroom record-keeping and organization routines. Implementation skills include those behaviors most directly identifiable as "teaching." The teacher must present material clearly at an appropriate level of difficulty, use effective questioning techniques, use instructional aids skillfully, and so forth. Assessment skills are necessary for diagnosing a student's reading level, for evaluating instructional material to determine its suitability for a given purpose, and for determining student mastery of specified objectives. Interaction skills enable the teacher to communicate positively and effectively with students, parents, community representatives, colleagues, and administrators.

CURRICULUM STRUCTURE: ACTIVITIES

For ease of presentation, the model professional core will be described as a sequence of twelve courses followed by a two-course sequence of directed teaching. Each of these courses is derived from the data base of required and desired generic competencies (See Chapters 3, 4, and 8). It should be noted, however, that this structure represents only one of several ways in which the competencies could be structured. A number of courses, for example, could be divided into several modules which might be interspersed with modules from other courses. The purpose of presenting the professional core in this manner is that the organization of competencies by courses seems to be both simple and defensible. The institutional policy governing many teacher education programs mandates the semester or quarter-hour system. Variations on this design can be developed by implementing institutions if circumstances indicate the need for modification.

As Figure 9.1 indicates, the suggested professional core course sequence is rather tightly structured. This serves a number of purposes. First, it is an attempt to standardize content without imposing unwarranted restrictions on the delivery technique, which is felt to be a prerogative of the instructor. Second, it avoids needless and wasteful repetition of material, particularly of theory. Since the curriculum is conceived of as a totality, overlap and gaps are minimized. A third advantage of the professional core structure is that field experiences are integrated with coursework throughout the program. Thus, the prospective teacher does not have to wait until his senior year to apply a skill he learned in his sophomore year.

The model professional core is structured so as to accommodate early entry; preferably, students can enter as freshmen. Because of the strong emphasis on early and ongoing field experiences, it is important that students begin their professional training as soon as possible. Certainly variations in the entry point are possible as long as the intent of the professional core is not compromised.

COURSE SEQUENCE AND OVERVIEWS

At this point, the suggested sequence of courses in the professional core is explained along with a brief description of each course. The interested reader may wish to refer to the data base of desired and required competencies (Chapters 3 and 4) to see how these discrete skills are built into the curriculum. Since a number of distinguishing features of the curriculum relate to the required fieldwork, this topic will be addressed separately following the course descriptions.

The initial course in the sequence is Teaching as a Profession. Because it provides an overview of the teaching profession, it should be taken during the student's first semester in the program. This course will give the student realistic information and experiences to assist in making a decision as to

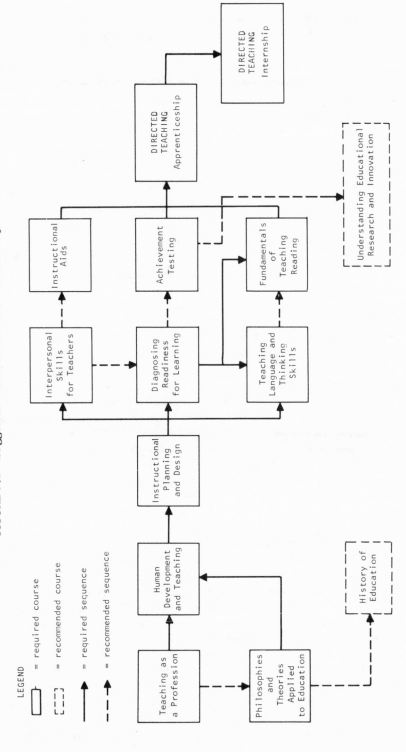

FIGURE 9.1   Suggested Professional Core Course Sequence.

LEGEND

☐ = required course

⌐‾⌐ = recommended course
⌊_⌋

↑ = required sequence

↑ = recommended sequence

Teaching as a Profession

Philosophies and Theories Applied to Education

History of Education

Human Development and Teaching

Instructional Planning and Design

Interpersonal Skills for Teachers

Diagnosing Readiness for Learning

Teaching Language and Thinking Skills

Instructional Aids

Achievement Testing

Fundamentals of Teaching Reading

Understanding Educational Research and Innovation

DIRECTED TEACHING Apprenticeship

DIRECTED TEACHING Internship

whether or not to pursue teaching as a career. This course will also provide the student with a practical framework for all subsequent coursework. This course introduces prospective teachers or those curious about the possibility of pursuing teaching as a career to an overview of the profession. The course content emphasizes a realistic rather than sugar-coated approach. Relevant data about the teacher's job as well as about education in general are covered. The intent of the course is to provide the student with information to enable him to make an informed decision early in his college training as to whether or not teaching is an appropriate career choice. This will hopefully avoid the all-too-common situation which occurs when students plan their undergraduate coursework with false expectations about their potential employability as well as about the realities of classroom teaching. The course includes a variety of field experiences, with an emphasis on visiting a range of public school settings (that is, urban/rural; elementary/middle/secondary; low/high socioeconomic areas, and so on). Content elements to be surveyed in the course include: school organization and administration, school finance, school law, community-school relations, teacher evaluation procedures, certification and recertification requirements, and professional organizations and benefits.

The second course in the suggested sequence is Philosophies and Theories Applied to Education. The course is depicted on Figure 9.1 as a concurrent or subsequent course to Teaching as a Profession. This course introduces the prospective teacher to some major philosophical and theoretical points of view in education. Covering philosophies and theories in a separate course is a rather novel approach at the undergraduate level. One reason this approach is recommended is that it enables students to see the relative contributions of various theories to the explanation of educational processes. In addition this approach will enable instructors of other courses to devote more time to the practical, "how-to" aspects of teaching, thus satisfying one of the basic goals of the job-related curriculum.

In this course, the student investigates the implications of various philosophies such as essentialism and existentialism for school curriculum. This avoids the fallacy of presenting various theories or philosophies as truths. Each theory is presented along with empirical evidence supporting or disputing its various constructs. This approach allows the students to assess the validity of each theory. Classroom applications of theories and taxonomies of motivation, moral development, intellectual development, learning, instruction, student management, and social processes are investigated.

An analysis of the content of various professional core courses revealed that the information to be covered in Philosophies and Theories is logically prerequisite to material in other courses. For example, an understanding of various philosophies of education will be useful background for the student in the History of Education course and will also help him/her understand various curricular emphases discussed in the Instructional Planning and Design course. The theories of Piaget, Freud, and Kohlberg will be useful background for the Human Development and Teaching course as will the work of Skinner, the Gestalt school and the Rogerian school for the Interpersonal

Skills for Teachers course. The team-teaching approach suggested for Philosophies and Theories will ensure expert coverage of each topic, thus allowing the instructors of other courses to concentrate on the operationalizations and applications of theories. The information in this course, together with that of Teaching as a Profession, will satisfy the NASDTEC Standard IId, requiring an "understanding of the foundations underlying the development and organization of education in the U.S."

The recommended course History of American Education could be taken any time in the student's course of study after he/she completes Teaching as a Profession. As mentioned in the above discussion, Philosophies and Theories could be a suggested, but not mandatory, prerequisite for this course. The practice of keeping prerequisites for recommended courses to a minimum will increase the flexibility of the overall curriculum by enabling students to fit recommended courses into their schedules whenever convenient.

The course History of American Education is designed to provide students with an understanding of significant influences on the historical development of the American educational system. One of the major purposes of this course is to enable students to assess the impact of this background on contemporary educational practices and trends. The history of American education is examined in the context of social, political, and cultural circumstances of various periods. Ways in which the clientele, purposes, and practices of education have changed because of these circumstances are also examined. The influence of major contributors to educational thought and practice is another area of investigation. While the content of this course is less directly applicable to classroom exigencies than is that of other courses, it is useful for teachers to have an overall perspective of education as an institution of American society.

Teachers also need to have an understanding of the social, emotional, physical, and intellectual characteristics of the students they will encounter. The course Human Development and Teaching is designed to provide prospective teachers with information about developmental patterns and their implications for learning. A knowledge of learners' characteristics at various developmental stages, however, is necessary but not sufficient. The prospective teacher must also be aware of variations in development which may be influenced by the students' cultural background. Also, although teachers need not be experts in human development, they should be able to detect major symptoms of exceptionality and make appropriate instructional decisions and referrals. Each content element in the course is considered in the context of its implications for teaching techniques appropriate to different-aged learners.

Human Development and Teaching is a pivotal course in this sequencing scheme because the skills and information it covers are vital to a number of other courses and also because it introduces the student to specific characteristics of learners at various age levels, thus giving the potential teacher an opportunity to rethink his/her intended teaching level before selecting an area of specialization. An understanding of the physical, mental, social, and emotional patterns of development of different-aged learners will be needed for the courses Interpersonal Skills for Teachers, Diagnosing Readiness for Learning, and Teaching Language and Thinking Skills. Also, the Human Development course introduces students to individual differences, multicultural differences, and exceptionalities. The specific implications of each of these will be developed in subsequent courses as they apply to teaching language and thinking skills, teaching reading skills, as well as to selecting and constructing achievement tests.

Because of the heavy emphasis on fieldwork throughout the professional core sequence, it is advisable that a course in Instructional Planning and Design be taken preliminary to any so-called "methods" courses. This approach will allow the prospective teacher to apply the skills he has learned in instructional design in a number of other courses before he begins the actual directed teaching phase of his preparation. An awareness of varieties of instructional objectives, materials, and techniques will give the student a more perceptive view of the classroom situations he observes and/or participates in during his subsequent training.

Instructional Planning and Design is intended to provide students with skills needed to plan effective instruction and to design appropriate instructional activities. Based on an assessment of the needs and characteristics of learners, the prospective teacher develops realistic instructional goals. Another fundamental skill area covered in the course is that of writing and sequencing objectives. The appropriate uses of various instructional strategies (such as, lecture, discussion, inquiry, simulation, and so on) are investigated. Students design alternative learning activities to accommodate varying learner needs and instructional objectives. Appropriate applications of various grouping patterns to manage student involvement are also covered. The prospective teacher gains proficiency in assessing learner feedback and in prescribing appropriate correctives to achieve stated objectives. Techniques for evaluating both student progress and instructional effectiveness are incorporated in the course content.

The course Interpersonal Skills for Teachers is suggested at this point in the sequence because the student will find communications and classroom management skills quite useful as he/she begins the intensive fieldwork associated with the remainder of the courses. While field experiences are an integral part of all of the courses, the student will be working directly with small groups of learners, implementing classroom activities, and working directly with public school teachers more frequently as the program progresses.

Interpersonal Skills for Teachers is designed to provide prospective teachers with the skills necessary for communicating with various populations encountered on the job and for effective classroom management. Prospective teachers practice basic communication skills for interacting with learners, parents, colleagues, and administrators. Appropriate verbal and nonverbal behavior in various situations is also explored. Students learn a variety of techniques for effective classroom management, including techniques for establishing a positive classroom climate, techniques for effective decision-making and problem-solving, class discussion methods, techniques for promoting positive self-image, and so on. Prospective teachers, however, also need skills to deal with the less appealing aspects of classroom reality. They need to know, for example, how to deal with conflict, resolve interpersonal problems, and deal with disciplinary emergencies. Teachers also need to learn how cultural differences affect students' behavior in the classroom and how to maintain interpersonal effectiveness in a multicultural setting. In short, the way a teacher relates to others is often the crux of his survival in the classroom and can be a gauge of his effectiveness.

The course Instructional Aids can be seen as relatively independent from other courses and therefore it may be advisable to allow the student to take it whenever convenient. However, the argument can be made that this course should be taken before the student enrolls in Diagnosing Readiness for Learning, Achievement Testing, Teaching Language and Thinking Skills, and Fundamentals of Teaching Reading because familiarity with materials and other aids will assist him/her in completing the instructional activities required in these courses.

Using instructional technology and human resources effectively in the classroom are skill areas teachers in training need to develop. In the course Using Instructional Aids, students learn to operate a range of audio-visual equipment and simple office machines (such as, duplicator, typewriter, and so forth). Where facilities are available, prospective teachers can also benefit from an introduction to the use of computers in education. Students also learn to plan and construct various instructional aids such as learning centers, bulletin boards, charts, and so forth. Criteria for evaluating the appropriateness of materials, such as textbooks, programmed materials, and workbooks, for a given instructional purpose are also covered. In addition, the prospective teacher learns techniques for taking advantage of various community resources in lesson planning. Techniques for coordinating plans with paraprofessionals and other resource personnel are also a part of the course.

In the last decade, the need for teachers to be able to assess students' readiness for learning has become increasingly apparent. All teachers, not just specialized personnel, should have the necessary skills to determine whether and when a student or group is ready to move on to the next skill, unit, topic, or activity. In this sense, readiness to learn is a generalized construct which is not limited to the early childhood period. While more attention has been focused on diagnosing readiness to learn at this stage of development than on any other, interest in individualized instruction and diagnostic/prescriptive teaching have made it crucial that all teachers develop these skills. In the course Diagnosing Readiness for Learning, the major factors which influence readiness are explored as well as major manifestations of learning characteristics and disorders. The student becomes familiar with the specific readiness skills and subskills as they apply to his intended area of specialization. Various types of informal and formal diagnostic instruments and techniques are investigated. Students practice selecting, administering, scoring, and interpreting the results of diagnostic instruments. The analysis of diagnostic findings for purposes of placement, prescribing appropriate instruction, and making referrals is another skill area covered in the course.

Diagnosing Readiness for Learning will provide the student with observational and diagnostic skills which will be useful in Teaching Language and Thinking Skills and in Fundamentals of Teaching Reading. This order is suggested because the former course will provide the student with a background on linguistics and cognition which will be helpful in the reading course.

A course in Achievement Testing is also included in the professional core. The ability to select or construct, administer, score, and interpret achievement tests has always been an expectation of the teacher. In recent years, moreover, the emphasis on competency-based education, criterion-referenced testing, and educational accountability has made it even more incumbent on training programs to provide teachers with essential skills in measurement and evaluation. Basic concepts and purposes of achievement testing are included in the course along with coverage of the relationship between objectives and test items. Students learn proper procedures for constructing various item types. Skills for using commercial standardized tests appropriately are also practiced. Procedures for marking students and reporting grades is another area of emphasis.

In the classroom, one of the teacher's most challenging tasks is to teach students to reason and to communicate their thinking processes effectively. In Teaching Language and Thinking Skills, students learn to apply procedures for teaching learners a variety of thinking skills necessary for concept formation. Essential to this is an understanding of the interrelationships between the learner's cognitive and language development as well as the influence of one's experiential background on this development. In the course, prospective teachers practice procedures for teaching learners: (1) to distinguish between denotative and connotative meanings of words, (2) to recall information, (3) to observe and compare, (4) to categorize, (5) to reason sequentially, (6) to reason causally, (7) to reason deductively, and (8) to reason inductively. The student develops a taxonomy of the mental processes listed above with accompanying words and structures that signal these processes. In addition, the student analyzes instructional materials and activities to determine the thinking processes they elicit from the learner.

The course Fundamentals of Teaching Reading is derived from evidence in the data base indicating that "all teachers should be teachers of reading." Prospective teachers are introduced to the skills and processes of reading and learn basic methods of teaching reading skills. Techniques for planning reading instruction and for incorporating reading and study skills in content areas are also included in the course. The entry level classroom teacher is not expected to be an expert in the diagnosis and remediation of reading deficiencies. He should, however, be able to make informed decisions about instructional strategies based on the reading levels and abilities of his students.

An understanding of the role of research in educational theory and practice is also useful knowledge for prospective teachers to acquire. The recommended course, Understanding Educational Research and Innovation, explicates the nature of the research process and provides a conceptual and procedural framework for examining its relevance to education. Students learn to critique research reports in various professional journals and other documents. Basic statistical concepts and their applications are covered. In addition, the prospective teacher develops a simple research design for testing innovations in the classroom. Through the experiences and content of the course, the prospective teacher learns how to compare new with traditional procedures and to draw defensible interpretations as to the relative effectiveness of each.

The Directed Teaching stage of the professional core is a two-sequence course that includes apprenticeship and internship. During the semester the prospective teacher serves as an apprentice, he assists a supervising teacher in carrying out supportive services in the classroom.

The student performs record-keeping duties, files materials, duplicates materials, and assists in general classroom maintenance. In addition, the apprentice practices supervisory roles such as monitoring study halls, corridors, cafeterias, playgrounds, and fire drills. The apprentice also assists with extracurricular activities such as field trips and student organizations. The apprentice also develops plans and materials for use during his internship. In short, the apprentice "learns the ropes" from the supervising teacher. This approach recognizes that many teacher's tasks which are not directly related to instruction can only be learned "on the job." By practicing these functions prior to the actual instructional phase of directed teaching, the student will be less likely to be overwhelmed by the demands of the student teaching experience.

During the internship segment of Directed Teaching, the student has an opportunity to integrate the skills he has developed in previous coursework and field experiences. Under the supervision of a cooperating teacher and a faculty member, the intern gradually assumes major responsibility for classroom teaching. The intern diagnoses readiness for learning, prepares lessons, teaches, provides supportive services, and evaluates achievement. The demarcation between the apprenticeship and internship phases is useful for student teachers, cooperating teachers, and learners in that it provides a symbolic change of status, thus smoothing the role transition.

INTEGRATING COURSEWORK AND FIELDWORK

A distinctive feature of the professional core is that a laboratory section is required for each course. Figure 9.2 relates appropriate professional lab-field experiences with professional core courses. The purpose of these labs is to facilitate the student's application of knowledge and skills covered in coursework. While this purpose is widely espoused as a part of conventional courses, it is rarely implemented. Because of the pressure to cover course material and the logistical difficulties of arranging field experiences, instructors fre-

FIGURE 9.2 Laboratory/field experiences.

Course Title	Visitations	Classroom Observations	Analysis, Critique of Teaching Practices, Materials, Tests, etc.	Demonstrations	Simulations, Role Playing, Micro-teaching, etc.
Teaching as a Profession	X				
Philosophies and Theories Applied to Education	X	X	X		
Human Development and Teaching	X	X	X		
History of American Education	X		X		
Interpersonal Skills for Teachers		X	X	X	X
Instructional Planning and Design		X	X	X	
Instructional Aids			X	X	
Diagnosing Readiness for Learning		X	X	X	
Fundamentals of Teaching Reading		X	X	X	X
Teaching Language and Thinking Skills		X	X	X	
Achievement Testing			X		
Understanding Educational Research and Innovation			X		
Directed Teaching: Apprenticeship		X	X		
Directed Teaching: Internship			X		

quently abandon their intentions to encompass field experiences in a course. In many cases, students are expected to arrange and execute field experiences on their own. This, however, can lead to public relations difficulties between sponsoring agency and school districts since the relative lack of organization and planning can be burdensome to administrators, classroom teachers, and prospective teachers alike. Assignments such as "make arrangements to go to a school, tutor a student with a reading problem for three weeks, and write a report on it" still too commonly pass for fieldwork. The lack of specificity, structure, and sensitivity in such assignments can render them dysfunctional to all participants.

The mechanics of implementing the lab sections must be carefully planned

FIGURE **9.2** **(continued)**

Production of Materials (AV, Tests, etc.)	Implementation/ Administration of Materials	Performing Instructional Support Tasks	Working with Individual Learners	Working with Small Groups of Learners	Working with a Whole Class
X	X				
X	X				
X	X		X		
X	X		X		
X	X			X	
X	X				X
X					
X	X	X	X	X	X
X	X	X	X	X	X

in relation to a number of factors. First, consideration should be given to the basis on which they will be organized, since this will influence many of the other criteria. It should be remembered that professional core courses are taught to a heterogeneous group of prospective teachers. Thus, the lab provides one means for the student to practice applying generic skills in specialized areas. That is, he applies these generic skills to the early childhood, secondary business, physical education, or other content.

Depending on specific conditions or needs, the labs can be organized in various ways. Regardless of the organizational approach selected, however, the lab setting should provide access to instructional materials and other resources for the prospective teacher. Supervision of the teacher-in-training as he carries out instructional and noninstructional tasks is also a requirement. Another fundamental role of the lab staff is to function as a liason between the sponsoring institution and the school district.

In some cases, a so-called "laboratory school" is available for the prospective teacher to practice professional skills. These schools are operated jointly by school districts and universities or may be under the direct auspices of the latter. Rising costs of maintaining such schools and other complications have, however, taken their toll. These "lab schools" provided prospective teachers with a theoretically ideal situation for using their newly acquired competencies in a school setting under supervised conditions.

One common criticism, however, was that the lab school too frequently existed in a kind of "hot house" environment removed from real world problems. Many such schools were populated by the community elite, such as doctors', lawyers', and professors' children. Supervising teachers were exemplary and the support provided the practicing teacher was atypical. Another concern which often beset the lab school was the "guinea pig" complaint. This criticism, which is a common criticism of practice and beginning teachers as well as of innovative programs, holds that students suffer when they are made the subjects of experimentation or practice. Despite the fact that enrollment in lab schools was frequently voluntary, the lack of continuity associated with frequent teacher turnover exacerbated this "guinea pig" effect.

Another possible organizational structure for accommodating field experiences is that of the individualized laboratory approach. The laboratory may be located in the preservice training institution or in a school district location. Students enrolled in any professional core course would develop a contract for accomplishing the required fieldwork. Laboratory staff would be responsible for making necessary arrangements with local schools, providing necessary materials and equipment, and supervising the prospective teacher's field activities.

While there are obvious advantages to this approach, such as the personalized nature of the program, certain disadvantages are also present. In many cases, the necessary personnel, financial, and physical resources simply are not available. A poorly staffed and equipped individualized program can be worse than none at all, since students are neither adequately supervised nor able to benefit from group interaction. If a well-staffed, well-equipped individualized laboratory is not feasible, another approach, perhaps less appealing but more workable, should be tried.

Another alternative is to arrange lab sections by area and level of specialization within each course. Using this approach, the prospective teachers will perform some kinds of lab assignments, such as simulations and microteaching, in the lab and others in the field. All students in a particular course, such as Fundamentals of Teaching Reading, would attend class sessions together but attend different lab sections. The exact breakdown of lab sections would depend to a great extent on factors such as the numbers and specializations of students in the class, the logical divisions of content, and school-oriented differentiations. In the reading course, for example, sections may be needed for early childhood, elementary, middle, and secondary levels. An alternate plan would be to retain early childhood and elementary labs, but differentiate middle and secondary on an alternative basis, such as content specialization. All middle/secondary teachers who might be directly involved in reading instruction (such as English majors) could comprise one section while all those who would be teaching peripheral reading skills in their fields of specialization could comprise another section. The flexibility of the small group lab permits the adjustment of the lab component to the "real world" requirements of the course content.

In some professional core courses, dividing students by area and level of specialization does not seem necessary. In the Teaching as a Profession course, an introductory survey of the profession, it seems unlikely that students would have selected an area of specialization at this point. Since one of the course objectives is to provide as wide a perspective about career options as possible, premature grouping is counterproductive. Other courses which would not necessarily require labs separated by specializations include History of American Education, Interpersonal Skills for Teachers, and Understanding Educational Research and Innovation.

The coursework and fieldwork encompassed by the professional core provide a foundation of generic skills needed by the entry level teacher. These skills, however central they may be to the professional development of the teacher, are not the entire teacher training program. In Chapter 10, Teaching Specializations, and Chapter 11, The General Education Component, we will describe the contributions of these components to the achievement of the ultimate objectives of the curriculum.

For each of the professional core courses, more detailed information and materials needed to facilitate instruction is available in the form of Teacher Resource Guides. Included in the guides are detailed course descriptions having general descriptive information, sequenced objectives, course content and instructional activities, recommended texts and other readings, course requirements and suggested dates, and scheduling of instruction by topic. Procedures and/or techniques for the evaluation of assignments including item banks, rating scales, or checklists as appropriate. All assignments and evaluation mechanisms are keyed to the course objectives and tables of specifications are provided for item banks. In addition, resources—texts, periodical references, exercises, tapes, films, and other materials which will facilitate the teaching-learning process—are recommended for each instructional topic. These guides were developed by subject matter experts in conjunction with curriculum and instructional design specialists and evaluators and can be used to implement the professional core courses as designed or to provide ideas and resources for comparable courses. The evaluation mechanisms designed to assess the attainment of professional core course objectives have provided the basis for the development of the Generic Competencies Examination for Teachers—an instrument originally designed for but not limited to teacher certification.

10

Teaching Specializations

The function of the professional core, as explained in Chapter 9, is to provide the prospective teacher with generic competencies which have been identified as essential for the entry level teacher to possess. Looking at the array of subjects taught in the public schools as well as at the range of student characteristics, one wonders whether generic competencies will suffice. Obviously they will not. The skills required for teaching students in auto mechanics to repair a carburetor differ considerably from the skills required for teaching first graders to distinguish among vowel sounds. While there are certain pedagogical techniques which can be applied to quite different subject areas, there are also unique concepts and procedures appropriate to each teaching specialization.

The term "teaching specialization" encompasses any field of concentration, discipline, or area of endorsement which can lead to certification as a teacher. In terms of the relative degree of preparation required for teaching specializations, we have divided our discussion into two sections: (1) the area of specialization or major concentration of coursework, and (2) the cognate area or minor concentration of coursework. The area of specialization is designed to provide depth in one discipline or breadth across a number of relevant disciplines (as for the elementary teacher). The cognate area, an option in the program, is complementary to the area of specialization. Its principal purposes are to provide career flexibility to the teacher and staffing flexibility to the school district.

Because of the recognition that generic skills need to be supplemented with specific skills, the professional core of the curriculum is designed to be interactive with the various teaching specializations. This is a departure from many conventional programs which promote an almost total separation between the two. Built into every course in the professional core are assignments and field activities to be applied in the prospective teacher's area of specialization. In the course Diagnosing Readiness for Learning, for example, all students will learn the common principles and generic procedures needed to assess informally students' readiness to learn whatever objective is to be taught. The student will apply or practice these skills, however, within the context of his intended area of specialization. The prospective secondary biology teacher, for example, will become familiar with the skills and subskills commonly taught in high school biology. He will also learn what mental or physical processes are required to execute these skills and will learn techniques for determining where individual students stand in reference to these skills and the processes. These diagnostic techniques will be used with "real" secondary biology students in actual classroom settings or in lab situations. An elementary education major in the same course will apply diagnostic techniques with learners at the grade level he intends to teach.

This approach may obviate the need for a specific course in "methods and materials" of a particular subject area. Because of NASDTEC/NCATE stipulations, however, these courses will most likely remain in the curriculum. The student's exposure through field experiences to methods as they are practiced and materials as they are used in the actual classroom will provide a more realistic orientation than has usually been the case in methods courses. Discrepancies between "the way it is" and "the way it should be" can be brought into the open and dealt with before the student begins his apprenticeship experience. Thus, much of the culture shock associated with student teaching can be circumvented.

CONSIDERATIONS IN DEVELOPING AREA OF SPECIALIZATION REQUIREMENTS

Establishing requirements for teaching specializations is complicated by the various dimensions of specialization. A prospective teacher specializes in terms of 1) age or grade level, 2) content area(s), and increasingly, 3) type of learner or teaching setting. The first dimension, that of grade level, is the most obvious and sometimes results in some rather misleading generalizations. It is often assumed, for example, that the secondary teacher needs less in the way of learning theory and other pedagogically oriented coursework than does the elementary teacher. Yet it is often secondary teachers whose commitment to "imparting subject matter" is jeopardized by a lack of instructional versatility. On the other hand, another common assumption is that elementary teachers need little in the way of academic background. Bulletin board construction, story telling skills, and a touch of Piaget will suffice, so this line of thinking goes. Yet, as Combs (1965) points out:

The elementary teacher has a specialty. It is teaching general education. For this he needs preparation in breadth over a number of subjects rather than depth in one or two, but few colleges are organized to provide this for him. Courses in the various subject-matter departments are generally designed with majors in mind and tend to become increasingly specialized, so that the student who should spread his attention over a number of areas can seldom acquire the kind of experience he needs. . . . The elementary teacher's specialization in general education is legitimate and necessary. It is a different order of specialization but surely not a less important one! The content required for general education is not less, only broader. (p. 44)

The third dimension of specialization, one which has come into prominence only in recent years, is that of providing prospective teachers with specialized skills appropriate to the kinds of learners and educational settings they expect to encounter. Building a base of generic teaching skills, this approach to specialization prepares teachers to work in contexts such as the following:

1.   In individualized settings

2.   In team-teaching programs

3.   In federal programs (such as Title I)

4.   In various communities (such as, rural, urban, suburban)

5.   In various socioeconomic settings

6.   In bilingual programs

7.   In multicultural settings

8.   In mainstreamed situations (that is, with learning disabled, educably retarded, visually impaired, and so on).

Many of the variables listed above have been virtually ignored in preservice teacher training. Yet the ability to adapt to one or more of these contexts is often critical to a teacher's classroom functioning. Today, specialization along these lines is a trend in undergraduate teacher training. In the job-related curriculum model, this dimension of specialization is accommodated through the careful structuring of relevant course and fieldwork and in the provision for a cognate area.

Not only are the dimensions of specialization a concern, but there are also significant issues to be considered within each teaching specialization. One of the basic determinations to be made in developing preservice programs is that of the scope and nature of the area of specialization knowledge needed by the prospective teacher. A crucial distinction must be recognized within each area of specialization. The NCATE (1977) standard concerning "Content for the Teaching Specialty" specifies these two kinds of knowledge: "One is the knowledge that is to be taught to the pupil; the other is the knowledge that may be needed by the teacher as a background for teaching his particular specialty" (p. 5). It is interesting, but not surprising, that NCATE mentions the teaching content component of the area of specialization first with almost incidental reference to background knowledge in the field of concentration. A look at college catalogs listing required courses for teachers, particularly secondary teachers, in various specializations will quickly reveal which side of this coin college faculties emphasize.

A frequent source of disillusionment for the beginning teacher is the realization that what he has been taught is not what he is supposed to teach. Most of the disciplinary content he has mastered, according to Smith (1969), must be put on the back burner when he enters the classroom:

> It functions in the teacher's mind as marginal knowledge, not as instructional content. Also, the subject matter actually taught to pupils is not always the same as that contained in the courses of the disciplines. . . . To go from the disciplines to the content of instruction involves a tremendous burden of translation. A teacher must sift out what is directly relevant to his work even for the purposes of his own interpretive background. Only in part can the content of the disciplines be adapted to the child's level of knowledge and experience. (pp. 119, 122)

In many professions, coursework in the major area is clearly and directly relevant to expected on-the-job performance. Health fields, engineering, social work, and other typical four-year preprofessional programs are generally quite focused in this respect. The prospective teacher, particularly an intended secondary teacher, finds himself in a quite different situation. In most institutions he must take virtually the same coursework as a liberal arts major in the field. This in and of itself is not necessarily detrimental. Indeed, many have argued that the teacher's subject matter background should be equal in all respects to that of the nonteacher.

The problem, rather, is that the prospective teacher rarely is provided a framework for differentiating between instructional content and background knowledge. This lack of differentiation leads all too frequently to the phenomenon of the high school teacher who wonders bitterly why the notes he painstakingly took from an outstanding professor are greeted with indifference or hostility when presented as a lecture to a high school class. The "blaming the victim" syndrome can occur when the teacher's training has not stressed the importance of communicating subject matter at an appropriate level of difficulty and of relating the subject matter to students' interests and to "real life" applications.

Another fundamental issue to be faced in attempting to develop a teaching specialization course of study appropriate to the needs of the prospective teacher is that of overt or covert conflict between education and disciplinary specialists. While NCATE refers somewhat glibly to the "joint responsibility for determining the content of a teaching specialty that is peculiarly relevant to teaching" (NCATE, 1977, p. 5), political realities and philosophical differences often make such a cooperative effort almost impossible. Not only is there a long-standing tradition on many campuses of mutual scorn between the so-called educationists and academicians, but there is also an increasingly urgent competition between them for students and resources. Donavan speaks of the "disciplinary chauvinism and/or myopia that pervades academe" and wonders what sort of "academic Sadie Hawkins Day" might overcome this impasse (Hunt, 1972, p. 221). In his critique of teacher education, Conant (1963) also focuses on this issue, particularly as it impacts on the prospective teacher when he takes courses in an area of specialization:

> Teachers are practitioners. Their concern is with the dissemination, application, and use of information. It is hoped they might be scholars too, but not in the same sense as one would expect of the student preparing to spend his life in research. This view of the uses of subject matter often lands the education student right in the middle of the practitioner-scholar controversy. . . . In all innocence he may find himself sitting in classes surrounded by students who see themselves as scholars, experts, and scientists and who hold education students in contempt. He may even be so unlucky as to find that the professor himself subscribes to such attitudes. (p. 48)

Another of the principal dilemmas in developing a comprehensive program spanning various teaching specializations is the difficulty of arriving at a consensus within each discipline or field. Controversies rage or simmer within numerous disciplines in the sciences, humanities, and social sciences as to what should be taught and how it should be taught. These concerns affect the nature of the college preparation the teacher receives and are even more evident and problematic in public school classroom application. In many fields, it seems, there is not a recognized "state of the art" but rather an ongoing and dysfunctional "debate of the art."

Another concern is the chasm between the recommendations made in "methods and materials" courses and the exigencies of classroom application. Teachers in training are frequently immersed in an approach to teaching subject matter which turns out to be counterproductive in the classroom. A typical example of this phenomenon is the prospective English teacher who has had little college level exposure to grammar of any sort. Literature is most likely the major emphasis of his coursework. The orientation in his required linguistics or history of language coursework is likely to be structural grammar. In the methods and materials course, he will be introduced to research findings which dispute the effectiveness of traditional grammar instruction. Yet, when this trainee begins student teaching, he usually inherits a traditional grammar textbook and students whose previous exposure, however inadequate, has been to traditional grammar. The student teacher finds himself in a quandary. To survive in the classroom he must renounce his disciplinary indoctrination. One can envision the "devil *vs.* angel" debate going on in his head, personified as the cooperating teacher against the college supervisor.

These issues provide a backdrop for the program design specialist's task. The process for determining areas of specialization should attempt to reconcile varying points of view which are inevitable within and among fields of concentration. The ultimate concern, however, should be that of developing teaching specialization requirements which will best prepare the prospective teacher to fulfill his classroom responsibilities.

A PROCEDURE FOR TEACHING
SPECIALIZATION PROGRAM DESIGN

Each area of specialization has specific requirements; these may vary greatly from one field of concentration to another. Thus, a procedure for determining what coursework, field experiences, and so forth should be included in any particular area of specialization is more useful than a description of a particular institution's requirements. This procedure can be followed by any institution seeking to initiate or revamp one area of specialization or to establish parameters for a number of fields of concentration. It should be noted that the procedures provided for determining areas of specialization can also be used to identify suitable cognate areas. It may be found, for example, that there is insufficient support for offering a particular area of specialization but that there is enough evidence of its viability to justify offering a cognate in the area.

Step 1: Identify Target Areas of Specialization

The first step in this procedure is to identify the target teaching specializations. It is becoming essential in today's era of retrenchment that teacher training institutions eliminate poorly functioning programs and initiate or strengthen those which the institution can operate effectively. An analysis of supply-demand projections in various fields of education is useful information for determining which areas of concentration should be offered. Projections of national and sometimes regional trends are available from sources such as the Research Division of the National Education Association (NEA), the Association for School, College, and University Staffing (ASCUS) Research Committee, and, of course, the United States Office of Education (OE).

While national trends provide a context, the state and local supply-demand picture is of more immediate concern to the decision-maker. Often, however, area-specific information of this type is not available. The investigator can get some indication of supply-demand trends by collecting and analyzing relevant data. Useful demographic data may be available through a number of government agencies.

Long-range plans developed by state departments of education, local school districts, and intermediate districts often provide indicators of curricular areas which are to be strengthened in coming years. Within a given institution's service area, for example, an analysis of the long-range plans of a number of school districts may indicate the need for more teachers in programs for gifted, vocational, and bilingual students. Pending state legislation and policies under consideration by local school boards can also provide indicators of the direction educational programs seem to be taking.

Another technique for obtaining information as to fields offering adequate potential employability is to survey superintendents, personnel supervisors, and principals in a particular service area. These officials can provide a field-oriented perspective of present and projected areas of over- and undersupply. This procedure is a useful check on the trends identified in other ways. Officials responsible for hiring teachers frequently have an almost intuitive grasp of present and future employment needs.

Another reason for soliciting the impressions of principals and other district officials is that they are usually keenly aware of identified or potential areas of deficiency in their programs or staffing capacity. Such deficiencies, for example, may be cited in self-studies or in evaluations conducted by regional accrediting agencies.

Equipped with this kind of information, the decision-maker will have a rational basis for determining which teaching specializations can and should be offered. It cannot be denied, however, that tradition (and the presence of tenured faculty) will play a large role in determining what specializations are offered. A small college, for example, may persist in offering a major in music education despite the fact that very few students enroll in the program. Such a school may have had, over the years, a fine reputation in music education. Changes in the student body and employment opportunities, however, may have drawn the potential music students into other areas. Maintaining the program, particularly because of the specialized skills and the equipment needed, can become a tremendous drain on the institution's already stretched resources.

This example points out the need for objectivity in establishing target areas of specialization. This is particularly true in light of the program-specific accreditation practices of NCATE. Weak programs hurt both the institution and its graduates. Target areas of specialization, then, should be limited to those which the institution can effectively operate and which promise a reasonable probability of employment opportunities for graduates.

Step 2: Determine Fundamental Content and Skills for Each Area

After possible areas of specialization have been identified, the next step is to survey practicing public school teachers in these areas to determine their perceptions of the fundamental content and skills prospective teachers need in order to perform effectively. One should expect, however, significant variations and even outright contradictions within each area of specialization. Although it may seem paradoxical, it is easier to secure agreement as to generic skills than it is to reach a consensus as to the appropriate content and skills needed to teach elementary social studies, for example. This, of course, is partly due to the different orientations which are evident in each discipline.

While practicing teachers are a primary source of information regarding appropriate area of specialization requirements, further screening steps are advisable. The program development specialist should realize that teachers may be attuned to both the "what is" and the "should be" in their generic skills. However, in their area of specialization it is probable that they will be more aligned to the "what is." Many practicing teachers might be out of touch with new developments in their fields of concentration. They might also be unduly influenced by the particular materials they have at their disposal. A teacher who has access only to traditional grammar textbooks, for example, may be reluctant to recommend that a prospective teacher be well versed in structural grammar even though he may realize its potential value.

Teachers' recommendations for the area of specialization tend to be limited by what they perceive as feasible in their own situations. ("Why teach a prospective teacher innovative methods when the other teachers don't know how to use them." "We'd like to try this method but we'll never get the board to approve the necessary textbooks," and so forth.) Because of a number of factors, classroom teachers tend to opt for the *status quo* in recommending an area of specialization preparation.

Step 3: Investigate Recommended Courses of Study for Each Area

The third step in developing areas of specialization programs is to obtain expert opinion as to an appropriate course of study for prospective teachers in each field. The most likely source of up-to-date, nationally representative opinion is incorporated in the guidelines for teacher preparation issued by many subject area professional associations. Most of these organizations have formulated recommended requirements which incorporate the findings of research in the field as well as the opinions of subject matter experts and practitioners. Most of these groups include classroom teachers in their membership as well as others in the field. The list presented in Appendix G includes some of the respected professional associations in various fields.

Guidelines provided by such associations, however, vary greatly from field to field. Some organizations present only general recommendations while others are quite rigid in their suggested requirements. In some cases, the guidelines represent a philosophical approach to the field which may or may not be realistic in particular local circumstances. For example, a strongly auditory foreign language emphasis in the preparation of language teachers may be unrealistic if prospective teachers are to teach in schools which do not have language laboratories or other appropriate equipment. Again, the "way it is" and "way it should be" are often quite discrepant.

Another source of comprehensive and up-to-date information regarding recommended courses of study is the opinions of experts in various subject areas. Experts may include practitioners of the field (such as chemists, writers, statisticians, and so forth) as well as professors in the various subject areas who are familiar with current practices and trends in the field. One matter which should be considered when assessing the utility of these recommendations is the relative success of various curriculum development projects which have used the "expert in the field" approach. For example, the so-called "new math" which has recently been abandoned by many schools, was developed by math theoreticians. Massive retraining programs were required to orient inservice teachers to the new approach. However, student weaknesses on standardized achievement tests in math, which stressed computational skills (such as with the "old math"), led to disillusionment with the new techniques. (One might argue that what was needed was not a return to the old math, but rather the development of tests which would measure the skills taught.)

Step 4: Filter Recommendations According to Established Standards

After the recommendations of various experts have been compiled, the next step is to filter these suggestions through NCATE and NASDTEC standards as well as any applicable state mandated certification requirements. One point program development specialists should be aware of is that many professional associations have developed their suggested programs in accordance with NASDTEC/NCATE standards. While this obviously is a convenience for program developers, it also has been a target of some concern. Much criticism of current teacher education programs has centered on the incestuous relationships which have developed among various professional and accrediting agencies, including NEA, AACTE, NCATE, NASDTEC, and certain disciplinary organizations. One report by the Study Commission on Undergraduate Education and the Education of Teachers (1976), for example, claims:

> The extant advice, recommendations, and guidelines from professional societies have their primary source in federally funded projects dating from the 1960's in which, for the most part, NASDTEC worked with a number of professional societies to develop guidelines for teacher education in various discipline-oriented specialties. The advice which is professional society-oriented almost always has to do with courses taken by teachers in arts and sciences to fulfill so-called "teaching majors." Some societies come perilously close to listing not only what departments must be present but what courses must be offered. . . . Such prescription not only has a strong effect on what courses will be offered within a "discipline" or department—and therefore also on what courses will be left out; the suggestion or prescription of what courses are to be offered inhibits, if it does not absolutely prohibit, interdisciplinary developments, particularly efforts to create some organic merging of the traditional functions of departments or of colleges of arts and sciences and colleges of education as they undertake task-oriented activities to meet the needs of clients in the field. (p. 117)

The guidelines of various associations, then, should be considered advisory rather than obligatory. Their applicability to the institutional and environmental context should be thoroughly considered.

Step 5: Synthesize Findings

The final step, and perhaps the most difficult, of this process is that of evaluating the various recommendations, reconciling them, and coordinating the resultant courses of study with professional core and general education requirements. This phase of the procedure should involve faculty responsible for professional training as well as representatives of each specific area of specialization. It is beyond the scope of this book to delineate particular courses appropriate to each area of specialization. It is hoped, however, that this suggested procedure will be useful in devising courses of study which meet the dual criteria of feasibility and relevance.

As mentioned above, the procedures used to determine area of specialization requirements can also provide information useful for targeting cognate areas. In the model job-related curriculum, a prospective teacher may or may not elect to add a cognate area to his area of specialization. Institutions seeking to adapt the model, however, will need to consider applicable institutional and state mandates in establishing cognate requirements. As presented in the model curriculum, a cognate consists of at least the minimum number of courses in a subject area required for certification. Thus, the traditional minor or endorsement in a field of study or a series of courses leading to a particular role specialization would constitute a cognate. The purposes of the cognate, in practical terms, is to increase the potential teacher's flexibility and thus enhance his employability. District officials responsible for hiring teachers frequently seek candidates who can fulfill more than one role in the school. Most of the cognates developed as part of the model curriculum are functional in nature as opposed to the more conventional disciplinary minor field. This is in keeping with the trend toward role specialization in public school systems. In team teaching or other differentiated staffing situations, the different cognate backgrounds of each teacher could contribute immensely to smooth and effective operations. Thus, benefits accrue for the teacher, in terms of increased employability, and for the school and student, it terms of more diversified competencies of the staff which can be translated into broader curricular offerings and supportive services.

DESCRIPTION OF SAMPLE COGNATE AREAS

While an exhaustive cataloging of possible teaching specializations is neither feasible nor appropriate, a brief description of sample cognate areas may provide the reader with a clearer understanding of their intent.

Eight new cognate areas were developed by the Job-Related Curriculum Project. The procedures described above were used to identify cognate areas which would enhance the prospective teacher's employability and add flexibility to the public school program. It should be reemphasized, however, that different cognates may be appropriate in other school or regional settings. The eight cognate areas identified by the job-related curriculum include:

1. Home-School Relations

2. Media Arts

3. Multicultural Education

4. Athletic Coaching

5. Reading

6. Rehabilitation Services

7. School Guidance

8. Special Education

Each of these areas will be described briefly to demonstrate that cognates or minors can be developed in areas other than the traditional disciplines (that is, English, social sciences, mathematics, and so on). Certainly, minors in traditional areas can be retained. They, along with the various areas of specialization, should be scrutinized periodically to see if they are actually filling a need in the schools.

A cognate in Home-School Relations is one of the recommended areas. While this field of study can supplement any area of specialization, it is a particularly useful adjunct to the Early Childhood major. By completing this cognate, prospective teachers become aware of family dynamics and their influence on the child's development. Working effectively with parents is another emphasis of this program. The suggested course sequence begins with the course Family Life Education: A Developmental Process. In this course, students investigate social policies which affect children and their families. The principles, practices, and content of the family life curriculum are explored with an emphasis on their implications for teaching. A second course, Parental Involvement in Education, examines various aspects of parent involvement/education programs. Research pertaining to family-school relationships is reviewed.

Additional coursework in Family Guidance strengthens the prospective teacher's ability to understand and work with the child and his family. Other courses appropriate to this cognate include The Psychology of Marriage and Sociology of the Family. A Practicum in Family Living Styles is also recommended to provide the student with exposure to a variety of family norms, values, and roles. Throughout this cognate sequence, the development of effective interpersonal skills is stressed.

Another cognate area with growing promise is that of Media Arts. Educational technology has tremendous potential for revolutionizing instruction. The application of performing arts techniques to teaching is also gaining wide support. Schools need personnel who are qualified to operate and care for a variety of audio-visual equipment as well as to plan and create instructional resources. Strong skills in this area enhance a teaching candidate's employability. To ensure a balanced yet cohesive background, prospective teachers should select courses representing at least three of the following areas: scripting, directing, performance, audio, video, photography, film, and graphics. Practical experience in using these skills in the school setting is a necessity. Prospective teachers must be aware of the logistical constraints and resource limitations they may have to contend with in the "real life" school situation.

The need for teachers who are aware of and able to accommodate the needs of students from a variety of cultural backgrounds has become increasingly apparent during the past two decades. Teachers need to develop skills for relating to students from different ethnic groups, socioeconomic groups, sexes, religions, lifestyles, and locales (inner city, rural, and so forth). Skills for facilitating positive intergroup relations among students are also vital. A cognate in Multicultural Education is designed to provide prospective teachers with the understandings and skills for effective teaching in a pluralistic school setting.

The first course suggested in the multicultural cognate sequence is Educational Anthropology. In this course, the prospective teacher is introduced to a rationale for a multicultural approach to teaching, classroom ethnography, bilingualism, communication across cultural boundaries, and learning style variations. The second suggested course, Teaching Multicultural Classes, provides the teacher-in-training with an array of competencies for effective teaching in the pluralistic classroom. This course emphasizes field experiences to give the student a "real life" perspective of the practical problems which may arise in the multicultural setting.

Cross-cultural counseling skills are also essential. In the third required course of this cognate, prospective teachers learn the conceptual and practical rudiments of counseling. In addition to general counseling skills, prospective teachers learn to apply techniques for working with members of various minority groups. Students also select a course in a particular aspect of cultural differentiation. A number of courses in the fields of sociology, anthropology, psychology, and ethnic studies relate to multicultural issues. The cognate sequence allows the student to select at least one additional course from appropriate options in these fields.

A number of recent changes in the role athletics plays in the school curriculum have converged to create a need for teachers with a background in techniques of coaching. One important trend, supported by Title IX legislation, is toward expanding athletic opportunities for female students. An increase in the popularity of so-called minor sports (soccer, track, and so on) is also changing the complexion of the school athletic program. An emphasis on physical fitness for all students seems to be supplanting the view that the major competitive sports should dominate physical education.

The cognate in Athletic Coaching gives teachers substantive knowledge in addition to whatever particular competencies they may choose to develop. A course in first aid and the care of athletic injuries should be required. This course will also stress protective practices so that injuries can be avoided. Students also take coursework in kinesiology and physiology. A course in coaching foundations including leadership theory, administrative and organizational functions, and techniques of coaching, is also required. Additional athletic participation and techniques courses can be elected to complete the cognate requirements.

Reading is a cognate area which complements almost any area of specialization. The gravity and pervasiveness of reading difficulties among learners has been and continues to be a major problem in American education. Increasingly, teachers are finding their lack of preparation in reading instruction a handicap, regardless of their teaching level or subject area. A cognate in reading increases the employability of a prospective teacher and provides him with skills that maximize his potential for success in today's classroom.

The professional core course Fundamentals of Teaching Reading is a prerequisite to the advanced coursework in this cognate. The second course, Diagnostic Techniques in Teaching Reading, provides the student with an array of formal and informal diagnostic techniques which can be used to identify individual and group reading abilities and deficiencies. As a sequel, Prescriptive Techniques in Teaching Reading enables students to pursue an in-depth study of some of the basic methods of teaching reading. Using diagnostic information, students plan and implement corrective and developmental instructional strategies. The coursework familiarizes prospective teachers with available materials as well as equips them with skills to design and create original materials and activities. Both of these courses incorporate fieldwork. A Practicum in Teaching Reading completes the cognate requirements. Students refine their competencies in teaching reading and apply these in a school setting.

A cognate in Rehabilitation Services recognizes the need for teachers to have specialized training to work with handicapped students. Public Law 94–142 makes this need even more dramatic. Public schools have long been geared to accommodating the "normal" individual; hence, teachers have traditionally had limited perspectives about the total range of needs of the handicapped/disabled learner. An introductory course such as Survey of Rehabilitation Professions provides an overview of the field of rehabilitation, including social, historical, and legal developments in the helping professions. A course covering the psychosocial aspects of disability and their implications for teaching is also recommended. General counseling techniques and their specific applications to handicapped individuals are also suggested as a course emphasis. In addition to field experiences in these courses, the student also should spend at least one semester in supervised experience in rehabilitation.

With a cognate in School Guidance, classroom teachers can develop an acceptable level of counseling skills. Interpersonal skills are not only crucial for teaching success but they also enable the teacher to deal effectively with parents and colleagues. The professional core course, Interpersonal Skills for Teachers, is prerequisite to this cognate sequence. Guidance Techniques for the Classroom Teacher builds on the fundamental communication and classroom management skills. A course in Counseling Theory and Techniques with an emphasis on classroom applications is also required. Depending on the prospective teacher's goals, he can select a course in a particular phase of counseling such as multicultural counseling or career development.

Special Education is another field which received wide support as a promising cognate area. Because of the mainstreaming which occurred as a result of Public Law 94–142, teachers need preparation for dealing with exceptional students. One course in the cognate is Educational Procedures for Integrating the Exceptional Student into the Regular Classroom. In this course, prospective teachers are familarized with materials and techniques used with the exceptional child in the least restrictive environment. A sequel course, Evaluation and Educational Planning for Mainstreamed Exceptional Individuals, concentrates on formal and informal assessment of exceptional learners and the development of Individualized Education Programs (IEP). The cognate also includes two survey and field experience courses, and providing actual experience in working with mildly and moderately handicapped individuals and the other in working with the severely and profoundly handicapped.

This brief review of possible cognate areas should provide the reader with a better understanding of the kind of flexibility cognates can provide both teacher and school. The generic teaching competencies developed in the professional core and the specific knowledge and skills developed through teaching specializations are critical to the professional preparation of the teacher. Additionally, it goes almost without question that the teacher needs an underlying foundation which is commonly referred to as a "general education." Issues associated with designing an appropriate general education component for the prospective teacher will be explored in the next chapter.

11

The General Education Component

The teacher education program, as we have repeatedly emphasized, must have as its central mission the provision of an adequate base of professional skills to prepare the entry level teacher to meet the demands of the classroom. The professional core, the teaching specializations, and the general education component must contribute to this end. In many conventional teacher training institutions, there is little or no planned coordination among these three elements of the curriculum.

The general education component of the teacher training program has as its purpose the development of a well-educated person or, more specifically, a well-educated teacher. Unfortunately, however, there is little agreement about the qualities or characteristics which distinguish the well-educated person. In addition, there is little consensus about the program or courses a college or university ought to offer in order to facilitate the individual's development of these characteristics. Without a clear definition of what is to be accomplished or how it is to be accomplished, institutions are obviously on shaky grounds in trying to evaluate or certify competence.

According to the Project on General Education Models (sponsored by the Society for Values in Higher Education, 363 St. Roman Street, New Haven, Conn. 06511), the cause of the American system of higher education's failure to produce the "well-educated person" resides in undergraduate rather than in graduate or professional training programs. Specifically, this problem can be traced to deficiencies in the general education component of undergraduate education. It is through this component that the student is expected to develop the sensitivities, appreciation, and knowledge that are the marks of an educated person, to become acquainted with his or her heritage, and to acquire the intellectual skills that allow him or her to continue learning beyond college. As implied by the term "liberal education," which is commonly used as a synonym for general education, this component theoretically liberates a person from narrow perspectives, ideas, and values. It is this area of the educational program that is supposed to open the mind to the complexities of the world, to foster the development of sophisticated intellectual and personal skills, and to promote the formulation of an individual philosophy of life.

Almost universally the course requirements of the general education component purport to broaden the student's understanding of the natural sciences, social sciences, and humanities. This function is acknowledged in the NASDTEC standards pertaining to general education for prospective teachers as follows: "Since general education is a developmental experience achieved with the maturation of the student, it shall be emphasized in the first two years of higher education, extended throughout the baccalaureate program, and continued in diminishing proportions into graduate study" (Standards for State Approval of Teacher Education, 1976, p. 15).

During the 1970's, an emphasis on career education has emerged. The problems already associated with general education have now been aggravated by the need to forge a link between vocational or professional training and "liberal" learning. The question is no longer "What constitutes a well-educated person?" but rather "What constitutes a well-educated accountant or engineer or teacher?"

DESIGNING A GENERAL EDUCATION COMPONENT FOR A PROFESSIONAL PROGRAM

For the last three decades, there has been a general feeling of dissatisfaction in higher education with the liberal arts or general education. There has also been a lack of agreement as to the definition of liberal arts. The appropriate distribution of course studies and proficiency requirements have been under scrutiny. Research on the organization and the transmission of knowledge has led to a questioning of the organization of academic disciplines at the college level. The recognition that just taking a prescribed number of courses does not constitute a liberal education emerged from these investigations. The emphasis has shifted away from the acquisition of content knowledge toward the development of cognitive and affective processes. Finally, there has been the call for relevance in education.

In response to this tumult in higher education, experimental colleges and innovative programs have been established. Some of the changes in the more traditional programs have included greater freedom of choice, fewer requirements, more relevant courses, alternative learning modes, and curricular experimentation. And still the consensus as to what constitutes an effective general education has continued to erode.

Trends in redesigning general education programs can be traced to a variety of sources. In this chapter, we will look at a number of these sources. General education requirements for prospective teachers have been influenced by NASDTEC and NCATE standards as well as by recent modifications in such certifying instruments as the NTE. Pacesetters in higher education, such as Harvard University and the University of California at Berkeley, have recently revamped their general education requirements. The thoroughgoing reappraisal of purpose and subsequent program restructuring these institutions have undergone will undoubtedly influence other institutions. We will also review the general education requirements of a number of teacher education institutions across the United States in order to get a comparative perspective. Recommendations derived from the data base of required and desired teacher competencies will also be considered.

NASDTEC STANDARDS FOR STATE APPROVAL OF TEACHER EDUCATION

According to the National Association of State Directors of Teacher Education and Certification, general education is based on those studies known as the liberal arts which include humanities, mathematics, the biological and physical sciences, and the social and behavioral sciences. The general education component should accomplish the following:

1. Stimulate scholarship that will give understanding to concepts not now extant and help prepare people for rapid adjustment to essential change

2. Foster individual fulfillment and nurture free, rational, and responsible adults

3. Cultivate appreciation for the values associated with life in a free society and for responsible citizenship

4. Develop leaders who are intellectually competent, imaginative, and vigorous

5. Contribute fundamentally to and give direction to the use of professional knowledge

6. Encourage discernment in examining the values inherent in foreign cultures to the end that a clearer understanding of other peoples will reduce world tensions

According to NASDTEC, the following broad areas of study should be addressed in the general education component:

1. Language skills as essential tools in communication

2. World literature with emphasis on, but not limited to, the writings of English and American authors

3. The aesthetic values in human experience expressed through the fine arts

4. The scientific and mathematical concepts upon which contemporary civilization depends

5. Contemporary world culture

6. Social, geographic, political, and economic conditions and their impacts on current problems in the nation and the world

7. The growth and development of the United States as a nation and its place in world affairs

8. The principles of physical and mental health as they apply to the individual and to the community

9. America's pluralistic culture and heritage

NCATE STANDARDS FOR THE GENERAL STUDIES COMPONENT

The National Council for Accreditation of Teacher Education recognizes that programs of general education vary widely among different institutions and suggests that general education be individualized according to the needs and interests of the student. According to NCATE, general education should include the studies most widely generalizable.

The NCATE standard for the general education component states that there should be a planned general studies component requiring that at least one-third of each curriculum for prospective teachers consist of studies in the symbolics of information, natural and behavioral sciences, and humanities.

CHANGES IN THE NATIONAL TEACHER EXAMINATION

The content of the general education component which is taught to teachers is partly determined by the subjects offered in the public schools. Traditionally these subjects have been and continue to be literature, history, languages, and fine arts. Literature and history now dominate the liberal arts program of the public school (Smith, 1971). History as it is taught in the schools is a mixture of political, social, and military history. Philosophy is almost entirely neglected except for erratic treatment in courses in literature. Fine arts is almost entirely neglected.

Part of the rationale for the National Teacher Examination is that it is based on the content of the program of teacher preparation which is itself presumably based largely on what is taught in the schools. The orientation of the general education subtests of the NTE is basically the same today as it was in the mid-1940's, although major changes are scheduled to be incorporated in 1981.

The competency areas tested by the National Teacher Examination are as follows:

1. Written English Expression: the correct and effective use of standard written English with emphasis on the problems of writing.

2. Social Studies: significant facts and concepts concerning basic subject matter from the fields of American history, world history, economics, geography, government, and sociology; interpretation of maps, graphs, cartoons, or short written passages.

3. Literature: major writers and their works from American and English literature, world literature, and classical mythology, including the author, the significance, and/or the content of a major literary work.

4. Music and Art: Music—an understanding of widely used music forms, terms, and instruments; familiarity with important composers, musical works, and performing artists.

   Art—the ability to recognize works that are either typical of a well-known artist or a particular culture; the characteristic works of broad periods of art history; an understanding of concepts or techniques basic to architecture, painting, photography, sculpture, and other art forms.

5. Science and Mathematics:

   Science: Biology—general knowledge of all biology, nutrition, photosynthesis; infection and disease, human physiology, genetics, and the important properties of plants and animals.

   Chemistry—familiarity with the properties of common elements and compounds, rate and yield of chemical reactions, chemical bonding, solutions, acids and bases.

   Physics—familiarity with the concepts and principles of velocity, acceleration, force, gravitation, wave properties, simple machines, behavior of gases, atomic phenomena, forms of energy and their conversion, and electricity and magnetism.

   Earth and Space Sciences—general knowledge of air pollution, natural and artificial satellites, the solar system, the structure and motions of the earth, erosion and weathering, rocks and minerals, and weather and climate.

   Mathematics: Knowledge of the number system and related operations, denominate numbers and measurement, geometry and mensuration, graphs and data, formulas and their evaluation; and modern concepts and techniques. (Commons Examination, 1974.)

The changes proposed for the National Teacher Examination are believed by the Educational Testing Service to reflect changes in the professional training of teachers. Specifically, emphasis in the area of written English expression is to be placed on general communication skills. The major change is to be one of orientation—the current form of the exam emphasizes the testing of content. The proposed form will place more emphasis on the testing of processes although within a framework of content.

HARVARD REVISES ITS "CORE CURRICULUM"

Harvard University began its search for a general standard or rationale for undergraduate education in the early 1970's. Harvard's Report for 1975–

1976 stated in very general terms the characteristics of the well-educated person of the late twentieth century. These are summarized below:

1. An educated person must be able to think and write clearly and effectively.

2. An educated person should have a critical appreciation of the ways in which we gain knowledge and understanding of the universe, of society, and of ourselves. Specifically, he or she should have an informed acquaintance with the aesthetic and intellectual experience of literature and the arts; with history as a mode of understanding present problems and the processes of human affairs, with the concepts and analytic techniques of modern social science; with philosophical analysis, especially as it relates to the moral dilemmas of modern men and women; and with the mathematical and experimental methods of the physical and biological sciences.

3. An educated American, in the last third of this century, cannot be provincial in the sense of being ignorant of other cultures and other times. It is no longer possible to conduct our lives without reference to the wider world within which we live. A crucial difference between the educated and the uneducated is the extent to which one's life experience is viewed in wider contexts.

4. An educated person is expected to have some understanding of and experience in thinking about moral and ethical problems. It may well be that the most significant quality in educated persons is the informed judgment which enables them to make discriminating moral choices.

5. Finally, an educated individual should have achieved depth in some field of knowledge. Cumulative learning is an effective way to develop a student's powers of reasoning and analysis, and for our undergraduates this is the principal role of concentrations.

The curriculum designed to encourage the development of the educated individual includes courses in each of five areas. The core requirements are as follows:

1. Literature and the Arts: one course in literature (examining important texts in a specific genre); one course in fine arts or music; and one pertaining to the "contexts of culture" which would be interdisciplinary emphasizing the social and historical contexts of art and literature.

2. History: one course concurrent with the historical orientation to present events; one course emphasizing an historical perspective on the past.

3. Social and Philosophical Analysis: one course in social analysis; one course in philosophical analysis.

4. Science and Mathematics: one course in physical science or mathematics; one course in biological or behavioral science.

5. Foreign Languages or Cultures: one course that would "penetrate deeply into selected aspects of the culture being studied."

In addition, the student is required to demonstrate a basic knowledge of mathematics through algebra and a reading competence of a foreign language. The undergraduate is also required to have one course in expository writing. (Harvard, 1978.)

NEW "BREADTH REQUIREMENTS" AT BERKELEY

The University of California requires that the undergraduate demonstrate competence in four basic areas. Specific course requirements are deemphasized.

1. English, Reading, and Composition: a sequence of courses designed for the purpose of developing facility in English, reading and composition, normally completed during the freshman year.

2. Quantitative Reasoning: the student will demonstrate competence in mathematics which ordinarily would "presuppose completion of approximately 3½ years of high school mathematics or the equivalent." This may be accomplished by an examination or by attaining a minimum grade of C- on any one college course from a list approved by the executive committee of the college.

3. Foreign Language: this requirement may be satisfied in any one of the following ways:

   a. By completing in secondary school two years of one foreign language acceptable in satisfaction of the requirements of the University of California and one additional year of the same language with minimum grades of C.

   b. By completing in secondary school two years of each of two foreign languages acceptable for admission to the University of California.

   c. By demonstrating equivalent knowledge through an approved examination.

   d. By completing in two foreign languages work equivalent to the second course of each as taught at Berkeley with a minimum grade of C-.

   e. By completing with a minimum grade of C- a college course of a level equivalent to the third course of a foreign language as taught at Berkeley.

4. Humanities, Social Science, and Natural Science: the student will complete at least eight courses, outside of the area of major, from the approved list. The student should complete at least two courses from each of the three areas—Humanities, Social Science, and Natural Science; if the student is a Letters and Science major, he must complete two courses from each of the two areas outside of his major and the remaining four courses from either or both areas outside of the major. (Berkeley, 1978.)

GENERAL EDUCATION IN TEACHER EDUCATION PROGRAMS

At the present time, few teacher education programs have devised general education requirements which vary substantially from those for other undergraduates. Establishing general education requirements has been regarded an institutional rather than a departmental prerogative. Historically, there has been much support for this approach since "general" education was viewed as that portion of the curriculum which was "common" to all graduates.

In many ways, this view has been reinforced by the organization of college curricula. Again using the pie analogy, the college curriculum was frequently sliced in half. Approximately one-half of the student's coursework was devoted to general education while the other half was concentrated in an area of specialization. Moreover, many institutions were rather rigid in their insistence that general education coursework precede area of specialization coursework. This separation was formalized in lower- and upper-division course schemes. In states where junior or community colleges are prevalent, the dichotomy was also enforced by systemic separation.

In recent years, however, there has been a considerable softening of these lines. Perhaps one of the major contributors to this change has been the increased flexibility of institutions of higher learning toward various alternatives to conventional coursework such as videotaped instruction, exemption through examination, life experience credit, and continuing education credit. The recent influx of mature students to the college campus, along with the influence of innovative programs such as University Without Walls, has led to a reassessment of the lockstep courses of study so widespread in the past.

Accompanying these changes has been the growing demand by business, industry, and even human service agencies for more technically competent employees. A number of employers found that entry level personnel had to be virtually retrained on the job despite graduation from programs which

TABLE 11.1 Relative Emphasis on Professional Coursework in Various Programs.

	required hours in professional coursework	per cent of total hours
Nursing	69	53%
Pharmacy (5-yr.)	86	51%
Business Administration	33	28%
Engineering	26	20%
Journalism	15	12%
Health & Physical Education	6	5%
Education	3	2%

Courses required of all undergraduates within the program and taught by that program's regular faculty.

were supposedly vocational or professional in orientation. The college community has responded to these criticisms by beefing up the professional skills emphasis of many programs, reducing general education requirements and elective options, and adding intern and extern programs. Some institutions have even experimented with the so-called "upside-down curriculum," which permits the student to take most of the professional coursework early in his program, then combine fieldwork with general education coursework during the remaining semesters.

While these trends are apparent in teacher education, they are not as strong as they are in many other professional preparation programs. To substantiate this claim, a number of professional programs were surveyed across a number of institutions. Each major or professional program was examined with regard to the actual courses required. Courses identified as or having a direct logical relation to the major were tabulated as required hours in professional coursework. Those general education and other incidental requirements which were designed to directly contribute to professional skills were categorized as supportive of the major area while those with no such direct relevance were classified as nonsupportive. Tables 11.1 and 11.2 reveal in one typical college the comparative emphases on professional coursework in various programs.

TABLE 11.2 Relative Emphasis on Supportive Coursework in Various Professional Programs.

	required hours		percent of total	
	non-supportive	supportive	non-supportive	supportive
Engineering	21–22	37–38	36%	64%
Pharmacy (5-yr.)	23	41	36%	64%
Health & Phys. Ed. . . .	40–48	15–20	72%	28%
Elementary Education . .	56–58	12	83%	17%
Early Childhood Educ. . .	48–51	9	85%	15%
Business Administration .	45–48	0	100%	0%
Secondary Education . . .	57–60	0	100%	0%
Journalism	73–76	0	100%	0%

Supportive and non-supportive courses required of all

program undergraduates and taught outside the program.

As these comparisons show, the student preparing to teach generally receives less in the way of professionally oriented coursework than does the prospective nurse, manager, or engineer. Appendix 4 presents a summary of the general education requirements of a number of teacher training programs. A survey of a number of programs in 1978 indicated that the percentage of credit hours allocated to general education requirements ranged from 25 percent to 54 percent of total credits required for graduation. Most programs required only slightly above the 33 percent level recommended by NCATE.

A common general education block is discernible in most undergraduate education programs. Prospective elementary teachers are frequently required to take additional coursework in various fields. This can be justified in terms of their need to function as generalists in the classroom. Secondary teachers ordinarily are not required to take general education courses beyond those required of liberal arts majors.

In terms of specific disciplines, teachers are typically required to take at least six hours of English. This minimum is often supplemented by required speech or literature courses. Most programs require at least one course in each of the following areas: math, natural science, health, and fine arts. Rarely are more than three courses required in any of these fields. Completion of four courses in the social sciences is a common requirement. Course selection is usually restricted to a list of recommended courses in a particular subject, but this list may range from two to a dozen alternatives. In a few cases, students may elect to take any course offered in a particular field.

GENERAL EDUCATION IN THE
JOB-RELATED CURRICULUM

As the above overview of trends indicates, institutions are becoming increasingly amenable to innovation in general education programs. There seems to be a movement toward modifying general education programs so as to make them clearly congruent with the philosophy and mission of the sponsoring institution. In some institutions, for example, this results in an interdisciplinary emphasis. In the model job-related curriculum, the primary function of the general education component is to ensure that the student acquires a liberal education that is supportive of his professional aspirations. The general education component represents an effort to link the professional training of teachers with liberal learning. Its purpose is two-fold. It provides the teacher with the knowledge (content) prerequisite to teaching the liberal arts courses in the classroom. Also, it has the function of preparing the teacher to be liberal and open in his/her thinking, to be aware of a wider world and wider contexts of life, and to have some understanding of the important moral and ethical concerns of life.

In designing a general education component for the model job-related curriculum, the data base of required and desired competencies was used as a reference point. Although the data base has the most direct impact on

TABLE 11.3 Comparative Chart.

NCATE Standards,
NASDTEC Standards,
General Education Component – Job Related Curriculum

NCATE	NASDTEC	GENERAL EDUCATION
Hours: 1/3 of required curriculum	Hours: not specified	Hours: 42 minimum
Symbolics of Information	Language Skills as Essential Tools in Communication	1 course: Literature and Rhetoric Public Communication
Humanities	World Literature: Emphasizing American and English	1 course: Critical Approaches to Literature Great Books of the Western World I Great Books of the Eastern World II Epic Poetry
	Fine Arts	1 course: Introduction to Art Teaching Second Languages to Young Children Introduction to Contemporary European Civilization Introduction to Music Introduction to Philosophy Philosophy of Education
	Contemporary World Culture	
	Growth and Development of the U.S.	1 course: Ethnology of Contemporary American Life Major Writers of American Literature American Drama Historical Geography of the United States The Geography of the American Future American National Government History of the U.S. from Discovery to the Present Day American Philosopy Community Organization
	America's Pluralistic Society	Educational Anthropology
	Scientific and Mathematical Concepts	1 course: Introduction to Computer Science Mathematical Analysis I Precalculus Mathematics Elementary Statistics

TABLE **11.3** (continued)

Natural and Behavioral Sciences	Social, geographic, political and economic conditions and their impact on world problems	1 course: Primates, People and Prehistory Principles of Economics Economics of Education Introduction to Geography Elementary Psychology Introductory Sociology
		1 course: General Biology Environmental Earth Science The Present Day Marine Environment Introduction to Physical Science I and Physical Science Laboratory I
	Principles of Physical and Mental Health	1 course: Introduction to Health Education Personal and Community Health Introduction to Human Movement I
		Psychology of the Exceptional Child
		Community Services for Children and Youth

the makeup of the professional core, it can also provide direction to decision-making about what the general education requirements should be. In some cases, competencies validated as "musts" can be acquired through the general education component. An example of such an item is the requirement that "the teacher *must* provide a proper model in verbal usage." Developing the prospective teacher's communications skills so that he can accomplish this is within the domain of general education.

Analysis of the "shoulds" of teaching will also yield implications for general education requirements. A number of desired skills, for example, relate to the prospective teacher's need to function effectively in a multicultural setting. This suggests that a course such as Educational Anthropology, which covers such topics as classroom ethnography, bilingualism, cultural minorities, and communication across ethnic boundaries, can satisfy the job-related mission as well as serving as a general education requirement.

The use of NASDTEC and NCATE standards as filters is another step in the design of an appropriate general education component. In this as in other areas, NASDTEC's recommendations are more specific than those provided by NCATE. Table 11.3 shows how the specifications of these two accrediting agencies are accommodated in a sample program.

It is in the area of general education that the greatest degree of flexibility in program design is recommended. One way of looking at the relationship between the professional core and the general education component is to see the two as complementary. The former provides the process, the latter provides the content. From this perspective the need for content will vary from one teaching specialization to another as well as between grade levels. The content needs of a fourth-grade teacher who may be teaching reading, grammar, arithmetic, social studies, and science will differ considerably from the needs of a ninth-grade physical science teacher. In addition, while teaching at the same grade level the general education needs of a tenth-grade teacher with five classes of social studies will be quite different from that of a teacher with five classes of home economics. Consequently, it is not possible to develop a sample general education component which will meet the needs of every education major. What we have done in the job-related curriculum is to develop a flexible set of recommendations for general education competencies for the prospective teacher. In addition, because of the structure of the academic program, we have expressed these competencies in terms of courses or credit hours. It is assumed that satisfactory coursework in these areas can be translated into competencies or knowledge in the subject area.

As indicated earlier in this chapter, general education is often an institutionally determined rather than a program-specific enterprise. Thus, the parameters of the existing program must often be accepted as givens. Within these parameters, however, the decision-makers can exercise influence to ensure that, wherever possible, general education experiences are supportive of the development of professional skills.

Thus, the professional core, teaching specializations, and the general education component each contribute in varying ways and degrees to the professional competence of the entry level teacher. The professional growth of the teacher, however, should be career-long. Designing inservice programs which accommodate the continuous development of the staff and the individual teacher will be addressed in the next chapter.

12

Designing Inservice Teacher Training Programs

In many ways, developing a preservice teacher education curriculum is a much simpler endeavor than that of developing a comprehensive inservice design. The structural characteristics of a degree program provide parameters which are not generally present in the inservice context. Also the preservice curriculum can be conceptualized holistically, whereas inservice training is rarely conceived of as a planned, unified entity. In most cases, it is easier to assess the prospective teacher's status with respect to desired outcomes than it is to assess those of the practicing teacher. Indeed, it is frequently difficult to agree upon a set of desired outcomes for a practicing teacher or for an entire faculty. Variations in teachers' backgrounds, training, assignments, and so forth compound the problem of designing relevant and effective programs. Furthermore, the conventional approach to inservice as a reactive, piecemeal conglomeration of activities is difficult to overcome.

A necessary first step in the design of inservice opportunities to meet identified individual and staff development needs is to clarify what is meant by inservice training. Traditionally, a variety of activities has been classified under the rubric of inservice education. Some definitions of inservice are so broad that they encompass almost any activity a practicing teacher participates in that can in any way be construed as potentially contributing to professional competence. Among these activities are the typical inservice workshops, attendance at professional conferences, visitations to other schools or programs, college courses, travel, professional reading, and so on. The problem inherent in considering any and all such activities as inservice is that the quality and interface of such experiences is not considered. The outgrowth of such a view is that anything scheduled during "inservice time" is considered to be inservice training whereas many such activities are merely time-killers and have no clear relation to job requirements. It is little wonder that there is so much criticism of inservice as worthless when it is as amorphous as presently conceived.

To standardize the terminology we will use to discuss inservice design, the following phrases will be defined: *professional development, teacher development, staff development, inservice program,* and *inservice session.* The first of these terms, professional development or growth, is a comprehensive construct. Conceptually, it ties together pre- and inservice teacher training as well as individual and staff development. All teacher education activities should be undertaken within the overall framework of professional development. As will be pointed out later in this chapter, however, the notion of a professional growth continuum underlying all teacher education activities is still largely theoretical but it is useful because it focuses on the holistic rather than the particularistic.

The term teacher development refers to those professional growth experiences which contribute to the increased competency of the individual teacher. These activities may be voluntary, such as professional reading, travel, and self-selected graduate coursework; or mandated, such as required coursework for certification renewal. In the individual level assessment of inservice needs, a profile of needed competencies is generated. (See Chapter 6.) Teacher development activities are those experiences which are selected with the aim of eliminating discrepancies between present and preferred competency profiles. In Section 2, Improving Teacher Competencies, specific procedures for improving the skills of the individual teacher will be discussed. If the procedures explicated later in this chapter are followed, a number of job-alike, school, and district level inservice activities will also contribute to teacher development, since they are predicated on the collective needs of individual teachers at a given organizational level.

Staff development refers to those activities which contribute to the increased effectiveness of working units within the district. In the problem identification process, commonalities were found in training needs at the district, school, and job-alike levels. Inservice activities at the staff development level are designed to provide training in those competency areas found to be common needs of the various working units. Staff development activities should also contribute to the cohesiveness of the particular organizational level, both in terms of agreement on shared goals, objectives, and procedures as well as in terms of improved interpersonal functioning.

Within this framework, the term inservice program means a planned, coordinated series of activities which contributes to professional development. The inservice program is a long-term design, spanning at least one and as many as five academic years. It encompasses a number of separate inservice sessions, each of which must contribute to the overall design. This conception of inservice is a dramatic shift from the conventional fragmentary approach.

Without a unifying program, the typical inservice session is reminiscent of a three-ring circus. Vying for the attention of teachers are three competing attractions, each tantalizing in promise but disappointing in delivery. Session A presents an elephant perched delicately on one foot. This performance is entitled "How to Implement Behavior Management Techniques in Your Classroom" or, more realistically, "How to Look Graceful While Playing the Heavy." In Ring 2 a juggler delivers a workshop on "How to Individualize Instruction" or, translated from educationese, "How to Balance the Diverse Needs of Thirty-five Learners Without Dropping Your Sanity." The third arena features a scantily clad performer who peddles a unicycle backwards while beckoning poodles to jump through fire-ringed hoops. This workshop is entitled "Strategies for Basic Skills Teaching," or, "How to Put the Thrill Back in Drill." Such sessions are often topical but ineffective because of their superficiality, redundancy, and impracticality.

In conceptualizing conventional inservice programs and alternative approaches, Jackson (1968, p. 19) uses the dichotomy of the "defect" versus the "developmental" approaches. In his aptly titled chapter, "Old Dogs and New Tricks," he maintains that inservice has traditionally been marshalled as a combatant in the war against teacher obsolescence. The assumption of inservice planners has been that teachers have defects which inservice sessions are supposed to repair:

> And what exactly are these defects? The most common one, it seems, is ignorance, arising from a lack of exposure to the latest developments in instructional techniques. Many teachers, so the proponents of this point of view would have us believe, have simply not kept up with what is going on in education. They do not know CIA from CAI or i.t.a. from IPI. They don't know what behavioral objectives are, much less how to write them. The mention of microteaching in their presence receives a blank look, as does interaction analysis. They associate discovery learning with John Dewey rather than with Jerome Bruner. In short, they are not "with it." (p. 21)

Despite Jackson's tongue-in-cheek treatment of the matter, it is clear that many teachers *do* have deficiencies in their preparation. In some cases, these deficiencies are a direct result of inadequate preservice programs. In other cases, new developments in education have made necessary the cultivation of new skills. It is more productive to accept this situation than to deny it. One way to ascertain the training needs of practicing teachers, as suggested in Chapter 6, is through paper and pencil testing and direct observation of teachers' performance of the competencies listed as "musts" of teaching. If the results of such assessments are used in a positive rather than in a punitive manner, most teachers can be expected to respond favorably. As a matter of fact, the concreteness and objectivity of such an approach is likely to reduce teachers' anxieties about supervisory and evaluative practices.

The developmental or professional growth model of inservice education can augment the defect model. Postulates of this model include the following:

1. Professional growth is a career-long process.

2. Thorough assessment and synthesis of both individual and staff development needs is essential (Problem Identification Stage).

3. The responsibility for making choices among an array of professional growth opportunities and for coordinating these choices must be shared (that is, by the individual teacher, the employing agency, and other appropriate actors such as institutions offering graduate work).

4. Inservice offerings must be conceived of and planned as a holistic program, rather than as a fragmented series of unrelated activities (Program Design Stage).

5. Ongoing evaluation of individual teacher and staff performance is a critical need, one which must be accomplished on a number of levels and through a variety of techniques (Program Effectiveness Stage).

6. The supportive function of supervision and evaluation must replace the present punitive orientation (Program Effectiveness Stage).

Recent literature on inservice education has claimed that the conventional dichotomy between pre- and inservice teacher education is both arbitrary and dysfunctional. Yet this division is a faithful representation of the traditional gap between these two phases of teacher education. One could hardly expect the situation to be otherwise, given the differences in roles, norms, and expectations experienced by the prospective teacher and the practicing teacher. The concept of a continuum of professional growth must be founded upon a developmental continuum of professional skills. To use the rhetoric of a continuum when the reality is one of fragmentation, however, is to perpetuate one of the fallacies that has long plagued teacher education: that is, the tendency to assume that reality will conform to the demands of euphemism.

The assumption that professional growth should be a career-long process requires little explanation. Some characteristics of the teaching profession, however, make this somewhat innocuous sounding statement difficult to implement. Because of the relative lack of staff differentiation among classroom teachers, vertical growth corresponding to that possible in business and industry is limited. At present, few districts have made provisions for merit pay, or recognition of exemplary teachers as "master" teachers. The role of department chairperson or team leader is frequently administrative, one which actually reduces contact hours with students. Ironically, the rewards available to effective or good teachers remove them from the classroom. The lure of professional advancement is too frequently out of the classroom and into the counsellor's office, principal's office, or curriculum coordinator's office. In addition to this problem, the concept of a smooth, sequential continuum of professional growth is attractive but often unrealistic. Specific circumstances, such as a personal move or other change in assignment, may require a teacher to learn a whole new set of skills. Thus, while professional growth may be conceptualized as a continuum, one should be aware that this is the ideal rather than the real.

While continuity in professional development is important at any stage of a teacher's career, it is particularly crucial for the entry level teacher. Even with the best of undergraduate preparation and successful practice teaching experience, the change in status from student to faculty member changes both the type and degree of supervision provided the beginning teacher. As a colleague rather than an intern, the beginning teacher faces a whole new set of expectations. Depending on the extent of responsibility, the individual assumed during student teaching, the full-time teachers' duties may seem to have increased exponentially. Yet the "sink or swim" philosophy often prevails, leaving the beginning teacher reluctant to seek help. To complicate the matter, new teachers in a school are often given larger classes and more difficult assignments than the more experienced teachers, who have already served their time as "low man on the totem pole." The informal seniority systems works against the beginning teacher in other ways. It is not uncommon to find the beginning teacher saddled with the largest class, the lowest tract, the fewest materials, and the oldest equipment.

The assumption that the entry level teacher is a finished product also impedes his professional development. Contrary to this belief, it should be recognized that no teacher at any stage of career development is a finished product. A stronger and more supportive supervisory system than is currently the norm is necessary to develop the potential of every teacher. One suggestion for transitional supervision which seems feasible in a number of situations is for the supervisory arrangement which prevailed during a teacher's internship experience to continue into his beginning teaching. Using this approach, school districts and preparing institutions would share the responsibility for providing supportive supervision to the teacher through at least the first year of full-time employment. Obviously, this arrangement is only feasible when the teacher's beginning employment is within the geographical area served by his or her undergraduate institution. Reciprocal provisions could be worked out to accommodate beginning teachers who enter employment in another area or state.

ESTABLISHING INSERVICE CONTENT PRIORITIES

In Chapter 6, procedures for identifying discrepancies between the present and preferred states of teacher and staff development were described. Commonalities among needs at the individual, district, school, and job-alike levels provide a starting point for designing long-term inservice program goals. It is not sufficient, however, to amass a laundry list of common needs and convert this into a series of inservice sessions. A number of decisions need to be made to establish relationships and priorities among the identified needs.

One of the foremost considerations is that of establishing a prognosis for reducing or eliminating a particular discrepancy. Too often, inservice programs have concentrated on trying to bring about changes which the teachers were either unwilling or unable to make. In some instances, teachers' affective inclinations against a particular change have been ignored. For example, a number of programs have attempted to instruct teachers in techniques of behavior modification. Many teachers, however, resist using these approaches because of philosophical disagreement, incompatible teaching styles, or negative experiences with these techniques. In other instances, the approaches advocated in inservice may have been supported by teachers but not supported by the institutional context. A prime example is an inservice emphasis on individualizing instruction despite inadequate instructional personnel and physical resources.

A review of previous attempts to reduce a particular discrepancy through inservice efforts is essential. If a particular inservice theme or skill has been pursued repeatedly with little or no evidence of success, the Sisyphus approach should be abandoned. It is possible that prerequisite knowledge, skills, or attitudes have not been established. When an inservice program has a history of ineffectiveness in terms of classroom application, it is likely that the teachers have more fundamental training needs that are being ignored.

ALTERNATIVES FOR STRUCTURING THE PROGRAM

Designing the professional growth program involves consideration of an array of factors which goes beyond concern with the inservice content itself. Many of these concerns require policy decisions. Significant alterations in the incentive system, for example, cannot be made without administrative and board approval. The program design specialist must be aware of alternatives for structuring the inservice program as well as cognizant of the opportunities and constraints present in the particular school district of interest.

One promising trend in professional growth is that of granting either graduate credit, salary advancement, or certificate renewal credit for participation in inservice programs. Such programs are often conducted under the joint auspices of a school district and a nearby university. In some of these programs, a kind of smorgasborg approach is used. The teacher can elect to attend and carry out the required activities of a variety of sessions on different topics, receiving a fraction of a salary advancement or graduate credit for each. This arrangement, of course, carries shades of the conventional piecemeal approach. The use of individual and staff profiles to structure the available options can help to eliminate this potential weakness.

More comprehensive training efforts are offered in some innovative inservice programs. Generally, these zero in on one particular set of competencies, such as classroom management skills. Teachers attend a series of related sessions throughout the year. Credit is awarded on the basis of contact hours *and* performance; that is, one must not merely attend, but must demonstrate an increased level of competence in order to be compensated. Classroom application is an integral part of such programs and, to the extent possible, follow up in the classroom is provided by the inservice staff. This kind of program is often tied in with the supervisory mechanism of the school.

One of the factors which has impeded the development and dissemination of quality inservice programs is the relatively insular way in which school districts are perceived and perceive themselves. Thus, District X's teachers may receive credit toward salary advancement for completing a District X-sponsored inservice program. However, this credit is not honored by District Y, despite the fact that it may offer a similar program. As inservice becomes a more highly respected vehicle for professional growth, it is likely that mechanisms will emerge for external, comparative criteria for the evaluation of district-sponsored programs. One can envision that new accrediting bodies will emerge. Additionally, it is likely that the increased standardization of inservice content and quality will lead to reciprocity among districts (and perhaps universities as well) in granting credit for inservice training.

Teacher Centers, formalized programs for inservice improvement of teachers, are another innovation. While the diversity of these programs is great, they are generally characterized by a higher degree of teacher governance than is generally the case. Usually they are operated with federal funding. Many are administered by local teachers' associations. Others are administered by districts. Many require that a group of teachers write a proposal outlining their own training needs. Competition for funds allows priorities to be established but can also run into political and practical difficulties. Teachers with the skills and fortitude to write fundable proposals, for example, may be much less in need of inservice than teachers who do not apply.

The Teacher Center concept generally includes a physical facility reserved for teacher training. Many such programs are of the ongoing "make and take" variety, providing a place where teachers can develop materials for their own classrooms. Modules on various teaching competencies, as well as protocol materials, are also available in many of these centers.

One approach to program design which is adaptable to most of the training content identified in Stage 1 is to develop a series of modules for presentation of the material. In the sense the term is used here, a module is a segment of an overall instructional unit. It covers at least one terminal objective and is coordinated with other terminal objectives relating to an overall competency area. Each inservice session could cover one module of the total program. These modules are not necessarily individualized (although they may include independent activities) because many relevant training experiences can and should be carried out in a group setting. However, the module must be a discrete segment of content and activities, the attainment of whose objectives can be assessed. The module should include objectives, alternative activities (such as, lecturettes, audio-visual presentations, group discussion, classroom performance activities, and so on), resources and materials (such as, filmstrips, protocol materials, professional journal articles, community speakers, and so forth) and evaluation techniques.

After a program has been designed to reduce the discrepancies found in the problem identification stage, concerns about implementation emerge. In contrast to the preservice teacher program, the inservice program must usually be sandwiched into the existing school schedule, a most challenging task. The one-hour, after school session, while generally ineffective, at least did not take up too much of the teacher's time, time which considering the content of many workshops, could have been spent more profitably in other ways. The design of professional development programs and attendant incentives, however, moves inservice from the realm of a pastime to that of a serious endeavor.

The portion of professional growth which is under the individual teacher's control, such as taking graduate courses or travelling, is dependent on circumstances such as convenience and financial exigencies. Individual choice is a prerogative of the adult professional. Thus, except for recertification requirements, districts have no leverage for forcing teachers to take a particular course which is perceived as contributing to professional growth rather than some other course, perhaps in a nonteaching-related area, or no course at all. The development of individual teacher competency profiles, accompanied by appropriate incentives, will do much to ensure that teacher development proceeds on a more coordinated basis, in harmony with staff development priorities. Linking training with supervision and evaluation will also encourage teacher development.

Some school districts have attempted to accommodate more intensive inservice programs by overhiring teachers. These teachers are used as a "floating faculty" to release a group of teachers for a week or two for inservice training. This approach may be disruptive to students' progress, however. Variations of this approach are likely to emerge in the near future.

Another arrangement which is promising is that of hiring teachers on a ten- rather than nine-month contract. A substantial block of time can be reserved for inservice training, generally prior to the beginning of school. In districts with year-long programs, even more flexibility is possible, with groups of teachers undergoing retraining during each academic session.

ALTERNATIVES FOR PRESENTING THE PROGRAM

Until the last few years, teacher involvement in inservice was generally that of the passive recipient of information. Their participation as planners and presenters was minimal. National trends toward increased professional autonomy have caused a dramatic change in teachers' individual and collective perceptions of their appropriate role in determining inservice requirements. Without exception, major authorities in the field of inservice cite increased teacher input in planning and implementation as a critical need. A number of studies of teacher attitude toward inservice confirm this conclusion. In a 1975 nationwide poll, NEA researchers asked a sample of teachers to indicate the degree of planning involvement they preferred. Fifty-six percent preferred programs planned by a group of teachers as contrasted with 25 percent for individual planning, 10 percent for school system planning, and 8.3 percent for local association planning (Inservice, 1976, p. 16).

The question of who should present inservice sessions is as controversial as that of who should plan them. The revolving-door phenomenon has been characteristic of inservice, as consultants "blow in, blow off, and blow out" (Erickson & Rose, 1976, p. 247). Regardless of the perceived expertise of the one-shot outside consultant, his perceived knowledge of local conditions and commitment to solving indigenous problems are questioned. The inservice consultant who "makes the rounds" of schools or districts gains the unfortunate reputation of a snake oil salesman. Despite the fact that his product may be of value, he cannot hope to sell it as a panacea. Without the time or follow-up opportunity to explain the subtleties or appropriate and inappropriate applications, the inservice consultant must capture the interest of potential users and hope that they will figure out proper dosages and potential side effects on their own.

A number of studies confirm the fact that teachers are increasingly questioning the credibility of nonteachers as inservice presenters, even if these consultants have had previous public school teaching experience. Reilly and Dembo (1975, p. 126) for example, gave a sample of one hundred elementary teachers a list of descriptions of thirteen potential inservice presenters. Respondents were asked to rate the confidence they would have in the opinions of each, relative to both cognitive and affective inservice topics. Experienced teachers were ranked highest for each of the two categories of inservice emphasis. Second and third places, respectively, were earned by the change agent (innovator) and the experienced professor. It is interesting to note that the "inexperienced teacher" was ranked fifth on both cognitive and affective lists, higher than such specialists as the school psychologist, child psychiatrist, neurologist, school social worker, or the ever-present publishing company representative.

In synthesizing the findings of five studies about inservice, Wilen and Kindsvatter (1978, p. 394) developed seven recommendations, two of which concerned the need for greater teacher input and involvement. Rubin cites a study conducted by Lawrence for the Florida Department of Education. The investigator analyzed ninety-seven studies of professional development efforts. One of the common findings was that "school-based programs in which teachers participate as helpers to each other and planners of inservice activities tend to have greater success in accomplishing their objectives than do programs that are conducted by college or other outside personnel without the assistance of teachers" (Rubin, 1978, p. 23). In a state-wide study conducted in Tennessee, 646 teachers responded to thirty-four Likert-type statements regarding inservice programs. Ninety-six percent of the respondents agreed with the statement that "teachers need to be involved in the development of purposes, activities, and methods of evaluation for inservice programs" (Brimm & Tollett, 1974, p. 522).

The inside-outside team approach is useful in the delivery of inservice programs and can be used quite effectively to pinpoint training priorities. The inside-outside or "cousin" team is essentially a problem-solving team composed of both representatives of the particular working unit or subsystem as well as members who are outside the particular working unit. Such a team, for example, might consist of teachers from various schools and levels of a district, central office representatives, and professors from a nearby college of education. Theoretically, a team composed in this manner combines the best of both worlds: it maintains the perceived credibility attributed to inside staffers who "know what our situation is like" with the perceived expertise of outsiders. Schmuck, et al. (1977) elaborate on the advantages of such a team in the context of organizational development:

> During most of the week, parttime cadre members are full-time teachers, counselors, principals, or central-office personnel, and this dual identity gives them several advantages of insiders and outsiders alike. First, each parttime specialist becomes a channel of communication between the cadre and the subsystem in which he or she holds a regular job. Second, each specialist becomes a source of support and expertise for other cadre members who are working with a group of which the specialist is regularly a part. Third, when they consult in subsystems to which they do not regularly belong, cadre members are in effect outsiders, with the result that their perspective on the clients' situation can be relatively unbiased. Clients tend to regard specialists from outside their own staff as having an expertise and competence that warrants much the same confidence as that usually accorded to a peer or to a consultant who receives a fee. (p. 527)

This team approach corresponds to the shared-teaching arrangement advocated for presentation of the preservice program. At the inservice level, it can be tied directly to supervisory functions, but not necessarily to individual teacher evaluation. Members of the problem-solving team should be trained in techniques of direct observation and clinical supervision. This will enable them to visit teachers' classrooms between sessions of the ongoing inservice program in order to observe how the teacher is incorporating new competencies into his or her teaching. Feedback from these observations can be useful in structuring future sessions as well as for monitoring individual teacher development.

Because of the wide variability in teacher and staff development needs, the design of inservice programs must be context-specific. Therefore, it is our position that advocacy of one inservice emphasis over another would not serve any useful purpose. By using the procedures described for evaluating program design, operation, effectiveness, and efficiency in the forthcoming chapters, inservice planners can improve the quality of professional growth opportunities for teachers.

13

Evaluating at the Program Design Stage

One of the difficulties commonly encountered in designing pre- and inservice teacher education is that of determining whether or not the program design is appropriate and adequate. The program design is a narrative and graphic representation of the program as conceptualized by its developers. It is essentially a blueprint which provides specifications for those who are to build or implement the program. The design describes the intended operation of the program. Then using the discrepancy approach, the evaluator can compare the actual with the intended system performance. In this manner, the program can be monitored to determine whether or not the goals are being achieved as intended.

The data base developed in the problem identification stage is the essential element of evaluation at the design stage. The data base is used to maintain a baseline for design performance and adequacy. In evaluating the design, the basic questions to be considered are: "Is this a good design?" and "Is this design adequate?" To answer these questions in the affirmative, the design 1) must be directly based on problems (needs) discerned at the problem identification stage, and 2) should be both structurally and empirically sound.

The data base developed at the problem identification stage is the basis for program design. The "existing state" defines the readiness of the participant to enter into the program and determines the initial learning activities to be undertaken by the program participant. The "preferred state" will be translated into the ultimate objectives of the program. The program activities will be designed to move the participants from the existing state to the preferred state.

Structural soundness in design is determined through the analysis of input, process, and output. These three design components must be examined to determine whether the components are adequately described and defined. Sufficient information must be provided in the design so that the evaluator will later be able to identify in what respects the program has not been implemented. Each of the components of the program must be broken down into the functions that take place as part of that component. The functions can then be broken down into even smaller units for analysis. In evaluating program implementation, the evaluator should be able to observe corresponding activitites in the field to compare the observed aspects of program functions and subfunctions with the standards provided for that aspect by the program design. The evaluator thus proceeds subfunction by subfunction through the program, comparing each with the design to establish congruency. The program design must be defined in sufficient detail so that it would be possible for the program staff to implement the program on the basis of the written design without additional explanation. The comprehensive blueprint or design of the program must include the objectives; the staff, students, media, facilities, and other resources which must be present before the objectives can be achieved; and the activities that form the process by which the objectives will be achieved.

It is essential that the design specifications be submitted to rigorous analysis by the evaluator for several reasons. The program design will be used as the standard against which program implementation and program effectiveness (Stages 3 and 4) will be evaluated. Only after the program design has been developed and evaluated, and any necessary adjustments have been made so that the design adequately reflects the needs assessment and the data base, can the design be used as a standard for evaluation of later stages of the process.

The analysis required for the evaluation of the program design will provide the program staff with information about needed resources, internal validity and completeness, and compatibility with existing programs. Also as a result of the design evaluation, the program administrator will have the data necessary to determine whether the financial resources available are adequate for the implementation and continuation of the program. Analysis of the design will reveal whether there exists an inconsistency between the program and another existing activity or program within the system. On the basis of these judgments, it is possible to continue the program through the program implementation stage. If the design cannot be adequately defined to provide this information, the program administrators are justified in deciding to terminate the program at the design stage.

In evaluating the program design, specific aspects of the program are of primary concern. The input component of program design primarily involves the selection criteria and organization of faculty and students or the way faculty and students are to be brought together so that instruction can take place. Considerations include the following: (1) student selection criteria and the mechanisms by which the student is moved through the program from admission to completion; (2) faculty and other staff selection and assignment criteria; (3) assignment procedures for dividing students among faculty and staff for different purposes; and (4) time schedules for duration and sequencing of instruction.

The process component may be classified under the general categories of curriculum, instruction, and nonhuman resources. In examining the curriculum, one looks primarily at content. This is the structure and body of knowledge which is described through the arrangement of topics into curriculum components and/or courses which will be covered as the individual progresses through the program. Each topic or course is further broken down into subheadings or course units. The subcategories should be sufficiently specific to provide the evaluator or evaluating team with sufficient information to develop course evaluation instruments and/or specifications for test item construction.

Instruction is basically those procedures which are used to facilitate learning. The instructional aspect of program design should include an outline of the proposed teaching activities by course subunit. The nature of the activities (such as, lecture, discussion, simulation, inquiry, and so on) should be specified. Planned interactions among faculty, students, and media should be summarized. Finally, learning principles pertaining to motivation, practice, and reinforcement which provide a basis for the instructional design should be discussed.

Nonhuman resources include space, special equipment, and expendables needed for the program. This category also includes the cost of the program. The money required for facilities, supplies, and personnel must not only be described adequately but should be allocated for specific purposes.

The output component of the program design is more closely aligned to the formulation of objectives—enabling, terminal, and ultimate. While there is much disagreement among evaluators and curriculum designers as to the specific format of the program objective, there is agreement that objectives should be specific and written in unambiguous terms. If the program design includes only broad, ambiguous goals, the evaluator should assume the role of assisting the program staff to revise these into precisely stated objectives.

Clearly stated, concise objectives serve many purposes. Most importantly, they make it possible for instructors to attend to important educational outcomes. They allow educators to distinguish between trivial and important changes in learner behavior as a result of instruction. In terms of measurement, they encourage the use of diverse and often sophisticated methods of making both qualitative as well as quantitative judgments of learner achievement. Measurement also implies accountability. Precisely stated objectives allow an instructor to be evaluated on the basis of his ability to effect the desired changes in a learner. Faculty and other instructional staff should not be evaluated strictly on their instructional methods or the means used in instruction. Many instructors may be misjudged simply because their preferred instructional techniques do not coincide with those currently in vogue. Precise objectives allow more meaningful evaluation because the instructional ends can be evaluated. It is fair as well as valid to assess instructor competence in terms of ability to effect specified behavioral changes in the student.

In evaluating program objectives, it should be remembered that they represent preferred levels of attainment. In designing the model job-related curriculum for preservice teachers, the basic source of objectives is the needs assessment and data base developed in the problem identification stage. Therefore, these data provide an absolute standard against which the program design and, specifically, program objectives can be evaluated. A logical analysis of the objectives will reveal their degree of congruence with the data base.

The program design must also provide procedures for evaluating the program. Using systems terminology, evaluation must be built into the input, process, and output components of the program. Evaluation in the input component involves selection and placement instruments and procedures for program participants, staff, and cooperating teachers as well as the assessment of the efficacy of the instruments and procedures. Evaluation in the process component requires the assessment of student-instructor interaction and, in general, a determination of how well the program runs. Input and process evaluation considerations are discussed in detail in Chapter 14, Evaluating at the Program Installation Stage. Evaluation in the output component requires that the attainment of program objectives be assessed. Evaluation of enabling and terminal objectives provides both process and output information. The assessment of objectives to make process and output decisions is discussed in Chapter 14 and in Chapter 16, Evaluating at the Program Effectiveness Stage.

In evaluating the design, requirements imposed on the program from external sources should be considered. For example, the standards of accrediting agencies play a role in both the design and the evaluation of a program design. Accreditation agencies charged with the responsibility of evaluating teacher education programs demonstrate varying degrees of specificity in their standards. These agencies often provide assistance in meeting accreditation standards. Obviously, it is preferable to design the program to meet the standards rather than to have to modify the program after it has been established. It should also be realized that the standards can be used to provide a measure of quality control in the design process. The National Association of State Directors of Teacher Education and Certification (NASDTEC) provides rather explicit and detailed standards for teacher education programs. The National Counsel for Accreditation of Teacher Education (NCATE) also provides standards outlining the desired minimum levels and direction for professional preparation for teachers. If a new program or program modification is designed using these standards as guideposts, the evaluation process should be somewhat simplified. Certainly, whether or not accreditation is an important concern in the program design process, NASDTEC and/or NCATE standards can provide one index against which program quality can be gauged. These standards were used as filters in developing the model job-related preservice curriculum, thus building into the design mandated specifications.

At the program design stage, it is often desirable to have input by representatives of any agencies which may ultimately have jurisdiction over the program. This will often take the form of review of project design by representatives of the State Department of Education. Input by these agencies during the design stage may insure greater cooperation at later stages than would be the case if the agency were brought in at the point when the program could be considered a *fait accompli*. The results of review by representatives of accrediting agencies, the State Department of Education, or institutional officials should be included in the evaluation report. This information should be available to the decision-maker in reaching a decision to continue, terminate, or modify the design.

At the design stage decision, three options are available to the program administrators. One option is to continue the development and implementation process with the proposed design. On the other hand, if the necessary resources are not available, if the program as designed is incompatible with existing activities, or if an irreparable discrepancy exists between the design and the data base, a decision to terminate the project may be reached. Finally, if the program design is found to be incomplete or poorly defined or if a rectifiable discrepancy exists between the program design and the data base, a decision may be reached to modify the design.

If the program decision-makers determine that modification is needed in the program design, it may be helpful to enter an inquiry procedure in which appropriate questions are used to determine the nature and efficacy of program modification. For example, if the design inadequacy is a matter of poor definition, the procedure may be as follows (Provus, 1971):

Is the problem properly defined?
If not, why not? (the point(s) of breakdown in design definition should be pinpointed here)
What correctives are possible? (This may require a detailed analysis of the problem in defining the program.)
Which corrective ideas represent the best solutions to the problem given the parameters of the program?
Which corrective is best? (This will involve the examination of values and other pre-established program criteria.)
Is the corrective adequately defined?
Has the corrective been installed?

A similar procedure can be followed in modifying a design that has been evaluated as incomplete. If the problem appears to be one of a major discrepancy between the design and the data base, the problem area will usually be in formulation of objectives—specifically, in terminal or ultimate objectives. They may not be consistent with or keyed to the data base or the enabling objectives may not be consistent with the terminal objectives. This inadequacy can be resolved using basically the same inquiry approach outlined for a poorly defined design. Needless to say, the modified program should be put through the same rigorous evaluation as the original program.

Ideally, at this stage of the evaluation process the decision-makers can work closely with the evaluator. The decision-makers should be provided with an evaluation report including the judgments and recommendations of the evaluator. The decision-maker may agree or disagree with the evaluator's interpretations. The decision-maker can request more information if he does not consider the data included in the report an adequate basis for making judgments as to the adequacy and appropriateness of the design. The final decision, as well as relevant comments on extraneous factors which influenced the decision, should be recorded as a supplement or addendum to the evaluation report.

PART IV: Testing and Achieving Solutions in Teacher Education

14

Evaluating at the Program Installation Stage

As the previous chapter pointed out, a thoughtful and well-constructed design is essential if the intent of the program is to be understood by those responsible for implementation. Yet even an ostensibly superior design may not result in a successful program. Or, if this hurdle is overcome, the program may run into difficulties after it is installed. Conducting evaluation activities concurrent with the installation and operation of the program can provide decision-makers with immediate and relevant information so that the program can be modified if necessary.

PROGRAM INSTALLATION: CONSIDERATIONS

Evaluating program installation involves the assessment of those activities and decisions associated with initiating the program or increments of the program. During the preservice teacher education program, installation is an on-going activity over a four-year program. In examining program installation, it is necessary to look at three basic components: 1) the feasibility of the installation; 2) the adequacy of recruitment; and 3) student-instructor activity. To evaluate these components, they are compared with the program standards as developed in the program design.

Feasibility

Examining the feasibility of installation should provide information as to which curriculum components should be installed and when they should be installed. This aspect of the evaluation may be considered a "minifeasibility study." The program has been designed within parameters of what the institution or sponsoring agency has identified as needs, that is, desired competencies for teachers. The needs assessment and resultant data base are used to develop design standard criteria. This standard has been developed with input by educational practitioners and experts in the field of education and represents an ideal or a criterion of desirability. In designing the program, the capabilities and resources of the sponsoring agencies are also taken into consideration. Therefore, while the data base provides the design standard for the program, the existing and projected resource base of the sponsoring agencies provides design parameters. At the point of installation, however, specific decisions must be made about the availability of the resource base and the resource needs of the program as proposed.

The program, if properly designed, includes a hierarchical arrangement of components, that is, courses, skills, or competencies. This curriculum structure represents limitations which must be considered when determining which components of the program will be installed. Given the basic curriculum structure as proposed in the program design, several factors will impact on the decision as to which components will be installed or the incremental scheduling of installation if the program is to be phased in.

The first factor to be considered is the availability of human resources—specifically, the instructional and field staff. The most obvious concern at this point is the availability of staff having the prerequisite skills to provide instruction and supervision for particular program components. However, the logistics of bringing students together with instructors with specific teaching skills may also be a consideration. The time and duration of interaction between students and staff with specialized skills or roles in the instructional process may place limitations on the program. In preservice teacher training programs, this is more likely to be a problem in determining which areas of specialization and possibly cognate areas will be offered as part of the program.

A second factor which may act as a constraint in program installation is the availability or unavailability of facilities. This includes space, special equipment, and expendables needed for the program. Buildings with unusual class or lab design as well as specialized equipment and materials may circumscribe the program offerings.

The third factor which must be considered is the cost of the curriculum components. This specifically involves the money required for facilities, maintenance, and personnel. Decision-makers must frequently make judgments about the appropriate allocation of finite resources. Given an estimated range of costs or specific cost estimates for each of the components of the curriculum, the most desirable level of funding for each component should be established. Some administrators may favor cutting corners in order to provide a wide variety of educational opportunities for the student. To others, it might be preferable to offer more limited choices with higher quality or more generously funded educational opportunities. This primarily involves a value judgment on the part of the administrators although the evaluator and, to a lesser extent, the program design specialists will play a major role in providing the information necessary for reaching decisions of this kind.

Recruitment

The second target of installation evaluation is the adequacy of the recruitment procedures. As part of the program design, selection criteria and recruitment criteria for faculty and/or instructors, students, participating teachers, and other program staff are developed. During the installation stage, it is necessary to examine the efficacy of the procedures and the criteria. This is partially a matter of determining whether or not an adequate staff has been procured for the program components scheduled for immediate installment. If not, the evaluator must determine if the proposed staff recruitment procedures have been followed. If the answer to this question is yes, then the recruitment procedures should be examined to determine why they do not result in a satisfactory staff.

For the most part, teaching staff needs will be determined by the specific design of the courses to be offered or by the diversity of topics to be covered in a single course. For example, the professional core courses Achievement Testing or Instructional Aids are relatively unidimensional. Either could be effectively taught by a single instructor. In contrast, Teaching as a Profession, because it provides an overview of the teaching profession and deals with a variety of topics, would benefit from the team approach to instruction. Some courses, such as Philosophies and Theories Applied to Education could be taught effectively by a single instructor. However, participation by faculty with a special interest in certain topics to be covered adds an element of vitality to the course.

A review of the table of specifications developed for each course to be offered will assist in the selection of teaching staff for the course. Specifically, the topics to be addressed and, to a lesser extent, the knowledge level at which the material will be taught can be matched to the known expertise and interests of the teaching staff. This procedure will facilitate the selection of appropriate instructors. Determining the appropriateness of staff skill or expertise is dependent on the particular role to be filled by the staff member. In evaluating teaching staff selection criteria, it may be necessary to observe the staff member in the classroom. It should be realized that an educational program can be worse than useless—actually damaging—if the staff is not properly selected. On the other hand, an excellent staff can do a great deal to salvage a poorly designed program. Care should be taken not to underestimate the importance of adequately evaluating the staff, student recruitment procedures, and selection criteria.

Student recruitment procedures should be examined in much the same manner as were the staff recruitment procedures. Depending upon the institution or sponsoring agency, minimum teacher-student ratios are often specified in order for a course or program to be implemented and/or continued. Again, this concern is a consideration in determining which components of the program will be installed or, if the program is to be installed incrementally, which components are scheduled for earliest installation. This aspect of the program feasibility study may be decided on the basis of preenrollment figures, preregistration, or *accurate* enrollment estimates. It is important that every effort be made to secure reliable data for this decision. It is potentially disruptive to the program to discover a miscalculation of student participation in the later phase of program installation.

Successful recruitment procedures, including publicizing the program, facilitating admission procedures, and possibly providing incentives for program participation, should in part eliminate the problem of underenrollment or underinvolvement. If the level of participation becomes a problem, then recruitment practices should be examined to determine whether they accurately coincide with the recruitment procedures proposed in the design. If the proposed procedures were followed and did not result in sufficient participation, then the procedures as designed may be weak and correctives should be applied.

It should be noted at this point that the projection of whether or not participation in a program will be adequate should not be based upon preregistration *per se*. The attrition or "participant mortality" rate can be calculated for the particular type of program and institution. This information should enter into early decisions about recruitment adequacy. Obviously, the degree and impact of attrition will vary from one situation to another. A three-day inservice program will have a very different attrition rate from that of a four-year program in an institution of higher learning. However, program administrators in both types of settings should have sufficient data to make decisions about present and projected participation.

The appropriateness of student selection criteria, like that of staff selection criteria, should not be determined until late in the installation stage. While closely linked to many aspects of the program, this is largely a function of four variables. The first variable is that of recruitment success. Overly stringent or inappropriate selection criteria at this point may result in difficulties in finding and attracting students to the program. However, this should only be a consideration after recruitment practices and proposed procedures have been subjected to careful study.

In the model job-related curriculum the course Teaching as a Profession serves as an additional screening device. During the course the student is exposed to a variety of activities which give him an orientation to the demands of teaching. Instruments are used to assess whether or not the student has realistic perceptions of teaching. Also, the student's attitudes toward teaching are measured. Based on this information about teaching and about himself, it is assumed that the student, with appropriate guidance, can make an early decision whether or not to continue preparing for the teaching profession. The course, in a sense, provides an opportunity for self-selection.

The second variable is the student attrition rate. Students who have been admitted to a program which is not appropriate for them will often recognize this early in the program and will choose to leave the program or will be eliminated from further participation through the normal measurement and student evaluation processes. An exceptionally high attrition rate—higher than normal for the type of program—may indicate problems in the selection criteria or in their application.

The inability of students to meet program objectives, particularly enabling objectives, is another indicator of weaknesses in the selection criteria. Assuming that the objectives are properly designed and are basically hierarchical in structure, if students are unable to achieve the enabling objectives, it is unlikely that they will be able to achieve the terminal or ultimate objectives. Obviously, there will be some students in every program who have problems with some of the enabling objectives. However, inappropriate selection criteria will result in widespread problems with objectives attainment. An examination of the attainment of enabling objectives will allow an early detection of this problem. However, it should be noted again that identification of faulty selection criteria and practices at this point in the installation—after the program activities are underway—can present serious problems in installing corrective actions.

The final variable in determining the adequacy of student selection criteria is that of student-teacher interaction. This is particularly the case in preservice programs, where appropriate attitudes toward teaching should be a consideration in selecting students. Prospective teachers whose skills and attitudes are not appropriate to the teaching profession may exhibit a different pattern of interaction with their instructors, supervising teachers, peers, and/or learners in the classroom or lab setting.

Student-Teacher Interaction

The third component of program installation is the level or quality of student and teacher activity. It should be possible to compare student-teacher interaction or level of activity to the program specifications developed in the program design itself. Comparison of program standard with actual performance may take several forms. Nonquantified measures such as visual verification of described behavior or quantifiable data at least at the ordinal level of measurement may be used. Although there has been some controversy associated with many of the instruments developed to document the nature of student-teacher interaction, many reputable instruments are available. Traditionally, the most reliable method of studying student and teacher activity has been the use of trained observers making repeated observations in carefully defined classroom situations. The observer must be provided with appropriate instruments having adequate and rational schemes for classifying student and/or teacher behaviors. The more precisely the observer can narrow his observations to specific types of behaviors, the more valid the resulting observations will be. When great variation exists between actual teacher behavior, student behavior, and/or student-teacher interaction and those behaviors prescribed in the program design, it becomes the responsibility of the evaluator to document the discrepancy between program performance and program specifications.

Various standardized instruments are available to measure classroom activity. One of these, Flanders Interaction Analysis Categories, can be found in Appendix I. In some instances it may be desirable to develop specific instruments for observing different aspects of the program. Tailored instruments may be constructed by the evaluator or by the program design specialist. See Appendix J for one example of possible format and content of an instrument for measuring student-teacher interaction. It should be noted that there are advantages to using an instrument specifically designed for the needs of the particular program being evaluated. However, if provisions cannot be made for establishing validity of the tailored instruments, it may be desirable to utilize a standardized instrument.

EVALUATING INSTALLATION

The data gathering process required for the evaluation of installation serves several purposes. It provides feedback to the staff during the installation process. It permits the identification of potential problems in the design and implementation of the program. It also provides information for program decisions.

In conducting the evaluation, there are several major considerations which will establish the direction for monitoring program activities. These have been discussed in the preceding section. Potential problem areas are identified and subsequently monitored. Among the areas which are particularly sensitive are the acceptance of change and support for the program by those involved in and/or affected by it, communications, student-staff interactions, logistics and scheduling, and adequacy of resources, physical facilities, and staff.

"Preprogrammed" decisions and the processes that provide the information necessary for these decisions are delineated. An example of these activities is the selection of students for the job-related curriculum program. This is basically a program installation decision although the preprogramming occurred during the design stage. This decision is projected well before the actual decision process takes place. However, selection cannot actually be made until the program has been publicized, students have been recruited, and applications accepted and reviewed. Then the program staff or administrator must select those students who most nearly meet the requirements outlined in the selection criteria. Such decisions imply detailed evaluation data requirements as well as advance structuring of the program design. Since this type of decision is generally essential to the operationalization of the program design, it has a major impact on the success of the program. The projection and delineation of preprogrammed decisions is therefore an important feature of the evaluation process.

Finally, as an important part of the evaluation, the main features of program design and the extent to which these are modified or deviated from in program installation should be observed and recorded. Later, this data may be valuable in understanding why program objectives may not have been achieved. This is particularly useful in identifying the stage which is at fault for deficiencies in the program.

It should be noted that the more adequate the problem identification and design evaluation, the more certain one can be of success during the installation stage. A rigorous application of evaluation techniques at the problem identification and design stages will minimize the problems encountered at the later evaluation stages. If program criteria and objectives are ill defined, the program is destined for failure since each stage builds upon the previous one.

Installation considerations will allow the identification of needed changes in the program. During the evaluation of program installation, basically the evaluator is testing for congruence between the observed aspect of the program as it is being installed and the standard provided for that aspect by the program design. The evaluator must proceed item by item through the program design as it is applicable to the installation. Because of the limited resources usually available to the evaluator, it may not be possible for him to test each item or variable in the program design. Consequently, it becomes necessary to select items to test on the basis of (1) the possibility of finding significant discrepancies between the particular aspect of the program and the actual performance of that aspect, and (2) the readiness with which that item or variable may be observed. The evaluator is trying to locate problems in the program. Identification of a malfunction of a specific component of the program during the installation stage allows early and, therefore, minimally disruptive program change and improvement.

In evaluating installation, an inquiry procedure very similar to that used for program design evaluation can be employed. The use of a question format simplifies the process and promotes the identification of problem areas. The appropriate starting point is with the following questions (Provus, 1971):

Has the program been installed?
If not, what should be done to install the program?
What are the alternate installation strategies?
What are the operational constraints on these strategies?
What are the best possible strategies (strategies with the least operational restraints)?
Which strategy is best?

If the program is installed, is there a discrepancy between the functioning program and the appropriate design standards?

What was the installation procedure used?

Where did the procedural breakdown occur?

What corrective alternatives are possible within the design parameters?

Which corrective alternative seems best?

Is the corrective adequately defined?

Has the corrective been installed?

Does a discrepancy still exist? (p. 190)

This inquiry procedure can be repeated until all sources of discrepancy between the program installation and the design standards have been satisfactorily controlled or eliminated. The content of the questions may vary depending upon the specific nature of the program and its design. The general format, however, is believed to be effective for achieving the desired purpose.

The evaluation of installation and of operations is generally conducted simultaneously. For the preservice program, installation is in fact an ongoing activity over the initial four years of the program. Each year an additional level of the program is installed. Consequently, program installation is being carried on concurrently with program operation. In addition, if problems are identified in either installation or operations and a decision is reached to modify rather than continue or terminate the program, the modification may take place either during installation or in operations.

In examining installation, the evaluator looks for a discrepancy between program installation and design standards for installation. Emphasis is placed on examining program feasibility, recruitment, and student-faculty interaction. The primary consideration at this point is installation fidelity. If a major discrepancy exists, an adjustment in installation allows the operating program to more closely approximate the program as designed. Any incongruence between design and installation which is left uncorrected will increase the discrepancy between design and operations. This allows the gap between design and performance to further widen at later stages.

15

Evaluating at the Program Operation Stage

Evaluation at the program operation stage is intended to insure that the program is functioning as it was designed. As discussed in Chapter 14, the evaluation of installation and of operations is generally conducted simultaneously. Operations data, like that resulting from installation evaluation, provides feedback to the program staff. Similarly, it permits identification of potential and existing problems in the program and provides information for decision-making. In general, installation and operations data are complementary. There are, however, two basic differences. First, different aspects of the program are examined when assessing the program operation. To evaluate program operations one examines instructional, population, and behavioral characteristics as well as the activities and decisions associated with the functioning program. This is discussed further in the following section. Second, evaluation of program operations is not initiated until the program (or the components of it which are to be evaluated) has been installed and is functioning. Thus, problems identified in the program are not simply the normal adjustment complications associated with installing the program.

PROGRAM OPERATIONS: CONSIDERATIONS

In examining program operations, it is necessary to look at both the total program and at its components. In the preservice program, the components of the program basically consist of the coursework and the fieldwork. These should be examined individually and then in their entirety as the total curriculum. At this point, it is essential to examine the interaction among learning activities to determine whether the components and lower level objectives do in fact comprise the desired learning experience.

Course Achievement

The use of enabling objectives provides a firm basis for making assessments and decisions about both the program and the students. The degree to which objectives are attained can provide reliable measures of educational output. Enabling objectives permit rational decision-making processes to be followed and provide a basis for informed choices, not only for staff but also for students.

During the program design stage, it is essential to ensure that the enabling objectives are well stated. It is also at this stage that the enabling objectives themselves are evaluated to determine their relationship to the needs assessment. At the program effectiveness stage, these objectives are now useful for evaluating the participant in the program as a product of the program.

It is recommended that as part of the program design specific evaluation mechanisms keyed to the enabling objectives be developed. Where indirect observation techniques are proposed for the assessment of specific objectives, test item banks may be developed as part of the program design. Other instruments needed for drawing inferences about program impact on the participant should be developed or selected (such as, standardized instruments) in conjunction with the enabling objectives.

Criterion measures for the evaluation of the attainment of enabling objectives may be categorized as standardized measures and scales, instructor-made instruments and devices, and informal projective devices. While standardized instruments are usually more useful for the measurement of terminal and ultimate objective achievement, some devices may be considered valuable for the measurement of enabling objectives. Some of these are discussed below:

1. Standardized self-inventories may be useful to examine changes in attitudes and values which represent the attainment of affective objectives. It should be noted that these often require pre- and post-testing procedures.

2. Standardized rating scales can be used for judging the quality of products such as compositions, lesson plans, media products, and visual displays.

3. Standardized tests may be useful for measuring the attainment of psychomotor skills and objectives related to physical competencies.

The more commonly used standardized achievement and aptitude scales have little practical value for measuring enabling objectives although they may be useful in making selection and placement decisions.

Instructor-made instruments are devices which are probably the most widely used and the most appropriate mechanisms for measuring enabling objectives. While the unimaginative instructor sometimes limits himself to one kind of test as a measure of achievement, there are in fact a variety of techniques which are quite functional for various types of enabling objectives:

1. The incomplete sentence technique is useful for measuring affective objective attainment. This technique involves the categorization of types of responses, their frequency of occurrence, and the interpretation of their meaning.

2. Teacher-devised projective devices such as role-playing, simulation of class-room encounters, case study interpretations, and similar activities are useful in reaching affective objectives. These devices are usually scored on the basis of the demonstration or frequency of demonstration of specific behaviors. The quality and intensity of emotional responses may also be assessed.

3. Teacher-made rating scales and checklists for specific behaviors in the class-room or in the lab setting can be used to assess cognitive and affective objectives.

4. Teacher-made achievement tests, both objective and essay, are particularly useful in evaluating the attainment of cognitive objectives.

A third category consists of these measurement devices which are not comfortably classified as either standardized or teacher-made instruments. These indicators of change in student behavior are often too informal to be useful for the purpose of officially certifying student achievement, that is, assigning grades. However, for formative evaluation, they may be valuable for projecting the extent to which enabling objectives are being met and for anticipating weak areas in student performance. These include a wide variety of observational methods:

1. Anecdotal records are useful for noting and recording behaviors which, particu-larly in terms of affective objectives, have been judged to be undesirable or highly desirable.

2. Assignments may be part of the formal or informal evaluation process.

3. Choices and changes expressed or carried out are useful when examined in terms of their appropriateness to identified affective objectives.

4. Attrition rate, particularly in regard to the number of drop-outs from a particu-lar course, may be considered a reflection on the extent to which objectives are being met or, more importantly, can be met by the students.

5. Demonstration of skills or new competencies, specifically those involved in learner-teacher interactions and interpersonal skills which cannot be readily measured by available instruments, may be considered an indicator of progress in attaining enabling objectives.

The selection and development of the appropriate instruments for measur-ing attainment of enabling objectives is only one step in determining program effectiveness. The actual scheduling of observation activities requires some skilled judgments on the part of the instructor. Frequently, measurement instruments are administered upon completion of a unit of study or at the point when a topic of instruction has been exhausted. Enabling objectives are often written to coincide with what the instructional designer considers to be a unit of instruction. Consequently, they are sometimes labeled "unit" objectives. While this particular approach may not always represent the most logical structure for information to be covered in a course, it does have the advantages of familiarity and common usage. It may be desirable to test upon completion of the instructional activities related to several enabling objectives or to observe progress after each individual objective has been addressed. This decision should be largely a matter of considering the nature of the course, the types of instrumentation proposed, and, to a lesser extent, the preferences of the instructional designer.

A more prominent controversy associated with postsecondary instruction today is the validity of cumulative final examinations as indices of behavioral change with respect to enabling and terminal objectives. Proponents of the use of task analysis in the construction of educational objectives state that terminal objectives generally are written at a different knowledge level than are enabling objectives. Consequently, the specific type of instrumentation needed to measure the attainment of terminal objectives will differ from that used to test the attainment of enabling objectives. The counterargument is that the subdivision of a learning task, for instance, breaking down the terminal objective into a logical hierarchy of subskills or enabling objectives, does not ensure that the higher level skill or task will be achieved. This has been one of the primary arguments against widespread use of task analysis in instructional design.

From the standpoint of the evaluator, the measurement of attainment of terminal objectives serves two important functions. First, it permits the determination of whether the instructional program has in fact brought about the behavioral changes specified in the objectives developed as part of the program design. Second, it is useful in determining whether the attainment of the subskills represented by the enabling objectives have resulted in the attainment of the terminal objectives. For example, if a student's performance on behavioral indices of the enabling objectives is satisfactory but his performance on an instrument designed to measure attainment of the terminal objective is unsatisfactory, it may be necessary to examine the relationships between the enabling and terminal objectives. It is quite possible that the subskills represented by the enabling objectives are not components of the skills represented by the terminal objectives.

It should be noted at this point that measuring attainment of the terminal objective does not necessarily correspond to the traditional cumulative "final exam." The typical final examination covers a sample of enabling objectives with appropriate items for testing attainment of those objectives. In this manner, the retention skills and perhaps the student's ability to second guess the instructor's choice of objectives is to be measured. A more appropriate final examination is an instrument that is specifically designed to measure the terminal objectives and consists of items or activities which were designed and constructed at the level appropriate for this purpose. It is not the purpose of this book to provide detailed instructions for test construction; however, several excellent texts are available for this purpose. A few of these are listed in Appendix K.

Having developed appropriate instruments for measuring objectives, the next steps involve the actual administration of the instruments and the use of appropriate statistical methods to analyze the resulting data. Administering the instrument is largely a matter of clear communications. Written instructions are mandatory to avoid misunderstanding or even confrontations with students who may believe that they were not made aware of the performance to be required. It is a common misconception that writing the instructions for an instrument is the simplest aspect of its preparation and administration. The same care should be used in writing the instructions as that which is used in the design of items or activities.

The selection and application of appropriate statistical techniques for analyzing the data provided by the measurement instrument is often simply a matter of counting the number of test items correct or the number of points accrued by the student as a result of a specified performance. Again, value judgments should be kept to a minimum. In other words, every effort should be made to ensure that the scoring procedures for any activity which is to be used as a measurement device be as objective as possible. Measurement and evaluation are two distinct activities. Subjectivity and value judgments should be limited as much as possible to the act of evaluation itself. The use of properly constructed objective tests—multiple-choice, matching, true-false, short answer supply-type formats—is certainly one means of ensuring objectivity in the scoring process. However, these formats are not always appropriate to the objectives being measured. The use of checklists, analytical scoring procedures for essay questions, and similar explicit scoring guidelines will assist in eliminating unreliable subjective judgment from the process. Several texts are available to provide additional information on scoring and statistical analysis. Among these are the texts listed in Appendix L.

Data on student achievement must be interpreted. This requires value judgments as to what constitutes adequate performance on the measures of attainment. On the basis of these interpretations, conclusions can be drawn about the behavioral changes or growth of the students as well as about the effectiveness of the program in bringing about these changes. The actual method used to determine what level of performance constitutes a minimal adequate behavior change is often a matter of personal philosophy on the part of the curriculum or instructional designer. Basically, however, the evaluator of student performance is making a comparison and from that comparison drawing inferences about the student's level of achievement.

To what is the student's performance compared? One approach is to compare the student's performance to that of other students. Another approach is to compare each student's performance to predetermined levels of achievement. This type of interpretation may be considered to provide information about absolute achievement since comparison is based on an absolute criterion. Much criticism has been directed toward the arbitrariness of using a predetermined level of achievement for grading purposes. However, criterion-related evaluation is conducive to determining the extent to which each enabling objective has been attained both by the individual student and by the class and group as a whole. It should be recognized that evaluation not only results in certification of student performance but also in the certification of program effectiveness. The preestablishment of desired levels of student performance also implies the preestablishment of desired levels of program performance. The latter is a very basic aspect of instructional design. The program designer specialist should have the expertise to determine the minimal acceptable levels of performance which might be considered indicative of competence in a particular area. More importantly, he should be sufficiently cognizant of the values implied as well as stated in the data base in order to incorporate them into the course evaluation procedures. For resources for marking and reporting systems see Appendix L.

Student-Instructor Interaction

In examining program operations, another consideration is that of student-instructor interaction. While achievement is the primary function of any educational program, the quality of the interaction between the instructor and the class and the level of the instructor's performance are important variables which affect student achievement. These variables are not directly examined in the measurement of the attainment of enabling or terminal objectives. There appears to be general agreement as to the importance of instructor performance both in preservice and inservice educational programs. However, there is much less agreement about the need to evaluate the performance of the instructor.

Indeed, the concensus completely evaporates when the issue of evaluation methods arises. Information to be used in the evaluation of instructors can be derived from department chairmen, deans, colleagues, committee evaluations, self-reports, student ratings, informal student opinions, grade distributions, course syllabi, course examinations, and even enrollment figures for elective courses. Obviously, criticism may be leveled at the use of a number of these sources of information.

No universally agreed upon standards of teacher effectiveness exist. However, research on instructional evaluation has resulted in the development of a general picture of good teaching. While no one list of teacher behaviors has been accepted as characteristic of the good instructor, specific cognitive and affective qualities seem to reoccur in research on instructor effectiveness. These can be categorized as competence in subject area, competence in instructional techniques, positive attitude toward students, and positive attitude toward subject matter. Since many educators believe that the ultimate criterion of an instructor's effectiveness is his impact on his students, it would seem that students can provide one of the most valid sources of information of instructor evaluation.

Student evaluation of instructors, however, demands the use of a carefully

constructed instrument. It is recommended that the instrument be administered twice during the semester or program term. If administered early during
the period, the instructor can use the findings to modify his performance
for the remainder of the program term. After the second administration,
the evaluation results may be placed in the instructor's personnel folder or
in a separate evaluation file.

There are several acceptable formats for student evaluation of instructor
performance. Student anonymity is essential for candid evaluation. It is desirable to limit the amount of writing required on the evaluation form. A standardized format may eliminate many interpretation problems. Sample formats
are provided in Appendix M. These may be used as constructed or as a
model to be adapted to the specific program for which they will be used.

Objectivity, reliability, and validity must be considered in the development
of instructor evaluation instruments. The use of a standardized format will
help to establish objectivity. Certain problems arise in trying to establish
reliability for this type of instrument. Probably the most cogent concern is
with the instrument's stability or reliability over time. If instructor performance changes, particularly as a result of an early administration of the evaluation instrument, student assessment of instructor performance will probably
change also. This will be reflected in lower reliability estimates. Internal
consistency is a second method of establishing reliability. This is generally
thought to be a weaker form of reliability. If the instrument is multidimen-
sional, that is, if it covers several factors such as competence in subject
area, competence in instructional techniques, positive attitude toward students, and so forth, reliability estimates based on internal consistency may
not be very high. Equivalent forms of the instrument may be used to establish
reliability if the characteristics of the instrument preclude the use of stability
or internal consistency. However, this procedure may be inconvenient because
equivalence between two forms of the instruments must be established. Instrument validity will probably take the form of face and construct validity.
See Appendix K for resources on instrument construction.

Judgment is essential in the use of student evaluations of staff. Instructors
who are having their first experiences with teaching should be evaluated
primarily with the purpose of providing information for improving their instructional techniques. Those teaching outside of their area of specialization
by administrative necessity or whose areas of specialization include courses
that are unpopular or academically strenuous face special problems in being
evaluated by students. Efforts must be made to prevent evaluation from taking
on unpleasant or punitive connotations. Emphasis must be placed on the
evaluation as a tool for improving instruction. Its role in merit increases,
promotion, and tenure decisions should be minimized.

A second important source of information for the assessment of instructor
effectiveness is evaluation by peers. This category includes colleagues, department chairmen, deans, or departmental committees. Unfortunately, evaluation
by peers tends to be biased in favor of the full professor or faculty member
with some standing in the institution or sponsoring agency. In many instances,

seniority is assumed to be equivalent to professional competence. To further complicate the matter, peer evaluations may tend to confuse teaching competence with one's professional reputation for research. Excellence in research should be considered independent of teaching effectiveness and should not be used as a criterion for evaluating classroom performance.

Peer evaluation of instruction may involve some form of classroom observation as a supplement to student evaluation. This is particularly useful when contradictory or negative judgments are expressed by students.

Several sample peer evaluation scales are provided. Again, it is preferable to tailor an instrument to the specific needs of the program. As is the case with student appraisal of teaching instruments, objectivity, reliability, and validity are important considerations.

Field Experiences

Assessment of how well the program is contributing to the achievement of enabling and terminal objectives is not complete until the student's field experiences have been examined. Ideally, field experiences bridge the gap between theory and practice. They allow the student to exercise his newly acquired knowledge and insights in a teaching-learning setting. One of the fundamental goals of the job-related curriculum for teacher preservice education is to integrate theory and practice through the integration of coursework and field experiences.

In recommending a procedure for examining the preservice field experience, it is important to realize that variations in the field experience will exist from program to program. To some extent these differences will result from variations in the administrative structures or policies of sponsoring agencies or institutions. In addition, each program is designed from a data base which is characteristic of the service area of the program. Obviously, the data base developed for a program which will produce teachers primarily for a major metropolitan area will differ from that attuned to the needs of rural communities. However, the major sources of variation in field experiences are, in fact, intraprogram differences. A number of factors impact on the evaluation procedure including the scheduling of the field experience—time of year, frequency and duration of the experience, the academic classification of the student, and the specific teaching situation in which the field experience occurs.

Assigned fieldwork, like more traditional coursework, is keyed to enabling and terminal objectives. Measuring the attainment of these objectives involves very similar processes to those cited previously. However, program staff and other individuals who share responsibility for assuring that program performance adheres to the standards established in the program design do not always have the same ability to control the field experience as they do with classroom experiences. Therefore, the initial step in evaluating the effectiveness of the field experience is not to examine the student's attainment of enabling objectives but rather to make certain that the particular education setting provides the student with the experiences and opportunities needed for the attainment of objectives. Student achievement cannot be assessed without first evaluating the opportunities that exist to foster achievement.

The most widely used mechanism for examining the field experience is the observational record. The most widely used records are usually booklets in which a trained observer can record what he saw and thought with respect to several specified topics of concern. While the topics and items included in the booklet will vary depending on the nature of the experience, documentation of the environmental conditions of the learning situation and of student behavior or performance in the setting are generally included. What the observer "saw" and what the observer "thought" must be treated separately. The record is not a grading scale but rather a device for recording observations. This is a fine distinction that must be maintained if the instrument is to serve its measurement function. For this reason, observations are recorded by checking the appropriate spaces and by anecdotal comments. As noted previously, evaluation or the exercise of a value judgment is an activity that is distinct from observation and measurement.

The observer may, in fact, be a program staff member or a cooperating teacher. In either case, however, the evaluation process should be carried out *with* the student not just *on* the student. Not only is the student being evaluated in terms of attaining the objectives but also the program is being evaluated.

Several sample formats from the Ohio Observational Record are included in Appendix N. These were designed primarily for evaluating the performance of practice teachers. They may be modified for use in other types of learning settings. Again, as with other evaluation instruments, objectivity, reliability, and validity must be considered in the development of a tailored scale.

Another viable source of information about the field experience is the student's assessment of its value. The student's evaluation of the experience as well as his self-evaluation of performance in the setting may be useful. A basic tool in the instructional process may be the analysis of problems encountered by the student in the field. The use of this device can be proposed as part of the program design. While its primary function is obviously instructional, its value as an evaluation instrument should not be disregarded. A format which may be useful in analyzing student problems is provided in Appendix O.

The Total Curriculum

The individual courses and their associated field experiences represent subcomponents of the curriculum. In examining the subcomponents, the evaluator assesses the extent to which enabling and terminal objectives are being attained. Instructor performance and student-instructor interaction are also observed. However, determining that each subcomponent independently is operating effectively does not assure that the total program is operating effectively. The ultimate test of program effectiveness will be the product evaluation discussed in Chapter 16. This involves determination of the extent to which the ultimate objectives are being attained by the program. However, there is an intermediate step between the observation of enabling and terminal objectives and the ultimate objectives. There remains a gap between the behavioral changes brought about by each independent learning activity and those brought about by the aggregate of the learning activities. This is the relationship between the subcomponents of the program and the total program.

Having looked at the learning experiences independently, it is necessary to look at the total curriculum. Several aspects of the curriculum must be considered. One is the scheduling and logistics, that is, whether or not the program actually runs smoothly. The course load demand on the student must also be examined. Individually, the course demands can be easily assessed by looking at group attainment of enabling and terminal objectives. However, the demands of the entire series of courses required for the student to keep pace with the overall program schedule may be overwhelming for the average or marginal student. Finally, it is assumed that the individual learning experiences are complementary. In a preservice program, coursework and fieldwork supposedly bridge the gap between theory and practice. Inservice activities theoretically carry over to application in the classroom. All learning activity— whether it is the more traditional coursework of the preservice program or the topic of the inservice program—should be structured in such a way that prerequisite activities are properly sequenced and both supplementary and complementary experiences are provided at the appropriate intervals. While this begins as a design problem, once the program is installed and operating, it becomes an evaluation concern. It is naive to assume that even in the most meticulously designed program adjustments will not have to be made in the field. So in examining the total curriculum, the interaction among the learning activities is a major concern. We must look at the program components and ask the question, Do we find interface or do we see conflict?

The examination of program scheduling and logistics is part of the effort to provide periodic feedback to the staff members responsible for implementing the program design. This is accomplished by identifying and continuously monitoring the use of resources, physical facilities, and staff with particular emphasis on scheduling. Regular meetings between the evaluator and staff will insure that the evaluator has the necessary information to determine if staff-student activities are running smoothly and if optimal use is being made of all available human and material resources. In the case of the inservice program, the program administrator should be able to provide the necessary feedback directly to the staff. Regardless of whether the administrator, evaluator, or program specialist assumes responsibility for this aspect of program monitoring, it is essential that continuous feedback about how the program is functioning be provided. How efficiently the program is actually operating in terms of scheduling and logistics is crucial during the early stages of program implementation. Later, as adjustments are made as a result of evaluation and the program becomes more structured, this aspect of the evaluation process becomes less critical. It should be realized that, except for blatant conflicts in the scheduling of learning activities and use of resources, all decisions for restructuring the program should be supported by the findings of the evaluation of enabling and terminal objectives.

The course load demand on the student is another very important consideration associated with program operations. In assessing this aspect of the program, the philosophy underlying the program is important. Most education programs, either preservice or inservice, attract participants with widely varying levels of ability, special skills or strengths, and interests and aspirations. Even within the range of minimum required entry skills, there is a great deal of variance. In assessing the extent to which the program or course load requirements on the student may be too demanding, first one must decide who the student actually is. It may be a matter of examining program demands on the average student. It appears to be a widespread practice to gear instruction to the average—whatever that may be interpreted to mean. On the other hand, in establishing selection criteria for the preservice program, one must look at the basic assumptions upon which the design of student selection criteria were based. It may have been assumed that there exists a high degree of probability that students who meet the minimal entry requirements can be developed or cultivated into adequate or competent teachers through the program. In this instance, the minimum entry requirements are probably rather high. Thus, fewer students meet the requirements and more consideration must be given to program demands on the marginal student. However, student selection criteria are often based on the assumption that the program itself will weed out those students who do not in fact have the aptitude to become teachers. Frequently, it is believed that it is more democratic to give as many students as possible an opportunity to enter the program regardless of how ill prepared they may be or how probable it is that they will drop out of the program before completing it.

In the case of the inservice program, a somewhat different consideration exists. The participants in the inservice program are practicing educators. Generally, the participants will be full-time classroom teachers, counselors, and school administrators. Often the program includes teaching aides. Occasionally, inservice programs are geared to the substitute teacher. Regardless of the emphasis of the particular inservice program, it may be assumed that all participants are practitioners. Basically, this means that all inservice participants have met the minimum requirements of their profession. They are not to be weeded out of the profession by the demands of the inservice program. They will merely benefit or not benefit from the program. The extent to which participants of the inservice program do not benefit or, worse yet, become disillusioned with inservice programs in general, may be taken as an indication of the value of the program rather than as an indication of the value of the participants. In assessing the demands of the inservice program, it is necessary to consider the performance of all participants—not just those who may be considered average or above average.

The second step in assessing the program demand on the participant is to establish a level at which the program may be considered excessively demanding. One approach to this problem would be to look at the average attrition rate of similar programs. The evaluator would become concerned only if the attrition rate of the program exceeds this rate. This is not a particularly desirable approach for a number of reasons. First, irreparable damage may have already been done to the program in terms of loss of promising students and inability to attract students in the future. Secondly, damage may have been done to the students who have been eliminated under these circumstances. Finally, if the new program is assumed to be an improvement over competing or previous programs, it is preferable to provide absolute criteria for evaluation rather than the relative criteria of comparison.

An approach more in keeping with this philosophy would be to preestablish a maximum percentage of students who could be allowed to fail to achieve the terminal objectives for a specified program period. The program period may be as long as a year or as short as one semester. However, if the specified percentage of students is exceeded, the curriculum demands for that particular period should be examined. The use of the attainment of terminal objectives allows the study of limited segments of the total program. Correctives and adjustments can be made before the problem becomes critical either for the program or for the student. Students, particularly those who fail to attain terminal objectives, provide a good source of information about the stringency of program demands. Obviously, these students should be provided with counseling and all other appropriate support to assist them in continuing in the program more successfully.

The actual establishment of a criterion level for determining the stringency of program demand is a judgment to be made by the decision-makers. The considerations in reaching this decision are very similar to those used to decide the level at which the program demands are to be geared. In the preservice program, if it is the function of student selection criteria to eliminate the less promising students, then the percentage of failure or those who do not attain terminal objectives that will be tolerated before the program comes under critical scrutiny must be very low. If selection criteria are not particularly stringent and it is considered a function of the program to eliminate the less promising, then the maximum percentage of failures tolerated may be considerably higher. These particular judgments are within the realm of the program decision-makers and/or the policy body of the institution or agency sponsoring the program. It is the responsibility of the evaluator to assure that, having established these evaluation criteria, the decision-maker is provided with sufficent information to make valid judgments regarding program demands.

Reliable sources of information for this aspect of the program evaluation are not limited to the end-of-term grades. Project staff, particularly those directly involved in teaching and otherwise interacting with the students, are an excellent source of information. They may not have the necessary combination of time and objectivity to conduct their own evaluation of the level of demand of the total program. However, their knowledgeability with the particular aspects of the program for which they are responsible and their familiarity with the problems and concerns of the student make their input essential. This aspect of the program should be discussed at periodic staff meetings. In addition, the evaluator should feel comfortable in making use of informal data-gathering techniques such as individual interviews, questionnaires, and suggestion boxes.

The third area to be considered in evaluating the total program is the interaction among learning activities. While many different types of learning experiences take place in the course of a teacher's preparation, emphasis must be placed on those activities which are controlled by the program. The job-related teacher education program, preservice or inservice, offers two basic types of directed learning activities—the classroom activity and field experience. Consequently, in examining the interaction among learning activities, it is necessary to look first at the interaction among classroom activities. Then, one should consider the interaction between class and field activities. Since the field activity in the preservice program is normally associated with the classroom or is undertaken with instructional staff direction, the first two considerations should preclude the necessity of examining the interaction among field experiences.

Compatibility and interface of learning activities are primarily based on three design concerns. First, in deriving ultimate objectives from the data base and constructing terminal and enabling objectives from the ultimate objectives, it may be beneficial to use task analysis, or some other analytic procedure to assure that the subobjectives are in fact component learning tasks of the overall objectives. Second, the design of learning activities to achieve the objectives at each level is a critical factor. This task falls within the realm of the instructional design specialist. However, specific learning activities must be keyed to specific objectives. While this method of instructional design minimizes any incidental learning which may be considered by some educators to be valuable in and of itself, it maximizes the probability that the identified learning objectives will be attained. Third, care must be taken in scheduling learning activities that prerequisite experiences are identified and provided at the appropriate time. Complementary and supplementary activities should also be recognized and considered in scheduling.

These design concerns should be examined and assessed during the program design stage; however, during the program operations, it is possible to observe how well this aspect of the design process functions in practice. Again, in obtaining information it is necessary to rely on the program staff, specifically the instructional staff. Using both the formal data gathering procedures of regularly scheduled staff meetings and periodic memos, questionnaires and the informal procedures of individual interview and open-ended reaction sheets, the evaluator can determine the first-hand experiences of the staff. Information about curricular weaknesses, conflicts, and other implementation problems can be obtained in this way. Before recommending modification of learning activities on the basis of these findings, however, it is essential that the attainment of enabling and terminal objectives be scrutinized to note supportive evidence for the identification of problems or conflicts in learning activities.

EVALUATING OPERATIONS

One of the most important aspects of the evaluation of program operations is the use of appropriate instruments. In collecting data, the evaluator should be flexible in the selection of instruments—formal and informal—including such methods as rating scales, records of staff meetings, suggestion boxes, Program Evaluation and Review Technique (PERT) schedules, both direct observation techniques and indirect instruments including Semantic Differential and other affective techniques, as well as cognitive instruments. The evaluator should be imaginative in the development and use of techniques to observe not only those variables which have been designed for observation but also unanticipated by important events.

In examining operations, the evaluator first examines the relationship between the program activities and the attainment of enabling objectives to determine whether the program is functioning properly and in accordance with the design. The major concern is the extent to which program components (instructional activities) are producing a satisfactory interim product: a student who is achieving the enabling objectives. It is at this point in the evaluation that preliminary measures of the product are made.

A second measure of the product is made because it is necessary to determine how effectively the program is producing students who have attained the terminal objectives. The inquiry procedures used in assessing installation are very similar to those used in assessing operations. At this point, however, administrative control over the program is more secure and staff knowledge of and skill in implementing the prescribed learning activities assures that it is the efficacy of the program that is being evaluated and not the smoothness of installation. Problems associated with student and staff selection, the development of appropriate evaluation instruments, and data analysis should have been resolved by this time. As a result, it is more probable that the evaluation findings at this stage are a result of the activities of the program itself and not of extraneous variables such as problems in instrumentation, data gathering and analysis procedures, or lack of program control by administrators or staff.

The use of terminal objectives in evaluating the interim product (the student) assures that the student has been given sufficient opportunity to familiarize himself with the demands and requirements of the program, to receive feedback on his own progress in the program, to avail himself of assistance in the event of academic or other adjustment problems, and to apply whatever correctives are recommended to stabilize and improve his own performance. Also, by evaluating on the basis of terminal rather than ultimate objective attainment, it is possible to identify and correct problem areas before irremediable damage is done to the program or to the students. The inquiry procedure recommended for evaluating program operations may employ any of the following questions:

Is the program achieving its terminal objectives?

Are student-teacher interactions adequate and appropriate for the attainment of terminal objectives?

Are the field experiences complementary to classroom activities?

Does the program "run" smoothly in terms of scheduling and logistics?

Are the program demands on the student excessive?

Is there conflict or interface between the learning activities?

If terminal objectives are not being achieved, why not?

What correctives are possible within the program design?

Which corrective appears to be the most effective?

Has the corrective been installed?

Is the corrective adequate in terms of achieving program design standards?

Does a discrepancy exist between the attainment of terminal objectives in the functioning program and that specified in the program design?

Evaluating program operations, unlike evaluating problem identification, design, or installation, is an on-going activity. This provides for continuous change and refinement of the program and for adjustment to the changing needs of those the program serves as well as technical changes in education. At the installation and operations stage, the decision-makers are faced with three decisions—to continue the program as is, to terminate it, or to modify the program. Modifications or refinements will be to the installation or operation of the program.

The evaluation of program operations is primarily aimed at ensuring that the program is functioning as intended. When discrepancies between design and implementation are identified, these should be remedied if at all possible. It is only when the program is operating according to specifications that its effectiveness can be judged. Trying to evaluate the effectiveness of a program before it is functioning as planned is like trying to judge the quality of a cake while it is still in the oven. Evaluating program effectiveness is essentially a process of certifying or attesting to the merits of the program. Care must be taken not to certify a program that is only half-baked.

16

Evaluating at the Program Effectiveness Stage

PROGRAM EFFECTIVENESS: CONSIDERATIONS

Does a particular teacher education program work? Is it successful in producing teachers who have mastered the skills needed for competent classroom performance? Questions of this variety can only be addressed once the program is operating according to the specifications in the design. In examining program effectiveness, the evaluator is in fact looking at the ultimate objectives to evaluate the educational program product—the student as teacher. This involves the measurement of attainments at the end of the program cycle. The program cycle for the preservice teacher education program is the period of time or the course of studies necessary to prepare the program participant— the student—to teach. The program or training cycle for the inservice program is the completion of a series of coordinated sessions which are designed to bring about a preestablished degree and type of professional growth. The general procedure for evaluating at this stage involves measuring the attainment of ultimate objectives and comparing these measurements with predetermined standards developed in the program design. As the reader will recall, the ultimate objectives are developed at the program design stage from the data base developed during problem identification. During program design, unacceptable levels of failure (to attain ultimate objectives) on the part of the program participants are established. These levels represent the predetermined standards against which the actual attainment of ultimate objectives will be compared.

In any educational undertaking, subprograms or program components can be identified. For example, in the preservice program individual courses and their associated field experiences constitute the program components. The structure of courses represents a chain of events that can be considered a flow of inputs to outputs for any series of learning activities. The ultimate objectives of the program are essentially the solutions to the problems identified at the problem identification stage. These objectives define the parameters of the individual courses; therefore, a clear understanding of the ultimate objectives is essential to the most effective partitioning of terminal and enabling objectives. At the level of individual program components, program effectiveness can be only partially determined. Program effectiveness is predicated on the degree to which ultimate objectives have been attained. The ultimate objectives are those which have been identified most "worth attaining" and for which all subprograms learning activity has been undertaken.

When looking at both program operations and program effectiveness, the primary consideration is the extent to which the objectives are being attained. To evaluate program operations, the functioning of the total program is examined. Many of the judgments at this point are based on monitoring all the aspects of the program as it functions. At the program effectiveness stage, on the other hand, the evaluator assesses the extent to which the program has been successful in effecting the desired changes in the participants.

During installation and operations, the focus is primarily on the extent to which the program activities and procedures are operating as intended. At the program effectiveness stage, the evaluator is interested in determining the extent to which objectives have been attained. At any point, one purpose is to identify the need for change or refinement in the program. Examination of installation and operations makes it possible to identify discrepancies between the program as it functions and as it was designed. Program effectiveness makes it possible to identify discrepancies between the actual program output—the entry level or retrained teacher—and the output as described in the program design.

In examining the attainment of ultimate objectives, it is essential to assess the performance of program participants in the public school classroom. The ultimate objectives relate to teacher effectiveness. Consequently, the procedure necessary for assessing the attainment of ultimate objectives requires the assessment of teacher effectiveness on the job. Specifically, two approaches to the evaluation of teacher effectiveness are considered. One approach to assessing the teacher's effectiveness is to use the progress of her students as the indicator. The second approach is to evaluate the performance of the teacher and the nature and level of student-teacher interaction directly in her classroom.

Many controversies are associated with the evaluation of teacher effectiveness on the basis of student achievement. Promoting student achievement is generally considered to be one of the principal functions of the school. Student achievement would seem, therefore, to be an appropriate yardstick for determining instructor effectiveness. There are numerous variables, however, which affect student achievement other than teacher performance. Among these are student cognitive and affective entry characteristics and the environmental conditions in which learning occurs. Since educational objectives are basically representative of changes in the student, evaluation becomes the process for determining the extent to which these changes are actually taking place. There are two important implications to this statement. First, the appropriate instruments to be used in this evaluation are those which measure student behavior. Second, it is not behavior *per se* that is being measured but the *change* in behavior. This means that at least two behavioral observations must be made—one at an early point in the instructional program, and another (or others) at a later time in the program. Ideally, observations would be made at a time after the instructional period is over to assess retention or the permanence of the learning that has taken place. For this reason, it is desirable that the system have an annual testing program so that permanent record of student progress can be maintained which would point out how well the student is attaining the instructional objectives and where the problem areas are occurring in the instructional program.

The process of evaluating teacher effectiveness using learner achievement as the primary criterion begins with the objectives of the instructional program. The objectives must be defined with sufficient clarity so as to enable the teacher to select properly and plan the learning experiences which will lead to the achievement of these objectives. It is then necessary to identify or develop evaluation procedures that will allow the observation of the various kinds of behaviors implied by each of the objectives. This may simply involve identifying the situation that will require the student to express the appropriate behavior. The next step in the procedure is to examine available instruments to determine which best sample the objectives to be achieved and devise the appropriate situations which will evoke the kind of behavior to be measured. At times it may be necessary to construct an evaluation instrument to measure attainment of a particular objective. In either case, the considerations of objectivity, reliability, and validity must be addressed. Several good texts are available to provide additional information on the topic of teaching for objectives. (See Appendix P.)

The instructional program will generally include several objectives. For each of these there will be at least two scores which represent the extent to which a student has attained this objective. A profile can be developed for each student describing his academic achievement. The student profile format should be sufficiently uniform over a period of years, so that the profile can be compared to those of preceding periods in order that student progress over time can be charted. The amount of student change that has taken place during the instructional period can be determined by comparing the results of several evaluation instruments given before and after the instructional period. Using this procedure, a pattern of academic strengths and weaknesses should appear. This pattern may or may not be related to strengths and weaknesses in the instructional program. A consistent pattern of strengths and weaknesses which can be discerned after a cross-student comparison of achievement during the instructional period may be taken as a strong indication of strengths and weaknesses in the instructional program. It then becomes necessary to formulate and test hypotheses about the reason(s) for this particular pattern of strengths and weaknesses. Learning activities can then be redesigned and taught to see if weaknesses in student achievement can be reduced. Persistent problems in overall student achievement despite correctives applied to instructional activities may be considered an indicator of teacher ineffectiveness. At this point, it becomes necessary to observe teacher activity and student-teacher interaction directly in the classroom.

This particular approach to assessing teacher effectiveness has several drawbacks. Little control is possible over extraneous variables that affect student achievement. Ideally the instructional program is designed to compensate for the more influential extraneous variables, particularly those which might be classified as environmental factors. The use of cross-student comparisons over a period of time, the academic year, is believed to be a control for many of the extraneous variables which might be categorized as personal factors. However, these assumptions may not be justified in reality. Second, the period of time required for initial evaluation, application of correctives to the instructional program, and a secondary evaluation may be inconveniently lengthy.

In fact, it may be the policy of the school district to provide the ineffective teacher with several opportunities to improve his performance before making a final judgment as to his effectiveness. This can have the effect of prolonging the program evaluation well beyond limits considered feasible. Nevertheless, if properly conducted this approach is one of the most valid procedures for evaluating teacher effectiveness. In addition, it allows evaluation to be built into the instructional planning process so that replanning, redevelopment, and reevaluation can form a closed cycle that will lead to continuing improvement in instruction over the years.

The second approach to evaluating the student as teacher involves the observation and assessment of teacher performance in the classroom. Teacher performance may be considered from two perspectives. One focuses on behaviors closely associated with the teacher's cognitive skills; it emphasizes his apparent knowledge of subject matter and his general ability to impart that knowledge to students. The second approach involves the observation of reciprocal contacts between the teacher and students. Teaching performance by definition is manifested within the context of social interaction. This interchange constitutes the act of teaching. Techniques for evaluating teacher performance are predicated on the idea that teacher-student interaction can be observed as a chain of events which occur one after the other.

Analysis of teacher performance may be conducted for different reasons. One is to assist the teacher in developing and refining his performance in the classroom. In addition, descriptions of interaction events, as well as extrapolation to the variables that affect the interaction, provide the basis for instructional theory, new instructional techniques, and educational outcomes. Finally, an important aspect of evaluating the extent to which a teacher education program has achieved its objectives is to evaluate the performance of its students as teachers in the classroom. This is particularly the case since the ultimate objectives of teacher education should be directly related to teacher performance. If the objectives are rooted in a data base of necessary and desired teacher competencies as in the job-related teacher education curriculum, it is impossible to evaluate the program genuinely without considering the job performance of the product—the student as teacher.

Different techniques for evaluating teacher performance in the classroom have been developed. Some are based on direct observation of classroom activity by an objective observer. Others recommend the use of somewhat less objective observers such as peers, students, or school administrators. Self-evaluation also has its functions.

Peer evaluators generally possess in-depth knowledge of the particular teaching assignment. This familiarity with the job tasks puts the peer evaluator in a position to assess the strengths and weaknesses of the instructional program. Accordingly, the peer is usually able to suggest strategies for overcoming the weaknesses. Peer evaluation may be less threatening than supervisor evaluation both on an individual basis and in terms of group morale. Certainly there are disadvantages to peer evaluation. The faculty *esprit de corps* and desire to maintain good relations with co-workers may invalidate or reduce the meaningfulness of evaluation. In addition, the fellow teacher often cannot view the instructional program from the larger perspective of the district or school needs.

Student evaluation has advantages not found in other types of evaluation. Many consider the student, the receiver of instruction, as the appropriate person to evaluate the teacher, the provider of instruction. Since students, particularly at upper grade levels, are exposed daily to a number of teachers, they are able to make comparisons of teaching skills and techniques. Of course, it should be noted that some students even in the upper grades are simply too immature to provide an objective evaluation. It is possible that those with a personal grudge against a particular teacher can persuade or pressure their classmates to join them in an unfair assessment of a teacher. Those teachers who are strict, assign more work, or teach a subject that is mandatory or unpopular may be at a disadvantage in terms of receiving a fair evaluation by their students.

Evaluation by supervisors usually assures that the evaluation is being conducted by a person who is at least minimally qualified in terms of training and job responsibility. Generally the staff supervisor has regular contact with staff members; consequently, he is able to make comparative, unbiased evaluations. Since he is in a position of authority as well as accountable for much of the acitivity undertaken in the overall instructional program, his evaluation is likely to have more impact and result in more changes than that of any other evaluator. On the other hand, the supervisor has often been removed from the classroom for a sufficiently long time to have become unfamiliar with current methodology and knowledge. He often has become a generalist who is not familiar enough with the various disciplines comprising the total curriculum to perform an informed evaluation. Finally, the supervisor's desire to avoid staff morale problems may color his assessment of staff performance.

An outside consultant may be the most objective evaluator available. He may be a staff member of an educational consultant firm, a faculty member of a teacher training institution, or a representative of another public agency concerned with the quality of the public school program. Generally, the outside consultant can provide a degree of expertise not available within the regular staff of the school district. He is likely to be familiar with current evaluation literature, models, and techniques. If a decision is reached *not* to engage a trained evaluator to conduct the evaluation, it is necessary that the individual who is assigned this responsibility be trained at a level of competence both in the use of the evaluation instrument and/or techniques.

The scheduling of evaluation varies depending upon the particular technique to be employed, the specific educational setting, and other factors that lend uniqueness to each instructional activity. For first-year teachers, it is reasonable to recommend one evaluation annually by students, three visits by the supervisor, and three peer evaluations. In some cases, the teacher's supervisory team from his internship period can continue working with him during his first year of employment. Another approach would be one evaluative visit when requested by the teacher, one evaluative visit at the request of the evaluator, and one unannounced visit. It is believed that this schedule will provide an adequate random sample of the teacher's performance.

The evaluation session often lasts one hour, a period that approximates the typical class period. This is suggested as a possible yardstick based on convenience, but flexibility is urged in determining the length of the observation period. The use of video tapes has the advantage of permitting mutal review and critique by the evaluator and the teacher.

In instances where the services of an outside evaluator are used and specifically where the technique of interaction analysis is utilized, the number of observation periods should be extended to a minimum of seven or eight. In this case the observation is being conducted with the consent and cooperation of the teacher. Therefore, the decisions to be made in terms of the specific activities to be evaluated, the environment in which the evaluation is to take place, and the scheduling and duration of the evaluation must be made with the cooperation of the teacher.

A number of excellent instruments have been developed for the purpose of evaluating teacher effectiveness in the classroom. Generally, they are based on the identification of activities in the classroom that reveal teacher competence. These activities may be classified under a number of topics or organized as questions. Some of the major concerns include the procedures used to stimulate students' thinking and synthesis of information, the teacher's recognition of and attention to the varying needs of different students, the teaching techniques employed, the climate and other affective characteristics of the classroom, and possibly the impact of teacher personality on student-teacher interaction. Among the classic teacher evaluation instruments that may be used directly or may be helpful in developing an instrument tailored to a specific academic program are the Ohio Teaching Record, the Furman University Observational Record, the Analysis of Student Problems of Teachers College of Columbia University, and the Michigan State College Teacher Observation Records.

The Ohio Teaching Record was developed at Ohio State University in 1940 and has been revised several times. Emphasis is placed on using the instrument as a mechanism for reporting what goes on during the observation period, rather than as a rating device. The Furman University instrument was developed as an adaptation of the Ohio Teaching Record. In many respects the two records are similar; however, the Furman instrument provides for summary evaluation of teacher performance in addition to the objective observational function. The Columbia University Teachers College instrument introduces a somewhat different approach to teacher evaluation. It uses teachers' statements of activities, problems, and needs faced in their practice as the basis for evaluation. Specific forms have been developed to record these aspects of the instructional activities that go on in the classroom. The Michigan State College Teacher Observation Record was originally developed for student teachers in vocational agriculture. This instrument introduces the use of daily teacher logs as well as the use of a daily activity chart which functions as a checklist of instructional activities organized under the objectives of the educational program.

It is recommended that these instruments not be used without modification as they have been designed by particular institutions for particular purposes. They should be used as references in developing an instrument that is designed specifically to meet the needs of the program being evaluated. At the product evaluation stage, the ultimate objectives of the program are being evaluated. Therefore, any instrument developed for use at this stage must be designed to assess the attainment of the ultimate objectives of the program. The specific instruments used to evaluate teacher performance must be keyed to the objectives of the teacher education program in which the teacher under observation was a student. Where the program objectives are based upon required and desired teacher competencies, the observation instrument must be designed to record activities in the classroom that reveal the presence or absence of these specified competencies.

A rather different approach to the evaluation of teacher performance is through the use of interaction analysis. Specifically, this technique requires that an observer sit in the classroom, view a video-tape or listen to a tape recording, and make a record of the discrete events that are going on in the classroom. There are a number of different instruments available for recording classroom activities. Usually these involve the use of sets of categories and checklists. In some instances, mechanical devices may be employed to facilitate and accelerate the recording process. Generally, the observer requires some training and practice prior to using this particular assessment technique. The necessary skills are relatively easy to learn. Unfortunately, interaction analysis has been rather widely misused. Efforts to use this technique directly for the evaluation of teacher performance have met with a notable lack of success.

Attempts to relate particular aspects of teacher performance to the academic achievement of students have been confounded by a number of variables. Among these are such personal variables as student aptitude, cognitive, and perceptual style, personality, sex, income level, ethnic background, and many other status, cognitive, and affective entry characteristics. Environmental variables including such factors as teaching techniques employed, subject matter or discipline, scheduling and duration of the class, and characteristics of the school and the community served also influence achievement.

The strength of interaction analysis is that inferences reached are based on events that can be said with a greater degree of certainty to have occurred than is the case with other more traditional observational techniques. Interaction analysis is primarily useful in the improvement of instruction. Second, it can be used as a tool for teacher training and finally as a way of predicting educational outcomes. Its value as an evaluation technique is predicated on the assumption that the design of the particular analysis record is based upon the program objectives. The instrument used to record classroom interaction must be designed in such a way that events are recorded which reveal the competencies underlying the objectives of the educational program. Through careful instrument design and skillful observation, it is possible to make valid inferences about the teacher's attainment of ultimate objectives from the chain of events being recorded. Several good texts are available on the subject of interaction analysis. (See Appendix Q.)

Regardless of the particular evaluator, technique, or instruments employed in evaluating teacher performance, the fact remains that it is the program that produced the teacher that is the target of the evaluation. The teacher himself is not the object of the evaluation. The purpose of the evaluation is to determine the extent to which the teacher, as the product of the educational program, has attained the ultimate objectives of the program under evaluation. A probable and desired by-product of the evaluation process is the improvement of teacher performance in the classroom. However, the primary purpose is to evaluate the effectiveness of the educational program and to provide information to aid in making decisions about the program.

EVALUATING PROGRAM EFFECTIVENESS

In evaluating program effectiveness, we determine whether the combination of learning activities undertaken as part of the educational program has resulted in a product which has met the ultimate objectives of the program. Having obtained information about product or teacher performance, specifically about the attainment of ultimate objectives, it is possible to use the inquiry format previously recommended for evaluating installation and operations. The type of inquiry may be as follows to review evaluation information of teacher performance:

Is the program achieving its ultimate objectives? or

Is there a discrepancy between the program standard (product as defined in the program design) and performance (the product performance in the classroom)?

If yes, which objectives are not being achieved?

What are the program learning activities related to the unattained objectives?

What correctives appear possible under the program?

What corrective appears most promising?

The specific line of inquiry should be developed in reference to the particular program being evaluated.

Unlike the decision point at previous stages, at the program effectiveness stage the decision-makers may be faced either with two decisions—continue the program as is or terminate it; or with three decisions—continue, terminate, or modify. In reaching a decision, at this point, the program administrator has all the evaluation information from the previous stages at his disposal. Assuming the evaluation process has been properly conducted at previous stages, it may be felt that a need for modification would indicate basic flaws in the program design and that, at this stage, changes in program design would be tantamount to the development of a new program. Those who advocate limiting the options at this stage to continue or terminate are trying to avoid what may be considered the traditional "Band-Aid" approach to program improvement. Due to the interrelatedness of the components program, a deficiency in one area and a resulting adjustment would probably effect undesirable changes in another area. From this perspective, it is preferable to redesign the program.

At the other extreme, it may be argued this is an unrealistic approach to improving teacher education. There should be a continuous modification of the program. This might be considered not only a means of overcoming deficiencies but also of refining the program and meeting the changing needs of its service area.

A more moderate approach to the question of modification and recycling in the evaluation process would be to reserve the option of modifying for relatively minor deficiencies. This might apply to repeated evidence of inadequate mastery of competencies in a limited number of categories or the absence of a basic skill which can be incorporated into the program with minimal repercussions. Again, as qualifiers such as "limited" and "minimal" imply, judgment must be exercised in determining whether modifications will affect the integrity of the program design. Widespread or serious deficiencies in program effectiveness should result in a decision to terminate the program and reenter the process either at the problem identification stage or at the design stage.

In the case of preservice education programs and on-going inservice programs, program effectiveness evaluation should be a continuous, regularly scheduled activity. Many of the accrediting agencies for teacher education programs require that the institutions or agencies sponsoring teacher education programs periodically evaluate the performance of their graduates in the field. It is recommended that an effort be made to evaluate an adequate sample of the teachers who are graduates of four-year teacher education programs on an annual basis. Unfortunately, the results of evaluation for many existing education programs are used primarily to maintain the educational *status quo*. It is merely data to be supplied to the accrediting agencies to meet their requirements. This is an unfortunate waste of a valuable resource for revitalizing teacher education and those organizations whose function is to prepare individuals to become educational practitioners. This data should be considered a means of keeping up with the needs and changes in the field of education.

If program effectiveness cannot be established, the program should be terminated and a new design developed. If the program is judged to be effective in solving the identified problem, the decision-makers may wish to view the program from another perspective. The efficiency of the program may also be a target for evaluation. While this type of evaluation has limitations when applied to educational programs, it does reflect some of the concerns expressed by the public and by decision-makers in today's era of accountability. Chapter 17 describes some of the uses and possible misuses of this approach to evaluating teacher education programs.

17

Program Efficiency: An Optional, Final Consideration

The program evaluation process developed for the assessment of the model job-related curriculum includes an additional stage, that of cost-benefit analysis. This evaluation can be conducted as a follow-up to the determination of program effectiveness. It is an optional procedure; therefore, only a few comments on the application of cost-benefit analysis to education are provided. During this phase of program evaluation, decision-makers are presented with alternatives to the program after it has been developed and piloted. Each alternative is examined with emphasis upon its potential for meeting the specified criteria which were developed from the data gathered during the problem identification stage.

Several techniques which have originated outside of the field of education have proven useful for this type of investigation. Among these are the Program Planning and Budgeting System (PPBS), the covergence technique, and cost-effectiveness analysis (Stufflebeam et al., 1971). In reaching consensus in instances where several decision-makers may be involved, the Delphi technique has proven effective. The Program Evaluation and Review Technique (PERT) is useful both in program design and in the comparison of program activities and incremental costs. These techniques were developed primarily for the business community to determine the efficacy of particular investment opportunities. They were later implemented on an impressive scale by the industrial sector and the military. More recently, the public sector, particularly federal and some state agencies, have found them useful in evaluating their programs.

One might wonder why cost-benefit analysis is recommended as the approach to final evaluation of a proposed education program. Simple profit-and-loss accounting might appear to be a more direct method for examining the value of a public investment such as a job-related teacher education program.

In cost-benefit analysis the concern is with the welfare of a defined society—not any smaller part of it. Unlike a private or even public commercial enterprise, a public educational program cannot be guided by the criterion of merely producing revenue that equals or exceeds its costs. Its activities cannot be guided solely by the profit motive. In evaluating an education program, a different sort of question is asked than is asked in the evlauation of a private enterprise. The concern is not with whether undertaking one enterprise rather than some other activity will benefit a set of investors. Instead, the issue is whether society as a whole will benefit by undertaking this project rather than by not undertaking it, or by undertaking one of a number of other projects.

In conducting a cost-benefit analysis, the evaluator must substitute the concept of social benefit for that of revenue. Rather than limiting himself to a consideration of fiscal costs, he extends his concern to the concept of opportunity lost. In place of the consideration of profit, he will examine excess social benefit over program cost.

It should be noted that the judgment which results from a cost-benefit analysis is not limited to a "correct" decision. Cost-benefit analysis in education indicates that given one set of factors several equally valid decisions are possible. The specific decision which will be made is dependent upon the perspective and values of the decision-makers. Frequently, the benefits or costs recognized by one set of decision-makers are not recognized as such by another set. Consequently, an inherent aspect of cost-benefit analysis is an examination of the decision-making bodies involved in the evaluation process and a determination how these decision outcomes would differ if made by a different set of decision-makers. In using cost-benefit techniques, the evaluator should use this information to determine the factors relevant to the specific decision to be made.

If the technique of cost-benefit analysis is to be applied to identify efficient educational programs, the following conditions must exist. The program to be evaluated and those which are proposed as alternatives must be sufficiently well defined and measured so that it is possible to identify input, process, and output at each program increment. In this manner, the cost as well as the impact of program increments can be determined. In addition, there must be an understanding of and agreement upon both the value and the measurement of the program benefits. Obviously these conditions are not often met in the evaluation process for educational programs. However, this is not to say that this procedure cannot be used under circumstances where the identified conditions can be met.

A major advantage of cost-benefit analysis is that it necessitates that the program decision-makers and staff define the program clearly by submitting it to functional cost-accounting procedures. While Stages 1 through 4 of the evaluation process presented in Chapters 13 through 16 require that the educational program be clearly defined, cost-benefit procedures make it necessary to look at cost increments relative to output increments. This is beneficial for future program design and modification whether or not the analysis is completed by comparison with similarly well-defined programs.

GENERAL COST-BENEFIT PROCEDURES

The first step in undertaking an effective cost-benefit analysis of any educational program is to acquire a clear understanding of what is meant by the term "benefit." The evaluator must think of the benefits in terms of the extent to which the program achieves the desired results. The desired results are the objectives of the program. These must be stated first and then operationalized in measurable form. Basically, these steps do not set the cost-benefit analysis technique apart from the evaluation process developed in the preceding chapters. The distinction becomes clear at the next step in the procedure. At this point, it is necessary to develop a set of weights that reflect some judgments about the comparative importance of each of the objectives.

It is assumed that finite resources exist for the implementation of the educational program. The weighting of objectives involves (1) the realization of alternative uses to which limited resources can be put, and (2) the identification of an existing pattern of demand for the resources. This existing pattern of demand reflects not only a specific desire for individuals with certain competencies in the field of education but also a decision to acquire and pay for the services of these individuals.

The drawback in applying cost-benefit analysis to the evaluation of educational programs results primarily from the fact that it has been underutilized in this area. Reluctance to use this technique is related to its primary emphasis on efficiency in the allocation of resources. When an education program is evaluated it is necessary to introduce the factor of social benefit into the cost-benefit equation to determine the appropriate allocation of resources. The simplest approach to the determination of social benefits is to think of them as reflected in the willingness of the public to pay for rather than do without the services derived from the program.

In identifying the benefits of the education program, it may be desirable to examine this aspect of program output by using several general classifications. First, benefits should be categorized as direct and indirect. Direct benefits are those which are the immediately observable outputs of the program— for example, a specific number of certified teachers over an identified period of time having skills and knowledge identified as desirable in the educational marketplace. Indirect benefits are those which are generated by either the stimulative effects of the direct outputs or the demand-inducing effects of the activities and expenditures of the program. Both direct and indirect benefits can be categorized as real or pecuniary. Real benefits consist of an increase in consumer satisfaction or a decrease in costs required to produce the product—the certified educator. A pecuniary effect represents an improvement in the well-being of some at the expense of the well-being of others. This involves a redistribution of wealth. An example under these categories is the change of status from student to educator (input to output), theoretically at the expense of the public. Finally, cost-benefit analysis involves the identification of tangible and intangible benefits. Tangible benefits are those which can be measured in dollar terms. Intangible benefits are those to which a monetary value cannot be attached. The following diagram presents a conceptualization of the task of identifying benefits:

Benefits

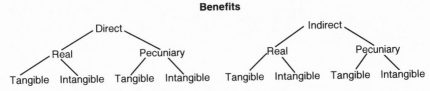

Program costs are calculated for the program operation period, although planning and installation of the program should also be considered. For example, the preservice program will probably cover a period of at least four years. The inservice program may be relatively brief and episodic in comparison. Unless specialized new facilities are required, capital (construction) costs will not be relevant in most program evaluations. The process of classifying program costs is very similar to that of categorizing program benefits. Included are considerations such as operation costs, the cost of lost opportunities, alternate choices on the part of program participants, human productivity (specifically, the loss of current production on the part of the program participants during the program, and so forth).

In cost-benefit jargon, public investment in a teacher education program is basically an investment in human capital. Analysis of the program in terms of both benefits and costs must be approached from this perspective. Measuring such costs and benefits poses all of the problems associated with the measurement of an abstraction. For example, program benefits to be reaped by society include not only higher output by the individual but also improvement of leadership abilities, and impact on students and others. Some effort must be made to bring these types of costs and benefits into the calculations as well as the more mundane and easily measurable characteristics.

As noted above, there are a number of problems associated with the use of cost-benefit analysis in education. The technique, if improperly applied, leads to vague results. However, the proper use of the cost-benefit approach permits placing expenditures in the educational sector on an equal footing with expenditures in other areas. This allows education to be viewed in a wider context of economic and social activities. This approach to the evaluation of educational programs in general, and teacher education programs specifically, can provide valuable insights into current issues such as the most equitable of financial resources for education between the public and the private sector. In general, the use of cost-benefit analysis can place educational planning on a more rational basis.

Improving Teacher Competencies

18

Identifying Problems in Professional Growth

In Section 1 of Improving Teacher Education, we illustrated the use of the problem-solving model in the development of teacher education programs. Program development is only one potential use of the model. Because the primary concern of this book is with the improvement of teacher education curricula, the development of effective pre- and inservice programs has been emphasized. However, in addition to the primary function of producing competent teachers, the teacher education program has the responsibility of determining whether its entrants are capable and certifying that its graduates are competent. This requires the application of the problem-solving model to the professional growth of the preservice education student and the inservice educational practitioner.

Decision-makers in teacher education programs must make a variety of judgments about their participants during the course of the pre- or inservice program. Three of these decision categories are discussed in this chapter: selection, placement, and diagnostic decisions. Chapter 20 focuses on instructional and remediation decisions. In Chapter 21, certification decisions are addressed.

SELECTION DECISIONS

The process for selecting students for a preservice teacher education program involves establishing criteria for probable success in the program. Presumably, general objectives for the program have been developed and defined. Appropriate sources of substantiation are identified as well as the instrumentation or other means for obtaining data on the program applicant. Finally, data collected on the individual can then be interpreted in terms of the objectives. The objectives used in the selection process may be labeled as the selection criteria. Thus the data collected at the problem identification stage are then compared to the selection criteria.

The establishment of selection criteria presupposes some concept of what characterizes a good teacher. Traditionally, laundry lists of qualities and virtues have been proposed as selection criteria. A survey of the literature would yield literally hundreds of these attributes: intelligence, scholarship, integrity, emotional stability, positive feelings for youth, respect for the individual, and a sound personal philosophy founded in knowledge and supported by conviction are among those commonly adovacated as fundamental. Obviously, any program would have problems finding sufficient applicants who meet these requirements. Unfortunately, many of these characteristics are difficult to observe or measure in a systematic manner. Some are to be developed as part of the educational program. Others can only be acquired through the experiences of a lifetime. In view of these problems, which characteristics should be addressed in the selection criteria? Indeed, is this list of desired teacher traits exhaustive?

Ideally, the selection criteria for a teacher education program would be directly linked to success in the program and causally associated with desired student outcomes in the classroom. Unfortunately, research has not conclusively isolated such characteristics. Because of this, the establishment of selection criteria for a teacher education program depends upon a number of factors. Obviously, the most important consideration should be the objectives of the program—the attainment of the required and desired teacher competencies. Expressed somewhat pragmatically, students should be selected who possess those characteristics that will enable them within a high degree of probability to achieve the objectives of the program. However, even in this calculated statement it is impossible to avoid a reliance on subjective judgment. Just what are the limits of a "high degree of probability" that the student can achieve satisfactorily? Here one can see that the establishment of selection criteria, like the establishment of program objectives is ultimately a question of value judgment and philosophy.

There are, however, some practical considerations which can objectify the establishment of selection criteria to some extent. The most important of these are the needs of the area to be served by the particular teacher education program. Obviously, a program that is designed around the identified needed and desired competencies of the educational practitioner has considered the needs of its service area. Its choice of students who can be expected to acquire or develop these competencies is additional evidence of its concern with these needs. This is the matter of supply and demand for educational practitioners. It should be the responsibility of the preservice program to assist in the placement of its graduates. Persistent long-term problems in placing graduates of a teacher education program may be taken as an indication of oversupply. A second, although less reliable indicator is teacher salary. While manipulation of entry requirements should never be based on these two indicators alone, they should certainly result in a careful examination of program admissions and area needs. To knowingly create an oversupply of teachers for the constituency served by the program is not meeting the needs of the service area itself, the profession, or the participants of the program. Selection criteria *per se* should be influenced only indirectly by supply and demand. However, long-term projections for the placement of program graduates should be considered in determining the number of eligible applicants to be accepted into the program.

Another factor which will affect the stringency with which selection criteria are enforced is the philosophy of the sponsoring institution in terms of its obligation to provide an educational opportunity to all who desire it. Those institutes who wish to open their doors to all students who seek an education must also exhibit a willingness and capacity to provide remediation for the more marginal participants or be willing to eliminate them at some later stage of the program. Essentially, to avoid compromising the program objectives, it becomes necessary to choose between limiting admission to the program to those who are more likely candidates for achieving program objectives or weeding out large numbers of candidates who should not have been admitted initially. The former choice involves the risk of depriving potentially good teachers of an opportunity to make their contribution to the profession and wasting a valuable human resource. The latter choice involves the risk of wasting the resources of both the program and the individual who has to be eliminated from the program. Obviously, this will not be an easy decision. It should be pointed out that the selection criteria for admission to a teacher education program are also dependent to a large extent on the selection criteria for general admission to the institution or agency sponsoring that program.

Another factor that will impact on the establishment of preservice selection criteria is the specific point in the student's academic career at which he seeks admission to the teacher education program. Generally, the design of the program itself will determine whether the student applies for candidacy during his freshman, sophomore, or junior year. Occasionally, a student will have completed several years of undergraduate and even graduate education before he determines his area of professional interest. Obviously, the years between eighteen and twenty-one, particularly if spent in an environment of intense intellectual stimulation and exposure to new experiences and ideas, can produce major changes in the student's attitudes, and intellectual and social competencies. Criteria which are reasonable and perhaps even liberal in evaluating the potential of a junior who is requesting admission to a teacher education program may be entirely inappropriate for the evaluation of a freshman.

Devising selection criteria for participants in inservice programs is generally less complicated than developing criteria for preservice programs. Frequently, the inservice program is designed to benefit all teachers in a particular school, geographic area, or particular specialty. Other inservice programs offer a variety of alternatives among which teachers select an area of interest or need. In this case, self-selection is operating. When competency profiles are developed for individual teachers (see Chapter 6), the indicators of need for particular professional growth experiences can be used as selection criteria. Obviously, singling out teachers for participation in a program on the basis of their need to cultivate or acquire competencies must be handled professionally and tactfully. Some inservice opportunities may be offered only to those who have earned or are supposed to assume advanced status as a result of training. For example, a group of teachers might be given release time and allowed to attend a professional conference. Objective selection criteria are critical in instances such as this in order to avoid repercussions from nonparticipants.

Having established selection criteria and determined what characteristics are indicative of an individual meeting those criteria, it becomes necessary to select appropriate instruments or methods to observe and measure those characteristics. It is impossible to recommend specific observation mechanisms for a program without knowledge of the selection criteria established for that program. At best it is possible to survey some of the instruments used by existing programs. The decision whether or not to use any screening or selection instrument should be made only after considering all of its strengths and weaknesses.

Probably the most widely used measures for preservice selection criteria are high school scholarship, generally as evidenced by grade point average and class rank, and intellectual ability and achievement in the form of college entrance examinations, scholastic aptitude tests, and other standardized achievement tests. In addition, many programs require that the applicant for admission demonstrate competence in reading, English, and areas of specialization. This may take the form of component area tests of widely used standardized instruments such as the Scholastic Aptitude Test. It may be a screening instrument developed specifically for the education program which establishes minimal functioning in academic areas considered essential to the attainment of the program objectives.

Some teacher education programs require the demonstration of appropriate speech and of suitable personality characteristics for admission. Generally, the vehicle for evaluating these characteristics is the interview. Qualities which may be considered in addition to voice and diction are use of English, social adaptability, enthusiasm, breadth of experience, emotional qualities, and personal appearance. Another mechanism sometimes used to obtain information on the personality and character of the applicant is rating by the applicant's high school principal or counsellor.

Having appropriate feelings toward children and youth is a teacher characteristic often considered in program selection criteria. A number of standardized instruments are available which purport to measure affect for the student. At least one teacher education program requires that its applicants have had at least one hundred hours of work experience with boys and girls in a social agency such as Scouts, 4-H clubs, or the YMCA/YWCA.

Closely related to positive feelings for youth is generally good mental health. There are numerous standardized instruments available which presumably measure the mental health or the psychological characteristics of the respondent. Psychological tests are available at various levels of sophistication and specificity. Many require interpretation by persons with expertise in the field of psychology or psychiatry. Several educational programs have required in the past or are presently requiring that the applicant undergo an interview with a psychiatrist or a psychiatric social worker so that a mental health rating can be obtained for the applicant.

Finally, there is generally concern that the applicant be in adequate physical health. Like many other selection criteria, this has come under scrutiny in recent years. Emphasis on providing equal job opportunity and general attitudinal changes toward the capabilities of the handicapped have resulted in an effort to remove unnecessary obstacles to their employment in professions previously closed to them. In establishing criteria for physical health, it is necessary to look at recent state and federal laws pertaining to the rights of handicapped persons and the policy of the sponsoring agency or institution. It is still common practice to require applicants to undergo a physical examination. It appears, however, that the function of the physical exam today is less one of eliminating applicants with correctable physical impairments than it is one of identifying the applicant with the raging case of tuberculosis.

PLACEMENT

Due to the diversity in entry characteristics among students, it is not always necessary or desirable to start each student at the same academic level. This is particularly the case with the general education component. Students who have transferred into the teacher education program from programs with similar requirements or who have completed demanding secondary programs may desire to exempt certain required courses. For those students who have taken postsecondary courses that can be certified as the equivalent of a required course in question, this presents no problem. However, students who cannot present adequate substantiation for a claim of academic equivalency for coursework should be given the opportunity to demonstrate their mastery of the course objectives. As a rule, the institution or program sponsoring agency will have specific procedures governing advanced placement. Consequently, teacher education program policy with regard to students exempting required courses should be coordinated with relevant institution policies.

Generally, one or more of the following procedures are recommended in obtaining advanced placement or exempting specific required courses. The verbal section of the college entrance examination may be used to determine advanced placement in introductory English courses. Similarly, advanced placement examinations associated with college entrance examinations may be used to obtain advanced placement in other areas such as history, biology, math, chemistry, foreign languages, or physics. The College Level Examination Program (CLEP) subject examinations offered in a number of different areas may be used to qualify the applicant for course exemption. The department in which the course is taught may be charged with the responsibility of developing, administering, and interpreting an instrument to establish that the student is qualified for advanced placement or course exemption.

In designing a preservice teacher education program, it may be desirable to provide the student with the option of exempting those courses the objectives of which he believes he has already attained—either through related academic work or through professional experience. In this case, it is unlikely that a suitable standardized instrument will be available and the program staff may be required to construct advanced placement or exemption instruments. Such instruments can be developed using item banks constructed to evaluate attainment of the terminal objectives for required courses. If the program emphasizes the attainment of skills, students who wish to exempt a course may be required to demonstrate mastery of skills through performance, such as conducting a lesson or constructing a test.

Placement decisions in the inservice program depend upon the availability of alternatives. In many cases, the constraints of the inservice context preclude the kinds of options which are possible at the preservice level.

DIAGNOSTIC DECISIONS

Selection and placement criteria are generally standardized; that is, they apply equally to all program participants. In contrast, diagnostic decisions are made in terms of an individual's performance of specific tasks within a course. Diagnostic decisions are based on identified discrepancies between an individual student's present performance and the preferred performance as stated in a particular objective or set of objectives.

The problem-solving model was applied in Section 1 of *Improving Teacher Education* at the macro or program level. It can also be applied at the micro level in diagnosing, prescribing for, and assessing the individual student.

Identifying problems at the program level is analogous to diagnosing the instructional needs of an individual prospective or practicing teacher. Designing programs corresponds to prescribing instructional activities to remedy deficiencies or to develop identified skills. The testing and achieving solutions stage can be compared to similar measurement and evaluation functions in the diagnostic-prescriptive model. Figure 18.1 depicts these relationships.

Each of the three stages of the problem-solving model involves three components—activities, evaluation, and decision-making. In diagnosis, these functions can be described as follows:

1. Activities—collecting information about the existing and preferred level of the professional characteristics under consideration.

FIGURE 18.1 Correspondence of Problem-Solving and Diagnostic Prescriptive Models.

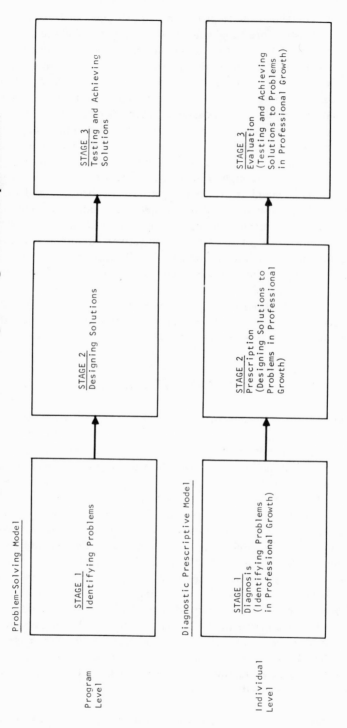

2. Evaluation—comparing the existing and preferred levels of the characteristic to determine whether a significant discrepancy exists between the two levels.

3. Decision-making—making a decision as to whether or not the discrepancy is sufficiently large to constitute a need and identifying in the prospective or practicing professional a pattern of strengths and weaknesses.

For our purposes, *assessment* is defined as the process of identifying the pattern of strengths and weaknesses in the individual. This includes his or her needs and personality characteristics, knowledge, skills, and the aptitudes necessary in reconciling the roles demanded by the environment to those which the individual is able to play. This definition has a number of important characteristics. First, it establishes the demands of the job as the criteria for the preferred state. In the model job-related curriculum project, for example, required and desired professional skills are explicitly identified. Criteria developed in this way are both concrete and objective, in contrast to their typical vague formulation. The present state, that is, the teacher's status in respect to these skills, is not limited to a few indicators but rather is determined by looking at the teacher as a whole package. While the term "to inventory" may seem rather commercial, it does convey the precise and comprehensive nature of the activities which should be done during any diagnosis or initial assessment phase.

It should be pointed out here that, with either a preservice or inservice teacher, the term discrepancy does not imply a deficiency in the sense that this term is frequently used in the diagnostic-prescriptive literature. The adult professional or preprofessional is not likely to have severe physical, intellectual, or emotional problems which interfere with his capacity to grow professionally. The aim of diagnosis is not so much to uncover shortcomings but to identify opportunities for further growth.

Another caveat should be recognized when the diagnostic-prescriptive approach is applied to professional growth situations. The diagnostic-prescriptive terminology borrowed from the medical profession may not transfer precisely to teacher education situations. For example, the term "to diagnose" implies discovering the cause of a particular difficulty. In education, particularly in retraining adult professionals, however, diagnosis is rarely concerned with etiology. Often, in fact, diagnosis concentrates not so much on finding a specific deficiency as on finding a pattern of strengths and weaknesses. Although teaching skills can be identified and catalogued as separate entities, they are rarely practiced in isolation. Indeed, the ability to blend, interweave, and coordinate a variety of teaching functions is frequently regarded as a hallmark of the effective teacher.

Professional growth for the preservice teacher can best be described as the process of "growing into the profession" or "becoming a professional." To the extent that the requirements for the teacher's job have been identified, the comparison of the individual's present to preferred performance is straightforward. The individual's present knowledge, skills, and attitudes are inventoried and compared to the required and desired teacher competencies. Discrepancies are then analyzed and prescriptions for eliminating them developed.

It is important to keep in mind that in regard to the preprofessional, diagnosis is only meaningful when it is conducted within a specific curricular framework. That is, the student's profile must be compared to the requirements of the program. Obviously, a well-designed program in place is essential. This is not to suggest that no modifications in the basic program can be made to accommodate individual differences. Rather, it is only within the context of a well-defined program that such decisions can be made on a rational basis. A failure to compare the individual's characteristics to specified program requirements and objectives can lead to diagnosis for the sake of diagnosis.

In dealing with teachers, especially practicing teachers, the diagnostic-prescriptive process must accommodate self-direction. Thus, a participatory procedure is needed to take into account the characteristics of the late adolescent and adult learners. Most decisions relating to professional growth are ultimately made by the individual teacher. Efforts to impose prescriptions without the cooperation and concurrence of a particular teacher are generally met with resistance. As professionals, teachers are entitled to and will benefit from participating in the identification of and reduction of discrepancies between their present and preferred levels of performance.

The traditional procedures used to gather data on teacher performance, that is, the infrequent but mandated visitation by principal or other supervisor with a rating scale and a license to pass judgment on the basis of an isolated observation, has made teachers justifiably uneasy about the term "teacher evaluation." Few supervisors have been adequately trained in observational and instructional improvement techniques, nor are they given adequate opportunity to follow-up any observed needs. Assessment of teacher performance has been essentially a necessary evil, becoming significant only when a case had to be made for dismissing a particular teacher.

The mastery learning model suggests itself as an appropriate diagnostic-prescriptive procedure for teacher education because of the fact that the identified competencies are essential. Merely covering these skills is inadequate; they must be mastered. That is, the entry level teacher should exhibit a measurable degree of competence in each area of the curriculum with emphasis upon those competencies to be developed in the professional core component. The hit or miss approach is no longer adequate to produce the kind of teacher the public school environment requires.

The mastery learning model is particularly adaptable to the data collection context of diagnosing for professional growth. While the precursors of this approach can be found in the 1920's (Winnetka Plan), the conceptual model was developed by Carroll in 1963. According to this approach, virtually all preservice and inservice teachers can and will master what they are taught if appropriate conditions for learning are provided. The mastery learning model posits that the degree of learning is a function of five factors:

1. Perseverance—the student's effort or sustained interest in learning; the amount of time spent learning particular material.

2. Opportunity to learn—the amount of time allotted by the instructor or program for the student to learn; logistical support for learning (availability of materials, and so forth).

3. Aptitude—the ease with which the student learns particular material or performs particular mental operations; inclination toward the particular subject matter.

4. Quality of instruction—the appropriateness, organization, and comprehensiveness of the instruction provided; suitability of teaching strategies, materials, media, and so forth.

5. Ability to understand instruction—the "match" between the student's learning style and the instructional delivery.

During the problem identification phase, an assessment is made of the student-oriented factors: perseverance, aptitude, and ability to understand instruction. The prescriptive stage focuses on manipulating those aspects of the model which the instructor can control, that is, the opportunity to learn and the quality of instruction. These factors will be considered in Chapter 19, Designing Programs for Professional Growth.

According to the mastery learning model, the higher the degree of perseverance, aptitude, and ability to understand instruction the student brings to the learning situation, the less critical are the quality of instruction and the opportunity to learn factors. Too frequently, according to mastery learning advocates, opportunity to learn is cut off before the student has had a chance to master the material or skill. Thus, he moves on to new objectives without necessary prerequisite knowledge and gradually builds a "cumulative deficit" of misunderstandings.

With the mastery learning approach, a level of desired competence is preestablished for each objective. Key decisions to be made are the determination of what constitutes mastery of each objective and what evidence of mastery will be acceptable. Initial instruction takes into account students' diagnosed aptitude for the subject, manifested or expressed interest in the subject (or anticipated perseverance), and ability to profit from various types of instruction. Of particular concern in diagnosing prospective and practicing teachers' readiness to master particular competencies are two factors: aptitude and interest. Aptitude refers to one's capacity for learning particular concepts, information, or skills. While aptitude is frequently interpreted as native or natural ability, it is also influenced by one's environment and background. Interest, or the willingness and motivation to develop a particular competency, is also critical. In the mastery learning model, interest is seen as perseverance. Interest can also be described as a "felt need." Simplistically, the two components of readiness can be visualized as a seesaw. A strong interest in learning to perform a particular skill may compensate to some extent for a limited aptitude in the skill area and vice versa.

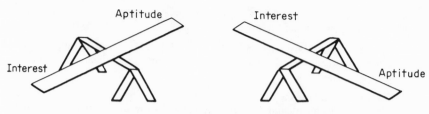

Readiness to learn, however, will be optimized when both aptitude and interest are present. To paraphrase an old adage, we might say "ready equals willing and able."

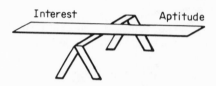

The individual's readiness to learn particular concepts, information, or skills must be considered in the problem identification stage. A particular deficiency may be quite apparent but if the teacher or prospective teacher is not at a stage of readiness to correct the deficiency, pointing it out may be futile. In some cases, a number of prerequisite skills will need to be developed before the identified deficiency can realistically be tackled. For example, a teacher who experiences difficulties with behavior management may need to work on a variety of interpersonal and instructional skills in order to reach a preferred level of performance. Simply identifying the manifestations of the deficiency is inadequate.

In both the preservice and inservice professional, the general process for identifying a discrepancy between the existing level and preferred level of competency is the same. It is in the interpretation of the discrepancy that the processes diverge. In the preservice program the discrepancy is interpreted in terms of the gap between the student's existing level and the preferred level already established as the objectives of the program. Generally, the

FIGURE 18.2 Diagnostic Discrepancy Analysis.

OBJECTIVE X:
Present Performance
Level

OBJECTIVE X:
Preferred Performance
Level

What is the magnitude of the gap between present and preferred performance levels?

What discrepancies are present in terms of related objectives?

What degree of readiness is apparent in the learner?

What patterns of strengths and weaknesses affect the learner's potential for reaching to preferred level?

minimum admissions or selection criteria to the program can be considered as the lowest possible existing level which can be demonstrated by an individual who has the potential to reach the preferred level. Obviously, this potential is considered in terms of program constraints such as opportunities for remediation and space within the program for participants as opposed to demand for admission. In most preservice programs, both the existing level for acceptance to the program and the preferred level are preestablished in terms of selection criteria and ultimate goals. The preprofessional essentially accepts the preferred level established by the program and must meet the existing level for entry into the program.

The inservice program is not conducted within the same parameters as is the preservice program. Specifically, a greater degree of flexibility is possible in establishing existing and preferred levels so that resulting discrepancies will impact more directly on program design. Since selection criteria may not be manipulable, the existing levels of the participants provide the starting point for program design. The preferred level may or may not have been preestablished; however, the discrepancy between the two levels will directly affect the planning of the vehicle to reduce the discrepancy. This is possible because of the smaller scale of the inservice program which allows more flexibility in attending to the needs of the individual participant.

Data collected on the individual will be examined two ways. The first is to determine whether a discrepancy exists between his existing level and the minimum acceptable existing level (selection criteria) of the program and the direction of that discrepancy. The size and direction of the discrepancy may result in 1) no admission, 2) regular admission, 3) conditional admission, or 4) advanced placement.

Second, the data will be examined to determine the nature of the discrepancy between the individual's existing level and the preferred level so that his specific program can be tailored as much as educational opportunities of the program sponsoring agency permit. Chapter 19, Designing Programs for Professional Growth, focuses on the prescriptive phase of the process.

19

Designing Programs for Professional Growth

The second stage of the problem-solving model, program preparation, corresponds to the prescriptive phase of the diagnostic-prescriptive process. The activities phase of this stage involves designing or prescribing programs to reduce the discrepancies identified during diagnosis and establishing procedures to ensure that the program will be implemented according to design specifications. The evaluation phase entails making a comparison between the actual implementation of the program and the prescribed program to determine whether discrepancies exist. The magnitude and seriousness of the discrepancy is determined during the decision-making phase. Judgments can then be made as to whether modifications should be made in the prescription.

PRESCRIBING LEARNING ACTIVITIES

The prescriptive phase of the diagnostic-prescriptive process involves the design of a plan for moving from a present to a preferred state of competence. It is, essentially, a plan for learning. In a sense, the entire preservice program can be considered a prescription for producing the kind of teacher required by the public school environment. Within the overall program, prescriptions are designed to facilitate the attainment of enabling and terminal objectives. Such prescriptions must take into account a wide variety of factors, including the diagnosed needs and characteristics of the individual, the available instructional resources, and feasible field experiences.

In Chapter 18, the diagnosis of individual characteristics and needs was stressed. At the prescriptive or instructional stage, however, it is often a practical impossibility to develop prescriptions for each teacher in training to master each specified competency. Indeed, such a task would not only be a logistical nightmare but would also be undesirable in terms of many program goals. If placement decisions have been made responsibly at the program level, refinements can be made at the course level by grouping students with similar discrepancy profiles.

Thorough and practical procedures for designing group instruction are described in *Mastery Learning in Classroom Instruction* (Block & Anderson, 1975). Many of the suggestions provided in this chapter are derived from the approach recommended by these authors.

In Chapter 17, we indicated that the student's aptitude for and interest in learning particular competencies should be diagnosed. At the prescriptive phase, the focus moves to the instructional program. A discrepancy has been identified through diagnosis. What learning experiences can be prescribed which will eliminate the particular discrepancy?

At this point, the characteristics of the instructional program must be assessed to determine their potential for reducing the identified discrepancy. This assessment process can be adapted to whatever level of specificity is desired. That is, one can apply the procedure for a specific enabling objective, for a cluster of related objectives, for an entire course, or for a total preservice program or inservice training cycle. The level of specification selected will depend upon the magnitude of the discrepancy, the relative importance of the particular concept or skill, and the ramifications of mastering or not mastering the skill or set of skills before moving on.

The variables included in the mastery learning model which can be manipulated as a part of the instructional program are the opportunity provided for the student to learn and the quality of instruction provided. The first of these variables has been operationalized by mastery learning theorists in terms of the time allotted in the course for the attainment of a given objective (Carroll, 1963). In developing prescriptions for mastery of particular competencies, flexibility should be permitted for accommodating the individual's rate of learning. Whenever possible, self-paced instructional materials can be used.

The first step in designing an appropriate prescription is to analyze the objective to be mastered to determine the mental or performance processes it requires. If the program has been designed according to procedures advocated in this book, each objective will clearly specify the intended mental or performance process. In the course, Interpersonal Skills for Teachers, for example, one objective may specify that the trainee *identify* characteristics of higher order questioning techniques. Another objective may require that the trainee *demonstrate* higher order questioning techniques. These two objectives require recall of information and application through performance respectively.

Once the required processes have been identified, they should be analyzed to determine the logical steps required to perform them. The process of task analysis is appropriate here, although the level of detail indicated will depend again on the complexity of the material to be covered and the magnitude of the learner's discrepancy. Task analysis is basically a procedure for breaking down a particular objective into the subtasks or steps necessary to master it. It should be realized that not every student will learn the material in precisely the same way. Nor does this logical analysis necessarily result in the best way of learning the material. What the procedure does accomplish is to make clear the kind of teaching sequence which is likely to lead to the mastery of the objective.

The next step in developing a prescription is to generate a variety of alternative activities for each subtask. These activities should, at this point, be stated in general terms. That is, the type of activity required should be stated in advance of the determination of what particular materials, media, or teaching strategies are available. This procedure is parallel to establishing design criteria at the program level. It provides a yardstick against which the particular sequence of activities can be measured. By generating so-called "ideal" learning activities, we will have specifications against which the actual activities can be evaluated. Characteristics of various media and materials and their applicability to different types of learning have been catalogued by a number of authorities including Cone and Gagné. The prescription designer should be familiar with the most appropriate uses of various media and materials.

The next step involves selecting among the activities generated in the previous step. Those activities which best meet the specifications for accomplishing the intended learning outcome are then refined. The logical sequence among the subtask activities is also restructured, if necessary.

The next phase in developing prescriptions involves an assessment of presently available resources in terms of their suitability for enabling learners to master a particular subtask. Thus, if the programmed-learning format was specified as the most appropriate way of conveying a particular concept, the program designer now seeks to locate programmed material relevant to the objective. If none is available, arrangements can be made to have the specified material developed, or an alternative activity can be substituted. The cataloging of available resources is essential, both for the original prescription as well as for possible corrective activities.

A number of considerations need to be taken into account when selecting and organizing a sequence of learning activities. One consideration is that of providing sufficient balance among types of activities. Activities can be varied according to degree of student involvement, duration, complexity, location, and intensity. A balance among presentational formats increases the probability that the prescription will accommodate varying learning styles and will maintain students' interest in learning.

Once the individual or group proceeds through the initial prescription, a formative test should be given (see Chapter 20 for more specific information about test construction). The results of this interim assessment are then reviewed by instructor and student. If the preestablished mastery level was not reached, corrective learning experiences should be prescribed. The extent of remediation necessary is indicated by the magnitude of the discrepancy between performance level and mastery level as well as through analysis of the relative importance of objectives not mastered. One important principle to be followed when selecting correctives is that they must be different from the original approach used. Thus, if a student did not master a particular concept through a reading assignment, it is unlikely he will do so through a different reading assignment. Perhaps an auditory approach would be more effective.

The approach used in the corrective must, then, be sufficiently different from the original activity to tap a different learning mode and to stimulate renewed interest. In many cases, prescribed correctives can be carried out independently by the student. Often, once one or two key concepts are mastered, supplementary concepts become clear and the misunderstandings are eradicated.

It is crucial that students be provided an opportunity to correct their mislearnings. If such an opportunity is not built into the training program, the phenomenon of "cumulative deficit" of learning may occur. Figure 19.1 illustrates the interdependent character of the job-related curriculum. Without

FIGURE 19.1   Professional Growth Requirements.

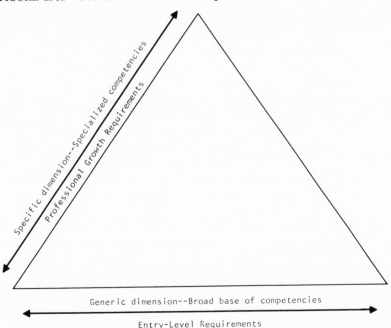

Specific dimension--Specialized competencies

Professional Growth Requirements

Generic dimension--Broad base of competencies

Entry-Level Requirements

a firm foundation of the basic concepts and skills, higher level competencies will rest on quicksand.

In the development of learning activities at the subtask level, one pitfall to avoid is that of losing sight of the overall goals of the curriculum. Specific learning activities should be designed so as to get the maximum possible yardage in terms of the ultimate objectives of the program. For example, one of the overall goals may be to produce a teacher with the ability to deal effectively in a multicultural classroom setting. In selecting activities for a course such as Instructional Design, this ultimate objective might be overlooked. If we keep in mind the need to reinforce the overall goals as frequently as possible, we might select multiculturally oriented activities to accomplish other objectives. This is accommodated in the professional core of the job-related curriculum through the horizontal and vertical relationship of competencies.

One of the major underpinnings of an effective diagnostic-prescriptive process is that of continuity. At the preservice level, this implies a strong and ongoing system of advisement. As recommended previously, the advisement pair or team, which includes a training institution representative and a public school representative, should track the student's progress throughout his preservice program and, if possible, into his initial professional assignment. This human dimension should be supplemented by programmatic continuity, including well-designed diagnostic techniques, a functional record-keeping system, and effective feedback mechanisms.

The purpose of the advisory-team approach is not simply to provide continuity in traditional advisement terms such as what courses the prospective teacher should take, what field activities he needs to participate in, and so forth. A more fundamental rationale for this approach is that the ongoing relationship between the teacher in training and his advisory team provides an opportunity for coherent diagnosis. During the years of contact between the advisory team and the student, a variety of data about the student's performance in various courses and in field activities can be collected. The participatory nature of diagnosis is enhanced when the advisory team works with the student to develop suitable prescriptions. Feedback, in this process, is not simply a matter of informing the student of a project or course grade. Instead, it is a process of integrating new information with previous information about the student's progress so that informed decisions can be made.

The competencies identified as required and desired represent a baseline of professional skills. As we discussed in Chapter 3, the function of the preservice curriculum is to provide teachers with these competencies so that they will enter the profession with the necessary entry level characteristics. This baseline also functions as a foundation upon which more advanced studies can be built. The competencies which comprise the professional core courses represent generic skills and, as such, are designed to provide breadth rather than depth. The entry level teacher needs a broad base of skills rather than extraordinary prowess in any one area. As the teacher grows on the job, he or she builds on the basic competencies.

The relationship between the professional core competencies and advanced teaching competencies can be visualized as a series of pyramids. At the base of each pyramid are the enabling objectives of the particular core course. Once this base has been mastered, the teacher can augment it with more specialized coursework in an area of choice. (See Figure 19.1.) Thus, any one of the professional core courses represents the bottom rung of a career ladder. If the practicing teacher chooses to specialize in a particular content area, additional competencies from selected pyramids can be used to supplement this area of concentration.

This vertical dimension leads to increased specialization or depth in a particular subject or skill area. Thus each pyramid represents a potential career ladder for the practicing teacher. For example, the basics of reading instruction are mastered in the Fundamentals of Teaching Reading course in the professional core. Building on this base, one course sequence will lead to certification as a reading teacher. Additional coursework will qualify one to be a reading consultant or clinician. The Interpersonal Skills for Teachers course represents the base of a pyramid leading to specialized skills in counselling and pupil personnel services. A career ladder growing from the course Diagnosing Readiness for Learning would prepare one to specialize in diagnostic work with exceptional students, such as the learning disabled. The course Instructional Planning and Design is a foundation for later specialization in instructional design and in curriculum development. From the basic competencies acquired in Using Instructional Aids, a teacher might specialize in media arts or in library science.

The design of inservice opportunities for encouraging the continued professional growth of teachers should take place within a dual context. As with the preservice teacher, one framework is that of the required and desired teacher competencies. An additional context is that of the curricular and instructional emphases at the applicable district, school, and job-alike levels. To the extent that there is congruence between teacher training center offerings and on-the-job needs, the professional growth program will have at least one of the basic requirements for effectiveness—relevance.

DESIGNING INCENTIVES FOR TEACHER PARTICIPATION IN INSERVICE

Prescribing professional growth activities for the practicing teacher is a more complex undertaking than prescribing for the preservice teacher. Teachers in a particular school or district often come from widely disparate backgrounds and vary considerably in their aspirations, skills, and openness to professional growth experiences. Another complication is inherent in the difficulty of scheduling and coordinating various professional growth activities. Traditionally, selection of postgraduate coursework has been the individual teacher's prerogative. Mechanisms have not been available to coordinate district-offered workshops, graduate courses, and other professional growth opportunities. Nor has there been a systematic diagnostic procedure which relates teacher performance to desired competencies.

Because of these conditions, teacher participation in the diagnostic-prescriptive process is essential. Whereas the preservice teacher generally needs to acquire the basic competencies to become a teacher, the practicing teacher needs to become a better teacher. Often, the teacher has a clear idea of what his or her needs are. Even when the practicing teacher has obvious deficiencies, the right to select a given path for improvement—or given adequate proficiency, to maintain the present level of functioning—should not be abridged.

The district or other training agency concerned with the professional growth of its staff must make adjustments in its incentive system so that the rewards for professional growth outweigh the rewards for complacency. In many school districts, the existing reward system is philosophically and practically incompatible with a professional growth-oriented inservice program. Because of the lack of differentiation of teaching roles at various career levels, the incentive system has too frequently had the effect of drawing competent teachers out of the classroom. Beyond the almost automatic salary increment system, there has been little to motivate the classroom teacher to excel within the teaching role. The titular and status rewards are largely administrative in nature. Thus, if we assume that the best or most highly respected teacher in a given department is rewarded by being elected or appointed department head, we face a common paradox. The administrative responsibilities the teacher takes on as a reward for good teaching are often accompanied by a smaller course load. Thus, the more experienced teachers often have less contact with students than do the less experienced.

As presently structured, many graduate programs in education also lure teachers out of the classroom and into the front or district office. Given the inelasticity of the school system hierarchy, one wonders how top-heavy districts will become before the folly of this trend becomes apparent. Opportunities for a teacher to advance *within the teaching role* should be emphasized rather than opportunities to abandon the classroom.

Some districts have instituted various gradations of the teacher's job description. In addition to the basic teaching role, it is possible to advance to master teacher, lead teacher, or some other status. In some cases, advancement is based on many of the same criteria as are presently used of certificate renewal and salary increments. In these situations, it is difficult to see how a new title will bring about any meaningful reassessment of the various career stages. On the other hand, a system based on merit may have a tremendous capacity for unleashing teacher potential. Such a system, however, would need to be carefully designed in order to avoid some rather obvious pitfalls. In a study of "Teachers' Preferences toward Alternative Systems of Salary Increment," for example, Bogie and Bogie (1978) found a general opposition toward merit pay in their sample of elementary school teachers:

Although presumably faced with increased public demands for accountability and heightened public scrutiny relating to the use of monetary resources, these teachers—irrespective of variations in socioeconomic characteristics—overwhelmingly opposed an increment system based on merit. At least some indication as to why this might be the case was gleaned from further analysis of survey results. Hence, when teachers were asked why they preferred one form of salary increments to the exclusion of another, those who favored uniform pay increments generally did so for one of two reasons: they either perceived merit systems as being "too political" or cited an absence of adequate evaluation techniques. (p. 218)

These researchers cite other factors in addition to those specified above. The essence of the concern, however, seems to reside in the fact that adequate criteria for assessment and an objective process for evaluation would not be used.

Prescribing professional growth programs for practicing teachers can follow much the same mechanics as used in developing preservice prescriptions. The importance of providing opportunities for career advancement and other appropriate and adequate incentives for participants, however, cannot be overestimated. Additionally, both pre- and inservice programs must be buttressed by a strong component of formative and summative evaluation. Recommendations for developing an assessment program compatible with the mastery learning approach are offered in Chapter 20.

20

Testing and Achieving Solutions in Professional Growth

The third stage in the application of the problem-solving model to improve teacher competencies involves testing the effectiveness of the prescribed program. During the activities phase, data pertaining to the effectiveness of the program—the extent to which the ultimate objectives have been attained by the individual for whom the program was prescribed—is collected. This data is analyzed during the evaluation phase. The final phase, decision-making, results in a judgment about the efficacy of the program. At this time, if the discrepancy between the participant's existing level and preferred level as represented by the ultimate objectives has not been adequately reduced, it may be necessary to modify the program. Such modifications will generally take the form of prescribed additional learning experiences.

In the job-related curriculum, remedial learning experiences for the preservice teacher will usually consist of predesigned educational activities. It is generally more economical to provide standardized alternate learning activities for individuals who are unable to achieve terminal or enabling objectives through the normal program. In situations where it is feasible to provide individualized instruction, an evaluation procedure more similar to the Lindvall and Cox (1970) model may be installed. This model provides for greater individualization in the design of learning activities and self-pacing on the part of the program participant. The Lindvall and Cox approach to evaluation with its emphasis on feedback and remediation may be more viable for inservice professional growth.

The ultimate test of the program's effectiveness resides in the competence manifested by its graduates or trainees on the job. It is unwise, however, to wait until the graduates are employed as teachers to evaluate program effectiveness. Information regarding student performance and perceptions of the training they receive must be collected and analyzed throughout their program. Likewise, the inservice professional growth program and its trainees should be evaluated consistently and continuously.

The evaluation component should be designed as an integral and interactive part of the total training program. A variety of instruments can be developed to assess trainees' mastery of objectives as well as to ascertain their perceptions of the effectiveness of the learning experiences. Feedback from each of these instruments can be used to modify training objectives and/or activities during the pilot phase. Once the program is installed in final form, minor revisions indicated by feedback can be made at appropriate points in the training cycle. Table 20.1 provides an overview of some of the common evaluation instruments, their format, sequence of administration, and purposes.

Data about trainee characteristics should be collected at the beginning of the training program. While the individual prospective or practicing teachers' anonymity must be maintained, results of both the pre/post cognitive and affective instruments can be correlated with a number of these characteristics. The purpose of this technique is to determine whether the training program has differential impact on specific individuals or staff units. Variables which might reasonably be expected to influence cognitive and affective scores include the following:

1. Length of time employed in the particular school

2. Previous teaching experience

3. Educational background

4. Previous job-oriented training experiences

5. Area and level of specialization (that is, job-alike category)

6. Organizational pattern (self-contained classroom, team situation, and so forth)

7. Age

8. Sex

9. Race

Standardized tests are used widely in primary and secondary school systems although less widely at the postsecondary level. Virtually hundreds of standardized tests are available to acquire different types of information about students at all educational levels. The standardized test is basically an instrument designed to measure a specific behavior or set of behaviors under standardized conditions. Standardized conditions are theoretically ideal conditions that vary little each time the instrument is administered. While these tests can be used for making instructional decisions as well as for administrative and counseling decisions, they are usually not suitable for evaluating the attainment of enabling and terminal objectives. For classroom teaching at

TABLE 20.1 Examples of Evaluation Instruments for Teacher Training Programs.

Type of Instrument	Format	When Administered	Purpose(s)
Cognitive Pretest (Form A)	Criterion-referenced objective items sampled from enabling objectives	Beginning of each course or inservice program	To determine entry level knowledge of trainees in relation to training objectives. To make adjustments in training experiences appropriate to needs of particular group.
Affective Pretest	"Disguised" attitudinal scale	Beginning of each course or inservice program	To determine entry level attitudes.
Formative Tests	Criterion-referenced tests sampled from objectives of each course	Completion of each course or program	To provide trainees with information about their level of mastery of objectives. To diagnose individual and group strenths and weaknesses. To provide feedback for possible course revision.
Cognitive Posttest (Form B Summative)	Criterion-referenced objective items sampled from enabling and terminal objectives	Completion of each course or in-service program	To determine individual and group gains from pre- to post-test. To determine individual mastery of training objectives. To contribute to overall evaluation of training effectiveness To identify individual and group variables which may influence cognitive gains.
Affective Posttest	"Disguised" attitudinal scale	Completion of each course or inservice program	To determine change in attitude. To identify individual and group variables which may influence affective gains.
Attitude scale Perceptions of Training Effectiveness	Likert-type (summated rating scale)	Completion of each course or inservice program	To determine trainees' perceptions of the effectiveness of training content, methodology, presenters, and logistics. To identify individual and group variables which may influence evaluation of training effectiveness.
Follow-up survey	Likert-type (summated rating scale) with open-ended items	Approximately six months after completion of training	To assess impact of training program on participants' perceived competency in the field.

the postsecondary level, a more appropriate use of the standardized instrument might be to supplement rather than to replace the instructor-made instrument. Standardized instruments which are selected to provide information for instructional decision-making must have high content validity, internal consistency, and must be keyed to the enabling and/or terminal objectives of the program. In addition, local norms must be used. A list of sources that can aid in the selection of standardized tests is provided in Appendix R.

Having made an observation and obtained measurements of student achievement of specified program objectives, it becomes necessary to place a value on those measurements. There are basically two approaches to this final step in the evaluation process. The first involves making a norm-referenced judgment in which the individual's score is compared with the scores of a reference group—usually his classmates. The second approach involves making a criterion-referenced judgment in which the individual's score is compared to a preestablished external reference. This may be a standard of performance identified by the instructor as indicative of mastery of the material or objectives. It may be a level of performance or behavioral characteristics of persons who are considered to have reached desired levels of proficiency in the learning task. Frequently, in establishing a criterion for this approach to evaluation, a combination of these two external references is used.

The approach to evaluation which is selected will depend on a number of factors. The specific type of behavioral change which is to be effected by the learning that is taking place will be an important consideration. The type of instrument to be employed, a factor interrelated with the type of behavior to be observed, will determine to a great extent whether the norm-referenced or the criterion-referenced approach is more suitable. However, the primary consideration will be the philosophy of the program administrators and teaching staff. The norm-referenced approach to instrument interpretation is usually most appropriate for making selection and placement decisions. If the program philosophy is one of establishing differences in student performance, it is likely that this approach will be used. Criterion-referenced interpretation is oriented toward the mastery of objectives by all program participants. Diagnostic decisions can be made frequently from the information provided by criterion-referenced test results.

In all instructor-made instruments as in standardized measurement devices, reliability and validity are a prime concern. Certainly, before using an instrument it should be checked for obvious flaws. The first step in assuring instrument validity and reliability is in meticulous design. Content validity, which is generally the focus of instruction-made instruments for student evaluation, can be established through appropriate design procedures. However, the establishment of construct and criterion-related validity requires the administration or repeated administration of the instrument. Certainly, reliability cannot be tested until the instrument has been administered. For detailed information on the psychometric aspects of test construction see Appendix S.

Because of the nature of the preservice program, it is likely that all trainees will be expected to master the objectives of the various courses. Hence, criterion-referenced tests are generally more appropriate than the conventional norm-referenced instruments. Criterion-referenced tests have several distinct advantages in competency or objective-based programs (Glaser & Nitko, 1971). These include the following:

1. They are constructed to yield measurements that are directly interpretable in terms of a specified domain of instructionally relevant tasks identified during the problem identification state.

2. They are constructed so as to provide diagnostic information which is useful for correcting individual and staff deficiencies as well as for making program modifications.

3. They tend to motivate trainees and reduce test anxiety since scores are compared with a mastery standard rather than compared with other trainees' scores.

4. They have, by virtue of the construction procedures, high content validity.

For these reasons, criterion-referenced tests can be used to measure trainees' mastery of intended cognitive outcomes. At least two parallel forms of each test should be developed, each measuring mastery of the entire range of training objectives in a particular course or inservice program. Form A can be administered as a pretest. These results can provide instructors with an overall profile of the entry level knowledge demonstrated by participants. Adjustments in training emphasis can be made appropriate to the diagnosed characteristics and needs of individual trainees as well as of particular working units. The posttest (Form B) can be administered at the completion of the course or training cycle. Comparison of these results with pretest results will be used to determine levels of individual and group mastery of training objectives. Additionally, the results will be interpreted as one indicator of training effectiveness. The appropriate test statistic for criterion-referenced items, an item sensitivity to instruction index, will be computed for each pair of parallel items so that any poorly functioning items can be revised. Trainees' gains in total score from pre- to posttest will constitute one measure of program success.

Appropriate levels of mastery of each objective as well as the relative importance of each competency should be determined prior to test construction. Mastery levels should be established in consultation with subject matter experts, representatives of the teachers to be trained, and district officials. A common practice, and one which seems applicable to this training context, is to develop an item bank simultaneously with curriculum development. To ensure content validity of the tests, tables of specification can be generated. These tables, which serve as "test blueprints," plot content elements (that is, the knowledge, concepts, and skills to be mastered) against the corresponding mental processes or performance procedures trainees are expected to perform on the content. If cognitive outcomes are to be assessed, for example, Handbook 1 of the *Taxonomy of Educational Objectives* (Bloom, et al., 1956) may be used. On a table of specifications, the intercept of each content element with a process element (that is, recall, comprehension, application, analysis, synthesis, or evaluation) represents a possible test item. This enables both inservice program and test developers to ensure a direct correspondence between instructional emphasis and testing emphasis. This procedure also allows the test developer to assign weights to various objectives so that their relative importance will be reflected in the apportionment of test items.

It is anticipated that some competencies will not be amenable to assessment through paper and pencil testing. Teachers' mastery of these performance objectives will be measured via checklists for procedures, rating scales for products, and direct observation for performance. A checklist, for example, might be used to determine whether or not the trainees followed recommended procedures for interviewing a parent in a simulated conference situation. Another performance objective might require the trainee (or perhaps a small group of trainees) to develop a plan for individualizing instruction for elementary math students. The plan thus produced would be evaluated according to preestablished criteria on a rating scale. Both checklists and rating scales can also serve as instructional tools since they clearly specify the suggested sequence for performing a given procedure and indicate the important properties a product should possess.

The steps in constructing a rating scale are similar to those for developing a checklist. The rating scale has an advantage over the checklist in that it allows the observer to make a judgment about the *degree* to which a behavior is present, not merely whether or not it is present. The performance or learning outcome must be specified. The steps or characteristics that comprise that behavior or outcome should be listed. At this point a scale for measuring each step or characteristic should be determined. Depending upon the particular performance that is being observed, the scale may take a number of different forms. These may be numerical ratings for evaluation or frequency, behavioral ratings, or descriptive ratings. Finally, the scales should be consciously arranged so as to discourage a response pattern on the part of the observer.

Formative tests should also be developed for administration during each training cycle. Items should be keyed to course objectives and will be cross-referenced on items on the pre- and posttests of the entire program. The "facet design" approach can be used in writing multiple-choice test items so that diagnostic inferences can be made from incorrect responses (Guttmann & Schlesinger, 1967). Using this approach, the foils or incorrect alternatives are developed by determining possible errors or misunderstandings. Thus, if a student selects one of the foils, the instructor will be able to make a diagnostic inference as to what led to this mistake. One useful way of developing such items is to administer short-answer completion items to a pilot group, tabulate and categorize their incorrect response, and use these common errors as foils on multiple choice items.

Formative instruments should be relatively short so that testing time does not intrude unnecessarily on training time. They serve three primary purposes. The first is to provide feedback to each participant about his/her level of mastery of the training objectives so that individual review can be undertaken if needed. The formative test results can also be used to diagnose specific individual or staff weaknesses or misunderstandings which may indicate the need for additional or corrective training experiences. The third use of these instruments is to assist in the evaluation of training effectiveness so as to make appropriate revisions in or to validate the program.

Regardless of whether an instrument is designed for instructor use as is often the case with checklists or rating scales or whether it is designed to be used by students, it is essential to have a set of instructions clearly specified. This reduces those errors which result from a misunderstanding as to how the instrument is to be used. A set of directions should also be developed as to how the instrument is to be scored. This set of directions need not be attached to the instrument itself but should be readily available for reference. In this way objectivity is enhanced.

Evaluation instruments can also be developed to measure the impact of the training program on participants' attitudes toward the usefulness of the competencies covered and their perceived mastery of training objectives. Because of the nature of the content, these instruments should be designed in such a way as to reduce the likelihood that trainees will be able to respond in a "socially desirable" way (that is, as they think they *ought* to feel rather than as they really do). A number of techniques for devising such an instrument are available. This type of instrument can be administered before and after the training cycle. An increase in positive affect toward the competencies covered in the modules can be considered one indicator of program effectiveness.

A Likert-type of summated rating scale can be designed to measure trainees' perceptions of the effectiveness of the training program. This instrument can be administered at the conclusion of the training program. The following list indicates some of the major categories and criteria which can be assessed by this type of instrument:

1.0 Content/Competencies
    1.1 Relevance to on-the-job needs
    1.2 Comprehensiveness of content
    1.3 Practicality of competencies
    1.4 Transferability to classroom situations

2.0 Training methodology
    2.1 Appropriateness of methods
    2.2 Adequate variety of activities
    2.3 Continuity of modules or activities
    2.4 Appropriateness of evaluation instruments
    2.5 Impact of materials

3.0 Instructors (Trainers)
    3.1 Credibility (perceived expertise)
    3.2 Familiarity with on-the-job problems
    3.3 Appropriateness of pacing
    3.4 Adequacy of feedback

3.5 Responsiveness to trainees' concerns
3.6 Use of relevant examples and demonstrations
3.7 Ability to maintain interest and involvement

4.0 Logistics
4.1 Scheduling of sessions
4.2 Adequacy of facilities
4.3 Adequacy of equipment
4.4 Appropriateness of incentives

The neutral point interpretation of individual scores (appropriate for this type of instrument) will enable evaluators to determine each trainee's attitude toward the overall effectiveness of the training program (Anderson, accepted for publication). A positive or strongly positive total group affect score will indicate trainee's assessment of the program as effective. Neutral or negative group affect will indicate the need for program improvement.

The construct validity of these affective instruments can be verified according to accepted logical and empirical procedures. The reliability of each instrument, for example, can be calculated by using the Cronbach alpha formula. If an instrument's reliability does not exceed a preestablished level, it should be revised so that adequate dependability of the instrument for measuring the attitudes under investigation can be assured.

In addition to pre- and posttesting of cognitive and affective objectives, a follow-up evaluation of the impact of the training program should be conducted using a randomly selected sample of former participants. The follow-up instrument should be administered after at least six months have elapsed from the conclusion of the training cycle. The purpose of this phase of the evaluation will be to determine the extent to which trainees found the program to be useful in helping them deal with the instructional problems they have encountered on the job. In addition to assessing the effectiveness of the program, participants' perceptions of the efficiency of the training program will also be solicited. Open-ended statements will be included so that former trainees can offer suggestions for improving the program. The results of the follow-up survey can be analyzed and used as input for revising the ongoing program.

Teacher performance in the classroom is obviously the most meaningful measure of a program's effectiveness. This represents the ultimate goal of any teacher training program. It is also, unfortunately, the most difficult to assess. Research attempting to identify teacher characteristics which bring about measurable gains in pupil achievement has generally been inconclusive (Gage, 1963). So many variables, other than the characteristics under investigation influence the instructional interaction between learner and teacher that it is almost impossible to ascribe student performance directly to any one or set of teacher characteristics. Nevertheless, in addition to the more traditional assessment procedures such as evaluation by principal, faculty advisor, supervisory teacher, or students, a number of rather sophisticated techniques have been developed to circumvent at least partially subjectivity in the evaluation process. The reader is referred to Chapters 14, 15, and

16 for a discussion of instruments and procedures for evaluating instructor performance in the classroom. Sample instruments for classroom observation may be found in Appendix I.

The importance of relevant and consistent evaluation of participant progress in any teacher education program should not be underestimated. Since the ultimate test of program success is in the performance of its products or graduates in the classroom, their progress toward attaining this goal must be systematically monitored. This and other distinguishing features of exemplary teacher education programs are discussed in Chapter 21.

21

Characteristics of Exemplary Teacher Education Programs

Throughout *Improving Teacher Education* we have used a problem-solving framework for developing pre- and inservice teacher education programs which will be effective in training teachers to meet the demands of today's classroom. We have tried to offer both a process—the problem-solving approach—and a product—the model job-related curriculum. This product can be installed as we have presented it or can be adapted to fit local needs. The problem-solving approach can be used to develop a teacher education program which will meet specific, indigenous needs. We believe that many institutions and organizations will want to apply the problem-solving procedures to educational contexts other than teacher education, such as administration, school program development, or program evaluation.

In this chapter, we review some of the characteristics which have been found to distinguish strong from weak programs. As a result of a rather extensive survey of teacher education programs, we have identified some features which are consistently evident in exemplary programs and often absent in poor programs. We have not attempted to present these as requirements but rather as recommendations. Also, we have tried to keep these suggestions as generic as possible. For this reason, specific programs which do or do not possess these characteristics are not identified.

EXEMPLARY PRESERVICE PROGRAMS

The most critical feature which distinguishes exemplary programs from others is that the curriculum is based on the professional skills or competencies required of all teachers. These generic skills are those which have been identified as essential for successful on-the-job performance. In addition, knowledge and attitudes supportive of the professional skills are specified. Professional competency is not clouded by general knowledge and attitudes appropriate for all humans to acquire.

It should be pointed out that most, if not all, teacher education programs include a set of objectives or competencies. In many cases, however, there is little evidence that these competencies are actually being taught or learned. Exemplary programs include specific provisions for learning essential professional skills. Three characteristics of such programs stand out:

1. Competencies are sequenced so that the more complex skills are built on less complex, prerequisite skills.

2. Provision is made for each competency to be practiced until mastery is achieved.

3. Provision is made for competencies to be integrated and applied. Relationships between competencies are taught and the prospective teacher integrates them in the public school classroom.

Programs which are effective in producing teachers with the necessary entry level skills are characterized by a relatively heavy emphasis on professional coursework. More than 30 semester hours (or the equivalent) are required in most of these programs for professional preparation. In some programs, different degrees of professional preparation are required depending upon the area of specialization. For instance, 36 semester hours may be required in the elementary education specialization while only 18 semester hours are required in secondary education specialization. However, in some cases the same competencies are taught even though different numbers of semester hours are devoted to teaching them. Variations within institutions notwithstanding, more than 30 semester hours of professional training are required in good programs.

Superior programs are also characterized by an obvious commitment to excellence in instruction. One indicator of this commitment is that specialists rather than generalists teach the course content. If a course covers a broad range of topics, different specialists are assigned to teach each topic (shared teaching). To cite an example from the model job-related curriculum, the course Teaching as a Profession might require as many as ten specialists to do justice to the broad survey of professional concerns. If the content of a course is clearly in a specific area of expertise, one instructor might be assigned to teach the entire course. An example of such a course from the job-related curriculum is Achievement Testing.

The instructional methods used do not seem to distinguish strong from weak programs. Many innovative programs are innovative only because they have changed *how* they teach in some modern way. There is no evidence that these technologies improve the quality of teacher training. There is some practical value in imparting information by means of media so that instructors can be relieved from lecturing to engage in instruction that machines cannot accomplish. Over-automated individualized instruction, however, can reduce student-teacher interaction to the detriment of learning.

While the emphasis on professional skill development clearly emerges as a distinguishing feature of exemplary programs, there is less evidence that variations in area of specialization or general education requirements make much difference in the overall effectiveness of the program. The argument as to how much training beginning teachers need in their area of specialization will never cease. Some observers believe that the entry level teacher needs only the minimum knowledge necessary to convey information to students. Others insist that the teacher should be a scholar or expert in the field of specialization. In our comparisons of programs, the number of courses required does not seem to set apart the exemplary program. What does seem to distinguish the strong program from the weak is that the former provides for the integration of area-of-specialization knowledge with professional skills whereas no such mechanism is apparent in the latter.

Despite variations in the number of general education courses required, there is a general consistency in the disciplines covered and the relative emphasis devoted to each. General education requirements range from approximately 30 to more than 70 semester hours. While general education requirements do not appear to distinguish exemplary programs, sound programs tend to be flexible in their course requirements and permit students to exempt courses by passing equivalency examinations.

Exemplary programs do not operate in a vacuum. They provide opportunities for students to be exposed to the realities of teaching early in their training so that they have a basis for deciding whether or not to pursue teaching as a profession. Not only the students but also the instructors are in continuous contact with public schools throughout the program. This helps to ensure that what is taught in teacher education courses has relevance to the real world of the classroom.

Field-based experiences are integrated with coursework in strong programs. Prospective teachers interact with public school teachers and students throughout their training. Provision is made for students to apply what they learn in their coursework in the classroom setting. In these programs, the ultimate evidence of the mastery of a competency is through classroom application. As the student learns competencies he integrates them in the classroom. This allows the student to assume increasing responsibility for classroom teaching.

The exemplary program also provides for early, continuous, and supportive supervision of students. Evidence shows that this promotes student satisfaction and discourages students from dropping out of the program. While the supervisory roles may vary from program to program, one approach has proven to be quite effective. Three advisors work with the student throughout his preservice training. A faculty advisor is assigned to the student as soon as he enters the program. This individual should be qualified to (1) give academic guidance, (2) teach advanced methods in the area of specialization, and (3) supervise student teaching. The faculty advisor must be from the student's area of specialization so that he can teach advanced methods, not merely those which are commonly used. A classroom supervising teacher in the student's area of specialization is also assigned to the student when he enters the teacher training program and continues to work with him until he graduates. The supervising teacher may or may not be the cooperating teacher during student teaching. The teacher helps the student apply in the classroom what he learns in coursework. The teacher also makes arrangements for the student to learn about school procedures and curriculum. The third member of the advisory team is a counselor who is assigned to observe, evaluate, and offer suggestions for improving the student's management of interpersonal relations in the classroom and school. In addition, the counselor may help the student adjust to teaching. Each of these supervisors is trained to observe and evaluate students' classroom performance against predetermined criteria.

Sound programs provide incentives for supervising prospective teachers in the public school setting. Teacher education faculty with supervisory responsibilities are compensated with pay supplements or reduced course load requirements. Those public school teachers who serve as advisors and/or cooperating teachers may receive additional pay as well as status. Status incentives include selecting outstanding teachers as supervisors and designating them as master teachers.

Sound programs incorporate systematic evaluation procedures for both participants and faculty. Student evaluation includes both formative and summative measurements and provides an objective basis for making selection, placement, diagnostic, and certification decisions. The evaluation of faculty is directly tied to their performance in terms of producing qualified teachers.

Formative evaluations are made periodically by course instructors to measure student progress toward course objectives. Students are informed of their progress and correctives are prescribed if they are not progressing adequately. This maximizes the probability that students receive the help they need to pass the summative tests.

Summative tests are constructed to assess the attainment of the competencies pursued in each course and in the program as a whole. These tests include both paper and pencil tests and observation instruments to assess students' on-the-job performance. The instruments are constructed by test development specialists in cooperation with subject matter specialists. This ensures adequate technical qualities such as content validity, reliability, and objectivity. Often the teaching and testing functions are distinct. The individuals who administer and score these tests are not those who are responsible for teaching the course.

The evaluation of faculty in strong teacher education programs makes clear the priorities of the institution. While research and administrative activities are also important, effectiveness in meeting teacher education goals is paramount. The quality of faculty teaching is systematically assessed and the evaluations are used to determine salary increases, promotion, and tenure.

Students periodically evaluate instructors via instruments which are specifically constructed to relate to the goals of the program. Faculty performance in the classroom is also evaluated on the basis of student achievement. This may be done using normative procedures. For example, faculty who teach the same course are compared with respect to the achievement of their students on the course summative tests. The evaluation may be based on absolute criteria established by an appointed faculty committee.

Teacher education faculty who supervise prospective teachers in the public schools are also evaluated by the school principal or a qualified delegate. These evaluations, along with those previously mentioned, are kept in the instructor's personnel file showing his performance in comparison to preestablished standards.

Evaluations are systematic and continuous. Competency standards are predetermined and explicit, and serve as criteria for evaluation. Evaluation data are recorded and available to the individual being evaluated and to the superior responsible for judging and certifying his competency. Feedback is given periodically to the individual and prescriptions are recommended for correcting weaknesses. Emphasis is placed on the improvement of performance. The individual is given sufficient opportunity to improve his performance before a judgment is made concerning his competency. These guidelines apply to the evaluation of faculty, staff, and students alike.

EXEMPLARY INSERVICE PROGRAMS

Sound inservice programs provide for the continuous professional growth of their participants. In so doing, they are characterized by a number of features which differentiate them from weak programs. Because of the diversity of inservice contexts, these characteristics can best be presented in the form of general recommendations applicable to the various circumstances in which inservice programs may be conducted.

Inservice program design should be based upon a systematic and comprehensive assessment of individual and staff professional growth needs. The assessment of professional needs should be conducted at regularly scheduled intervals in order that the changes in staff as well as changes in the needs of continuing staff members throughout the school system will be recognized and will impact on inservice planning. Instruments and techniques used for assessing staff needs should be based on the competencies required and desired of the educational practitioner.

Inservice programs should provide for removing deficiencies in present functioning, upgrading existing skills, and acquiring new professional competencies. The design should minimize duplication through the logical sequencing of skills. Provisions should also be developed for assessing both mastery and integration of skills.

Practicing teachers should participate in both planning and presenting the inservice program. They should also have a primary role in evaluating the effectiveness of the program. Their assessment of the quality and relevance of the program can be used in revising the program. Incentives for participation should be established.

The inservice program functions most effectively when linked with the supervisory mechanism of the school or district. This linkage permits classroom follow-up to determine if the skills covered in inservice are being used appropriately in the classroom. Participants can also be evaluated to assess the attainment of competencies pursued in the program and to determine whether the objectives of the particular program or increment of the program were met. Summative tests can be constructed which will assess the attainment of competencies addressed by the program. These tests should be developed by test development specialists in cooperation with inservice training specialists.

In general, inservice programs are not as systematically organized as preservice programs. Preservice programs extend four years within the framework of a structured curriculum. Course requirements tend to be defined and courses tend to be sequenced. In contrast, courses, workshops, and symposiums offered for inservice training are often not formally knit into a curriculum and often reflect the fad of the day or the bias of local educators responsible for inservice planning. We suggest that inservice training can benefit from formal organization geared to ensure that practicing teachers learn the basic professional skills they did not acquire in preservice training. In addition, the curriculum organization should provide practicing teachers with the opportunity to build on these basic professional skills so that they may develop more specialized expertise in areas of their choice.

In Chapter 19, we indicated that the courses in the professional core (described fully in Chapter 9) develop a broad base of competencies needed for entry into the teaching profession. We suggested further that the competencies acquired in many of the professional core courses provide the foundation for the development of more specialized competencies. We cited the examples of how the basic course Instructional Planning and Design provides a foundation for specialization in instructional design and curriculum development. We indicated further that the professional core course Fundamentals of Teaching Reading provides the foundation for a reading specialization that might lead to certification as a reading teacher.

School districts can use the professional core courses to identify the basic entry level skills that are required in the teaching profession. Practicing teachers can be given diagnostic tests to determine their strengths and weaknesses with respect to these basic skills. We have completed diagnostic tests for this purpose as well as instructional prescriptions to remediate weaknesses. The districts, then, can provide incentives and opportunities for remediating the weaknesses. This can be accomplished in conjunction with universities, if at all feasible.

Incentives and opportunities to develop further expertise can be provided to teachers who have mastered basic entry skills. Districts can identify career opportunities in various areas of specialization so that teachers may see where opportunities lie. If a group of teachers shows interest in a specialization, the school district can identify course sequences at accessible universities that lead to advanced competency.

Finally, strong inservice programs include provisions for enabling teachers to keep abreast of research that has implications for the improvement of instruction. Periodic symposiums should be held at which teachers are informed about instructional practices supported by research findings. At the end of Chapter 4 we stressed the importance of basing instruction on scientific evidence and we mentioned some significant research findings and their implications for instruction. Teachers should not only learn about significant findings but also they should learn how to apply them in their classrooms. These symposiums can be more effective if teachers are trained to interpret and evaluate research evidence. This requires that the teachers have mastered the skills in a course such as Understanding Educational Research and Innovation, which is in the professional core. When educators are trained to understand research evidence, they are less gullible and less inclined to adopt the fad of the moment. They are more inclined to request evidence when a new instructional program is proposed and are able, from the evidence, to see whether or not a proposed instructional method should be adopted.

We hope that pre- and inservice program designers will find the preceding recommendations helpful in developing and revamping teacher education programs. By applying the problem-solving techniques described in previous chapters, programs to improve teacher education can be implemented. Our experiences in designing a model job-related curriculum and in observing other successful programs have shown us that relevant and effective programs are possible. As we enter an era of increasing demands upon our teachers and our public schools, we hope that institutions and organizations involved in teacher education will find the recommendations and resources provided in this book helpful in bringing about necessary and desired changes.

Appendixes

APPENDIX A

I. OBSERVATIONAL DATA SOURCES

Altman, H. Teacher-student interaction in inner-city and advantaged classes using the science curriculum improvement study. *Classroom Interaction Newsletter,* 1970, *6*(1), 5–16.

Bellack, A. A., Hyman, R. T., Smith, F. L., Jr., & Kliebard, H. M. *The language of the classroom.* (Final report, USOE Cooperative Research Project, No. 2023). New York: Teachers College, Columbia University, 1966.

Dahllof, U. S., & Lundgren, U. P. *Project compass 23: Macro and micro approaches combined for curriculum project analysis: A Swedish educational field project.* Paper presented at the annual meeting of the American Educational Research Association, Minneapolis, 1970.

Dunkin, M., & Biddle, B. *The study of teaching.* New York: Holt, Rinehart and Winston, 1974.

Fortune, J. C., Gage, N. L., & Shutes, R. E. *The generality of the ability to explain.* Paper presented at the American Educational Research Association, Amherst, Mass., 1966.

Furst, N. The effects of training in interaction analysis on the behavior of student teachers in secondary schools. In E. J. Amidon & J. B. Hough (Eds.), *Interaction analysis: Theory, research, and application.* Reading, Mass.: Addison-Wesley, 1967.

Gump, P. M. *The classroom behavior setting: Its nature and relation to student behavior.* Final report, Contract No. OE-4-10-107, U.S. Bureau of Research, H.E.W., 1967.

Lohman, E., Ober, R., & Hough, J. B. A study of the effect of preservice training in interaction analysis on the verbal behavior of student teachers. In E. J. Amidon & J. B. Hough (Eds.), *Interaction analysis: Theory, research, and application.* Reading, Mass.: Addison-Wesley, 1967.

Lorentz, J. L. *The development of measures of teacher effectiveness from multiple measures of student growth.* Paper presented at the annual meeting of the American Educational Research Association, New York, 1977.

Lundgren, U. P. *Frame factors and the teaching process: A contribution to curriculum theory and theory on teaching.* Stockholm: Almgrist and Wiksell, 1972.

Mueller, D. L. Observing student teachers in a competency-based program. *Peabody Journal of Education,* 1976, *53*(4), 248–253.

Park, C. B. The Bay City experiment as seen by the director. *Journal of Teacher Education,* 1956, *7,* 101–110.

Perkins, H. V. A procedure for assessing the classroom behavior of students and teachers. *American Educational Research Journal,* 1964, *1*(4), 249–260. Also reprinted in R. T. Hyman (Ed.), *Teaching: Vantage points for study.* Philadelphia: Lippincott, 1968.

Power, C. N. *The effects of communications patterns on student sociometric status, attitudes, and achievement in science.* Unpublished thesis, University of Queensland, Australia, 1971.

Resnick, L. B. *Teacher behavior in an informal British infant school.* Paper presented at the annual meeting of the American Educational Research Association, New York, 1971.

Richey, R. W. *Planning for teaching.* New York: McGraw-Hill, 1968.

Soar, R., Coker, H., & Lorentz, J. *Using process product relationships as the basis of describing effective teacher behavior.* Paper presented at a meeting of the American Educational Research Association, New York, 1977.

Sorber, E. Classroom interaction patterns and personality needs of traditionally prepared first-year elementary teachers and graduate teaching interns with degrees from colleges of liberal arts. *Classroom Interaction Newsletter,* 1967, *2*(2), 51–55.

Tisher, R. Verbal interaction in science class. *Journal of Research in Science Teaching,* 1971, *8*(1), 1–8.

II. TEACHER REPORT DATA SOURCES

Heinbach, A. *Job analysis of elementary school teachers and some implications for competency-based teacher education programs.* Unpublished doctoral dissertation, McNeese State University, Lake Charles, La., 1974.

Manatt, R., Palmer, K., & Hidlebaugh, E. Evaluating teacher performance with improved rating scales. *NASSP Bulletin,* 1976.

Survey of high school educator opinion, 1975–1976. Columbia, S.C.: South Carolina Education Association.

III. COMPETENCY LIST INFORMATION

Hall, G. & Jones, H. *Competency-based education: A process for the improvement of education.* Englewood Cliffs, N.J.: Prentice-Hall, 1976.

Houston, W. R. *Exploring competency-based education.* Berkeley, Calif.: McCutchan, 1974.

Manatt, R. P. *Developing a teacher performance evaluation system.* Des Moines: Iowa Association of School Boards, 1976.

Schmeider, A. A. Profile of the states in competency-based education. *PBTE: Performance Based Teacher Education,* 1974, *3*.

Schmeider, A. A., Mark, J. L., & Aldrich, J. L. *Competency-based education: A briefing package.* Unpublished draft, U.S. Office of education, 1975.

APPENDIX B

General Survey Form

Name: _____

Address: _____

Telephone Number: _____

Position: _____

Agency or School Where Employed: _____

If you are employed in a school, indicate whether it is an elementary, middle, or secondary school: _____

* * *

Skills

The teacher-in-training should learn to <u>do</u> the following. List the most important skills the teacher-in-training needs to learn.

[1. through 20.]

* * *

Knowledge

The teacher-in-training should acquire the following knowledge. List the most important subject matter the teacher-in-training needs to learn.

[1. through 20.]

* * *

Attitudes

The teacher-in-training should develop the following <u>attitudes</u>. List the most important attitudes a teacher-in-training needs to develop.

[1. through 20.]

Note: The symbol * * * indicates separate pages.

APPENDIX C

Data Collection Instruments

Faculty Interview Schedule

1. What skills, attitudes, and knowledge are important in the teacher?

2. Are you aware of any job descriptions of the teacher's job?

3. Are you aware of any data sources that indicate the skills, knowledge, and attitudes the teacher-in-training should learn?

4. What field-based experiences should the teacher-in-training have?

5. Are you aware of any job-related teacher education programs which have been implemented into the new curriculum?

6. Are you aware of any developmental activities in the college that might be incorporated into the new curriculum?

7. Do you know of any courses ouside the college of education which are job-related or supportive of teacher education?

8. Are there any other recommendations you would like to make?

APPENDIX D

Source Competency Lists

Thirteen teacher competency lists were used as sources of desired attitudes, knowledge, and skills for the Generic List of Teacher Competencies.

The lists cover a range of intended applications. Some lists were developed as a basis for reworking of certification requirements for graduates or for teachers (such as, Carroll County and Hawaii). Others were developed with revision of a particular college's program in mind (such as, Boston, Florida State, and the South Carolina C.O.P.E. program), or as a guide for district-wide or state-wide curriculum revision (such as, Michigan, Michigan State/Lansing, Wayne State). Still others are of a nonspecific, model or experimental nature (such as, Georgia, Ohio State, B. Joiner, L. Lessinger, L. Peter).

The following information is presented:

1. The *source.*

2. The *development director(s)* (the actual title varied), as we were able to ascertain from the publication itself, or from other material.

3. The *title* of the publication, the date and publisher. Words such as "mimeograph" indicate a rather informal printing, intended for limited circulation, was used.

4. *Addresses* of publisher, compiler, or both, which should enable the reader to contact persons involved for more information.

5. A short statement indicating the *intended use* of the list, in the developers' own words whenever possible.

COMPETENCY LISTS CONSULTED

List:	Boston College
Development Director:	Lester E. Przewlocki
Publication:	*Providing specialized preparation for regular education personnel,* 1977, mimeograph
Address:	School of Education, Boston College, Chestnut Hill, Mass. 02167
Purpose:	"The major aim of the planned revised curriculum is to equip students not only to graduate with a college degree and a teaching certificate, but also to be equipped with the knowledge, attitudes, and skills necessary to enter various areas in the field of human services."

List:	Carroll County, Georgia
Development Director:	Homer Coker and Joan G. Coker
Publication:	*Carroll County generic competency areas, teacher behaviors and student outcomes* (1974: School of Education, West Georgia College)
Address:	School of Education, West Georgia College, Carrollton, Ga. 30117
Purpose:	"The major objective of the Carroll County Competency Based Teacher Certification project is the development of a system for the recertification of experienced classroom teachers which is a potential

alternative to the program-approved approach currently in use in Georgia."

List:	Florida State University
Development Director:	Norman R. Dodl
Publication:	1971: mimeograph
Address:	College of Education, Florida State University, Tallahassee, Fla. 32306
Purpose:	The "structuring of a teacher education program around measurable performance criteria and organized to permit self-pacing and program entry at any point. . . ."

List:	University of Hawaii
Development Directors:	M. Collins, L. Murayama, P. Whitesell, and R. Will
Publication:	*Goals for a performance-based undergraduate teacher education program* (1972: University of Hawaii)
Addresses:	Office of Personnel Service, State Department of Education, P. O. Box 2360, Honolulu, Hawaii 96804; University of Hawaii, Honolulu, Hawaii 96822
Purpose:	A "statement of performance-based goals applicable to graduates of the College of Education was prepared. . . . The statement specifies achievable and measurable skills the graduate should be able to demonstrate. . . ."

List:	University of Michigan
Development Director:	Stephen A. Roderick
Publication:	*Final report of a competency-based teacher education project focusing on the directed teaching experience* (1977: University of Michigan)
Address:	School of Education, University of Michigan, Ann Arbor, Mich. 48104
Purpose:	The project "had as its major thrust, the development and refinement of competency-based teacher training programs in elementary and secondary education."

List:	University of South Carolina—Community and Occupational Programs in Education
Development Directors:	W. Jackson Lyday and H. Larry Winecoff
Publication:	1975 mimeograph
Address:	C.O.P.E., University of South Carolina, S.C. 29208
Purpose:	Basis for the C.O.P.E. program, which is designed to prepare educational leaders and managers in the fields of Community-based Education including adult education, career education, community education, continuing education, cooperative education, cooperative extension service, industrial training, leisure education, technical education, and vocational education.

List:	Michigan State University and Lansing School District
Development Directors:	H. Kennedy, L. Dean, R. Chamberlain, D. Freeman, R. Hatfield and P. Slocum (for MSU); D. Schulert, L. Graham and G. Iverson (for Lansing)
Publication:	*Development of a competency based teacher education program focusing on the directed teaching experience.* (1976: Michigan Department of Education)

Addresses:	School of Teacher Education, Michigan State University, East Lansing, Mich. 48824; Lansing School District, 519 W. Kalamazoo St., Lansing, Mich. 48933
Purpose:	The "development of a competency-based program which provides for instruction in the directed teaching experience of undergraduates enrolled in a teacher education program."

List:	Ohio State University
Development Director:	James B. Hamilton
Publication:	Performance-based teacher education modules (1977: AAVIM)
Addresses:	Center for Vocational Education, Ohio State University, 1960 Kenny Road, Columbus, Ohio 43210; American Association for Vocational Instructional Materials (AAVIM), 120 Engineering Center, Athens, Ga. 30602
Purpose:	"The competencies upon which these modules were based were identified and verified through research as being important to successful vocational teaching at both the secondary and postsecondary levels of instruction. The modules are suitable for the preparation of teachers in all occupational areas."

List:	Lawrence J. Peter
Publication:	*Competencies for teaching: teacher education* (1975: Wadsworth)
Address:	Wadsworth Publishing Co., Inc., 10 Davis Dr., Belmont, Calif. 94002
Purpose:	The last in a four volume series, offering "a complete system of competency-based teacher education." Apparently not institution-specific, it "can be implemented by a department of teacher education within its existing budgetry and time limits."

List:	University of Georgia
Compilers:	G. F. Shearron and C. E. Johnson
Publication:	*Specifications worksheets for behaviors drawn from educational principles* (1969: Georgia Education Models Bulletin 69–21)
Addresses:	College of Education, University of Georgia, Athens, Ga. 30601; Program and Staff Development, Department of Education, State Office Building, Atlanta, Ga. 30334.
Purpose:	One of a series of four bulletins. The goal was "developing and operating a model and exemplary program for the preparation of elementary school teachers."

List:	University of South Carolina—Burnett Joiner, Jr.
Publication:	1975, Ph.D. dissertation
Address:	Thomas Cooper Library, University of South Carolina, Columbia, S.C. 29208
Purpose:	To "investigate an alternative model of providing teaching and learning experiences which was more performance-oriented than some of the traditional programs that have been prevalent in past years for undergraduate teacher education students."

List:	Leon M. Lessinger
Publication:	*A job description for the school teacher.* (1977, working draft)
Address:	College of Education, University of South Carolina, Columbia, S.C. 29208
Purpose:	A model job description tells "*what* is to be done by the teacher, viewed here as a manager, and spells out the authority and responsibility associated with doing it."

List:	Wayne State University

Development
  Directors: R. Richey, R. Alec, and F. Cook
Publication: *Project EXAM: Final report* (1977: Wayne State University)
Address: Wayne State University, Detroit, Mich. 48202
Purpose: "The purpose of the project was to develop a directed-teaching objec-
                tive-referenced assessment instrument to measure exit competencies
                of secondary preservice teachers."

APPENDIX E

Questionnaire

This questionnaire was designed by the Job-Related Curriculum Project. The purpose of the questionnaire is to find out more about teachers' views of current inservice training programs.

As used in the questionnaire, the term "inservice session," means any planned presentation or workshop sponsored by a district (or school) for the purpose of improving the teaching skills of its professional staff. Teachers are required or expected to attend these sessions as part of their duties.

You will note that the questionnaire does not ask for your name or for the name of your school. Your responses will remain anonymous.

PART I: The following statements are opinions about inservice training. There are no "right" or "wrong" responses to any of the statements. Please put a check mark in the space which tells how strongly you agree or disagree with each statement.

Please work carefully and quickly. Do not spend a long time on any one item.

1. The suggestions inservice consultants make are practical.

   STRONGLY   CAN'T   STRONGLY
   AGREE _____ AGREE _____ DECIDE _____ DISAGREE _____ DISAGREE _____

2. Teachers could use the time spent in inservice sessions more profitably in other ways.

   STRONGLY   CAN'T   STRONGLY
   AGREE _____ AGREE _____ DECIDE _____ DISAGREE _____ DISAGREE _____

3. Inservice consultants show an understanding of classroom realities.

   STRONGLY   CAN'T   STRONGLY
   AGREE _____ AGREE _____ DECIDE _____ DISAGREE _____ DISAGREE _____

4. The teaching skills I would like to improve are not covered in inservice sessions.

   STRONGLY   CAN'T   STRONGLY
   AGREE _____ AGREE _____ DECIDE _____ DISAGREE _____ DISAGREE _____

5. Inservice consultants use relevant examples and demonstrations.

   STRONGLY   CAN'T   STRONGLY
   AGREE _____ AGREE _____ DECIDE _____ DISAGREE _____ DISAGREE _____

6. I learn useful teaching techniques in inservice sessions.

   STRONGLY   CAN'T   STRONGLY
   AGREE _____ AGREE _____ DECIDE _____ DISAGREE _____ DISAGREE _____

7. The topics covered in inservice sessions are classroom-oriented.

   STRONGLY   CAN'T   STRONGLY
   AGREE _____ AGREE _____ DECIDE _____ DISAGREE _____ DISAGREE _____

8. Attending inservice sessions is just another requirement--teachers
    really do not expect to get anything out of them.

    STRONGLY   CAN'T   STRONGLY
    AGREE _____   AGREE _____ DECIDE _____   DISAGREE _____ DISAGREE _____

9. Inservice sessions give me new ideas about how to motivate my students.

    STRONGLY   CAN'T   STRONGLY
    AGREE _____   AGREE _____ DECIDE _____   DISAGREE _____ DISAGREE _____

10. The information presented in inservice sessions helps me do a better job
    as a teacher.

    STRONGLY   CAN'T   STRONGLY
    AGREE _____   AGREE _____ DECIDE _____   DISAGREE _____ DISAGREE _____

    PART II: Please complete the following statements.

1. The best way to improve inservice training would be to _____

    _____

    _____

    _____

    _____

2. Teachers would benefit from additional training in the following skills:

    _____

    _____

    _____

    _____

    _____

                    THANK YOU FOR YOUR ASSISTANCE

APPENDIX F

Open-Ended Questionnaires for Assessing Overall Curriculum

<u>Job-Related Curriculum Questionnaire</u>

Please read and evaluate our proposed job-related undergraduate curriculum and share your reactions with us by completing the following questionnaire.

As you complete the questionnaire, keep in mind that you are reacting only to the proposed <u>content</u> of the new curriculum. After we have revised the content we will consider how the content should be taught. You will note, however, that one item asks you to recommend methods for teaching the new curriculum.

Name _____

Date _____

Position _____

District (or organization)
you are representing _____

* * *

Do you believe our project to develop a more job-related undergraduate teacher education program is needed in South Carolina?
(Check one of the following):

yes_____

no_____

Please explain your response below.

Note: The symbol * * * indicates separate pages.

The content of the general education group of courses, (check one of the following):

is acceptable as described._____

        needs revision._____

If you checked "needs revision," please indicate below the revisions you suggest.

* * *

The content of the professional core group of courses, (check one of the following):

is acceptable as described._____

        needs revision._____

If you checked "needs revision," please indicate below the revisions you suggest.

* * *

The content of the early childhood education specialization courses, (check one of the following):

is acceptable as described._____

        needs revision._____

If you checked "needs revision," please indicate below the revisions you suggest.

* * *

The content of the elementary education specialization courses, (check one of the following):

is acceptable as described._____

        needs revision._____

If you checked "needs revision," please indicate below the revisions you suggest.

* * *

The content of the middle school education specialization courses, (check one of the following):

is acceptable as described._____

needs revision._____

If you checked "needs revision," please indicate below the revisions you suggest.

* * *

The content of the secondary education specialization courses, (check one of the following):

is acceptable as described._____

needs revision._____

If you checked "needs revision," please indicate below the revisions you suggest.

* * *

The content of the rehabilitation services specialization courses, (check one of the following):

is acceptable as described._____

needs revision._____

If you checked "needs revision," please indicate below the revisions you suggest.

* * *

RECOMMENDATIONS

Develop follow-up research to determine the most effective courses and to determine additions and deletions as changing conditions make this necessary.

Conduct research to show what competencies correlate with effective teaching.

* * *

APPENDIX G

Professional Associations

The following associations provide guidelines and information useful for the development of teacher education programs:

American Alliance for Health, Physical Education and Recreation
1201 Sixteenth Street, N.W.
Washington, D.C. 20036

American Association of Physics Teachers
Graduate Physics Building
SUNY at Stony Brook
Stony Brook, New York 11794

American Chemical Society
1155 Sixteenth Street, N.W.
Washington, D.C. 20036

American Council on Industrial Arts Teacher Education
c/o Louis J. Pardini
Division of Technology
Arizona State University
Tempe, Arizona 85281

American Home Economics Association
2010 Massachusetts Avenue, N.W.
Washington, D.C. 20036

National Art Education Association
1916 Association Drive
Reston, Virginia 22091

National Association of Biology Teachers
11250 Roger Bacon Drive
Reston, Virginia 22090

National Council for the Social Studies
Suite 400
2030 M Street, N.W.
Washington, D.C. 20036

National Council of Teachers of English
1111 Kenyon Road
Urbana, Illinois 61801

Updated addresses for these associations may be found in the current edition of *Encyclopedia of Associations.* Mary Wilson Pair (Ed.) Vol. 1 National Organizations of the U.S., Detroit: Gale Research Company.

Summary of General Education Requirements at Selected Teacher Education Programs

For purposes of comparison, we outline here the general education programs of other colleges of interest, where copies of these programs were available to us. The colleges on the list either identify themselves as "competency-based," or were designated as such by the U.S. Office of Education (Competency-Based Education: A Briefing, unpublished 1975 draft).

The following abbreviations are used:

Hum = Humanities (defined as art, music; some colleges include literature, foreign language, philosophy)

SSci = Social Sciences (defined as sociology, anthropology, political science, history; some include psychology, philosophy, and geography)

PSci = Physical Science (defines as physics, chemistry, and geology; some include engineering, mathematics, and geography)

NSci = PSci plus biology or other life science

H&PE = Health and Physical Education

We have used descriptors as specific as possible. Thus, SSci is broken down to Hist, Socy, and Anth if the college does so, but grouped as SSci if not specified.

Where a requirement is "12 hours in at least two different areas" of some larger heading, it is reported as 12(/2).

Summarized are:

TOTAL = total program hours required for a bachelor's degree, these are semester hours unless designated "qh" for quarter hours. An equivalence in semester hours is given for qh, considering a qh to be 2/3 a sh.

GEd = total hours given to general education.

%GEd = percent of total hours given to general education.

We focus on those hours required of all prospective teachers at the respective colleges. Several colleges require additional courses in English, math, science, history, and so forth for prospective elementary teachers. These requirements are noted, but not elaborated upon.

GEORGE PEABODY COLLEGE FOR TEACHERS—Nashville, Tenn.
accredited: NCATE, SACAS, APA
   Engl 8, Speech 2, Literature 3, Art-Music 3, Phil 3, H&PE 6, Math 3, NSci 8, SSci 9(/3)
   The Elementary Ed. program prescribes an additional 23 in these areas.
   TOTAL: 120 sh   GEd: 43 sh   %GEd: 36
FLORIDA STATE UNIVERSITY—Tallahassee, Fla.
accredited: NCATE
   (Quarter hours) Engl 9, Hist 9, SSci 12(/2), Hum 12(/2), NSci 13(/3), Math 4.
   TOTAL: 180 qh (= 120 sh)   GEd: 59 qh (= 40 sh)   %GEd: 33
UNIVERSITY OF TOLEDO—Toledo, Ohio
accredited: AACTE, NCATE
   (Quarter hours) Engl 15, SSci 13, Hum 6–8, Psyc 4, NSci 3–4, Math 3–4, H&PE 3.
   Elementary programs require an additional 49 qh in Speech, SSci, NSci and Hum.
   TOTAL: 192 qh (= 128 sh)   GEd: 47–51 (= 30–33 sh)   %GEd: 25–26
UNIVERSITY OF HOUSTON—Houston, Tex.
accredited: NCATE, SACAS, AACTE, NCA

Engl 9, SSci 6, Hist 6, NSci & Math 12, H&PE 2, electives outside Educ 9
TOTAL: 123 sh   GEd: 44 sh   %GEd: 36
UNIVERSITY OF OREGON—Eugene, Ore.
accredited: NCATE
Engl & Hum 15, NSci & Math 9, SSci 9, H&PE 11 (for BA/BS)
Engl & Hum 18, NSci & Math 18, SSci 18, H&PE 11 (for BEd)
Elementary Ed. majors take additional Hum.
TOTAL: 120 sh   GEd: 44, 65 sh   %GEd: 37, 54
WEBER STATE COLLEGE—Ogden, Utah
accredited: NCATE
(Quarter hours) Engl 9, Communications 3, H&PE 5, PSci 9, Biol 9, Psyc 3, SSci 6, Hum 9, others 4.
24 additional qh required for BA rather than BS.
Early childhood requires 11 additional qh in General Ed.
TOTAL: 183 qh (= 121 sh)   GEd: 57 (= 38 sh)   %GEd: 31
SYRACUSE UNIVERSITY—Syracuse, N.Y.
accredited: NCATE
Early Childhood Education and Elementary Education programs are in different departments, coordinated by the College of Education. The General Ed. requirements differ.
Early Childhood: Engl 6, NSci, Math or ForL 12, Nutrition 3, SSci 6, Psyc 3, Hum 12(/2).
Elementary: Six "groups" are designated; students must complete 6 sh in five of these groups, and 6 more in four of the five. The groups: A. Engl and Hum (must be elected); B. ForL and Literature; C. Phil and Religion; D. NSci; E. Math; F. SSci.
TOTAL: 124, 120 sh   GEd: 42, 54 sh   %GEd: 34, 45
UNIVERSITY OF MICHIGAN—East Lansing, Mich.
accredited: NCATE
(Quarter hours) American Thought & Language 9, NSci 12, SSci 12, Hum 12, other 15.
Elementary Ed. requires additional General Education.
TOTAL: 180 qh   GEd: 60   %GEd: 33
UNIVERSITY OF WISCONSIN—Lacrosse, Wisc.
accredited: NCATE
Engl 6, Speech 2, NSci & Math 12(/2), Hist 6, SSci 6, H&PE 2, Hum 9–14(/2).
TOTAL: 120 sh   GEd: 43–48   %GEd: 36–40
UNIVERSITY OF GEORGIA—Athens, Ga.
accredited: NCATE
(Quarter hours) Engl 10, Literature 10, Math & NSci 20, SSci 10, Hist 10, Psyc 5, Hum 5, Speech 5.
TOTAL: 180 qh (exclusive of basic Engl, Math, Phys Ed and ROTC) = 195 qh
actual GEd: 75   %GEd: 38

APPENDIX I

Sample Standardized Classroom Observation Instruments

FLANDERS' INTERACTION ANALYSIS CATEGORIES* (FIAC)

Teacher Talk	Response	1. <u>Accepts feeling</u>. Accepts and clarifies an attitude or the feeling tone of a pupil in a nonthreatening manner. Feelings may be positive or negative. Predicting and recalling feelings are included. 2. <u>Praises or encourages</u>. Praises or encourages pupil action or behavior. Jokes that release tension, but not at the expense of another individual; nodding head, or saying "Um-hm?" or "go on" are included. 3. <u>Accepts or uses ideas of pupils.</u> Clarifying, building, or developing ideas suggested by a pupil. Teacher extensions of pupil ideas are included but as the teacher brings more of his own ideas into play, shift to category five.
		4. <u>Asks questions</u>. Asking a question about content or procedure, based on teacher ideas, with the intent that a pupil will answer.
	Initiation	5. <u>Lecturing</u>. Giving facts or opinions about content or procedures; expressing his own ideas, giving his own explanation, or citing an authority other than a pupil. 6. <u>Giving directions</u>. Directions, commands, or orders to which a pupil is expected to comply. 7. <u>Criticizing or justifying authority</u>. Statements intended to change pupil behavior from nonacceptable to acceptable pattern; bawling someone out; stating why the teacher is doing what he is doing; extreme self-reference.
Pupil Talk	Response	8. <u>Pupil-talk/response</u>. Talk by pupils in response to teacher. Teacher initiates the contact or solicits pupil statement or structures the situation. Freedom to express own ideas is limited.
	Initiation	9. <u>Pupil-talk/initiation</u>. Talk by pupils which they initiate. Expressing own ideas; initiating a new topic; freedom to develop opinions and a line of thought, like asking thoughtful questions; going beyond the existing structure.
Silence		10. <u>Silence or confusion</u>. Pauses, short periods of silence and periods of confusion in which communication cannot be understood by the observer.

*There is <u>no</u> scale implied by these numbers. Each number is classificatory; it designates a particular kind of communication event. To write these numbers down during observation is to enumerate, not to judge a position on a scale.

(Flanders, 1970)

APPENDIX J

Sample Format and Content
of Observation Instruments

Excerpt of a Form for
Student-Teacher Interaction

Instructions: Using the symbols shown below, make a
notation every three (3) seconds for
ten (10) consecutive minutes to indicate
the nature of the behavior occurring at
each 3 second interval.

Legend: Teacher behavior:
1 = Asks a question
2 = Gives instructions
3 = Provides information
4 = Reflects student comment

Student behavior:
5 = Asks a question
6 = Answers a question
7 = Provides information
8 = Etc.

Other:
9 = Silence

Date _____   Hour_____

Class _____   Instructor_____

Observer _____   First Recording_____Time_____

_____

_____

_____

(Gephart, 1974)

APPENDIX K

Test Construction Texts

Adkins, D. C. *Test construction: Development and interpretation of achievement tests.* Columbus, Ohio: Merrill, 1960.

Ahman, J. S. & Glock, M. *Evaluating pupil growth: Principles of tests and measurement.* Boston: Allyn and Bacon, 1971.

Cooper, J. O. *Measurement and analysis of behavioral techniques.* Columbus, Ohio: Merrill, 1974.

Ebel, R. J. *Measuring educational achievement.* Englewood Cliffs, N.J.: Prentice-Hall, 1965.

Gronland, N. E. *Measurement and evaluation in teaching.* New York: Macmillan, 1967.

Lien, A. J. *Measurement and evaluation of learning.* Dubuque, Iowa: William C. Brown, 1976.

Lindvall, C. M. *Measuring pupil achievement and aptitude.* New York: Harcourt, Brace and World, 1967.

Mehrens, W. A. & Lehman, I. *Measurement and evaluation in education and psychology.* New York: Holt, Rinehart and Winston, 1973.

Popham, W. J. *Evaluating instruction.* Englewood Cliffs, N.J.: Prentice-Hall, 1975.

Sawin, E. I. *Evaluating and the work of the teacher.* Belmont, Calif.: Wadsworth, 1969.

Schoer, L. Q. *Test construction: A programmed guide.* Boston: Allyn and Bacon, 1972.

APPENDIX L

Texts for Scoring and Evaluation

Ahman, J. S. & Glock, M. *Evaluating pupil growth: Principles of tests and measurement.* Boston: Allyn and Bacon, 1971.

Ebel, R. J. *Measuring educational achievement.* Englewood Cliffs, N.J.: Prentice-Hall, 1965.

Gronland, N. E. *Measurement and evaluation in teaching.* New York: Macmillan, 1967.

Lien, A. J. *Measurement and evaluation of learning.* Dubuque, Iowa: William C. Brown, 1976.

Mehrens, W. A. *Readings in measurement and evaluation in education and psychology.* New York: Holt, Rinehart, and Winston, 1976.

Miller, D. M. *Interpreting test scores.* New York: John Wiley and Sons, 1972.

APPENDIX M

Sample Instrument for Student Evaluation of Instructor Performance

MICHIGAN STATE UNIVERSITY
TEACHER EVALUATION SHEET

Major_____Sex_____ Class_____Grade Point Average_____

DIRECTIONS: It is the desire of your instructor to achieve the best possible instructions in this course. To help accomplish the purpose, this evaluation sheet was devised to obtain a systematic poll of student opinion. Carefully consider each question, then record your judgment by encircling one of the letters A, B, C, D, E, for each item. A blank space has been provided at the end for adding comments you wish to make.

1. Were important objectives met?	The course is an important contribution to my college education	Contributes about as much as the average college course	This course doesn't seem worthwhile to me
2. Does instructor's presentation of subject matter enhance learning?	Presentation very meaningful and facilitates learning	Presentation not unusually good or bad, about average	Presentation often confusing: seldom helpful
3. Is instructor's speech effective?	Instructor's speaking skill concentrates my attention on subject	Speech sometimes invites attention on speaker rather than subject	Speech usually distracting, concentration very difficult
4. How well does the instructor work with students?	I feel welcome to seek extra help as often as needed	I feel hesitant to ask for extra help	I would avoid asking this instructor for extra help unless absolutely necessary
5. Does the instructor stimulate independent thinking?	Instructor continually inspires me to extra effort and thought beyond course requirements	In general, I do only the usual thinking involved in the assignments	I seldom do more than rote memory work and cramming
6. Do grading procedures give valid results?	Instructor's estimate of my over-all accomplishment has been quite accurate to date	Instructor's estimate of my accomplishment is of average accuracy	I feel that the instructor's estimate is quite inaccurate
7. How does this instructor rank with others you have had?	One of the best instructors I have ever had	Satisfactory or about average	One of the poorest instructors I have ever had

Comments:

(favorable)

(unfavorable)

LIST OF CHARACTERISTICS OF EFFECTIVE TEACHING

Course Content and Presentation

Contrasts implications of various theories
Presents origins of ideas and concepts
Presents facts and concepts from related fields
Talks about research he has done himself
Emphasizes ways of solving problems rather than
  solutions
Discusses practical applications
Explains his actions, decisions, and selection of topics
Seems well read beyond the subject he teaches
Is an excellent public speaker
Speaks clearly
Explains clearly
Gives lectures that are easy to outline
Reads lectures or stays close to notes (Negative)
Assigns text, but lectures include other topics
Makes difficult topics easy to understand
Summarizes major points
States objectives for each class session
Identifies what he considers important
Shows interest and concern in quality of his teaching
Gives examinations requiring creative, original thinking
Gives examinations having instructional value
Gives examinations requiring chiefly recall of facts
  (Negative)
Gives interesting and stimulating assignments
Stresses the aesthetic and emotional value of the
  subject
Is a dynamic and energetic person
Seems to enjoy teaching
Is enthusiastic about his subject
Seems to have self-confidence
Varies the speed and tone of his voice
Has a sense of humor

Relations with Students

Is careful and precise in answering questions
Explains his own criticisms
Encourages class discussion
Invites students to share their knowledge and experiences
Clarifies thinking by identifying reasons for questions
Invites criticism of his own ideas
Knows if the class is understanding him or not
Knows when students are bored or confused
Has students apply concepts to demonstrate understanding
Keeps well informed about progress of class
Anticipates difficulties and prepares students beforehand

Relations with Students (Continued)

Has definite plan, yet uses material introduced by
    students
Provides time for discussion and questions
Is sensitive to student's desire to ask a question
Encourages students to speak out in lecture or discussion
Quickly grasps what a student is asking or telling him
Restates questions or comments to clarify for entire class
Asks others to comment on one student's contribution
Compliments students for raising good points
Doesn't fully answer questions (Negative)
Determines if one student's problem is common to others
Reminds students to see him if having difficulty
Informs students of coming campus events related to course
Encourages students to express feelings and opinions
Relates class topics to students' lives and experiences
Has a genuine interest in students
Relates to students as individuals
Recognizes and greets students out of class
Is valued for advice not directly related to the course
Treats students as equals

Characteristics of a Majority of BEST and WORST Teachers,
But More Typical of BEST

Discusses points of view other than his own
Discusses recent developments in the field
Gives references for the more interesting and
    involved points
Emphasizes conceptual understanding
Disagrees with some ideas in textbook and other readings
Stresses rational and intellectual aspects of the
    subject
Stresses general concepts and ideas
Seems to have a serious commitment to his field
Is well prepared
Gives examinations stressing conceptual understanding
Gives examinations requiring synthesis of various
    parts of course
Gives examinations permitting students to show under-
    standing
Is friendly toward students
Is accessible to students out of class
Respects students as persons
Is always courteous to students
Gives personal help to students having difficulty
    with course
Has an interesting style of presentation

(Hildebrand, Wilson, & Dienst, 1971)

UNIVERSITY OF SOUTH CAROLINA
COLLEGE OF EDUCATION

COURSE AND TEACHER RATING SCALE

This scale is designed to collect information about the course you are about to finish. The information you provide is completely anonymous. You should not put your name or any other information that identifies you personally on this form or on the answer sheet you will use to record your responses to the questions. The combined information from you and the rest of the class will be given to the course instructor.

Please begin by filling in the following information on your answer sheets:
Faculty identification number - put in columns 71-72,
Campus identification number - put in columns 73-74,
Course prefix identification number - put in columns 75-76,
Course number - put in columns 77-78-79,
Section number - put in column 80.

Your instructor will tell you what numbers to use for this information.

Directions for Questions 1-32

For questions 1 through 32, you will read a statement that describes the characteristic of a teacher or some activity teachers do when they teach. For each statement, you are to indicate the extent to which your teacher possesses the characteristic or does the activity described in the statement. Indicate the extent to which you think each statement describes a characteristic of your teacher or an activity your teacher performs on the following scale:

0) Strongly Agree   1) Agree   2) Disagree   3) Strongly Disagree
   (SA)   (A)   (D)   (DS)

For each question you should fill in the space that corresponds to your response to each question. Answer question 1 in column 1, question 2 in column 2, and so on. Directions for questions after number 32 are given with those later questions.

01) The instructor chats with students before class, after class or during breaks.

    0) SA   1) A   2) D   3) SD

02) The examinations are of reasonable difficulty.

    0) SA   1) A   2) D   3) SD

03) The instructor's presentations are well-organized.

    0) SA   1) A   2) D   3) SD

(Over)

04) The instructor said he/she would meet with any student who had difficulty with the class.

   0) SA   1) A   2) D   3) SD

05) The instructor understands the major issues, concepts, and problems in his/her major field.

   0) SA   1) A   2) D   3) SD

06) The instructor has command of the subject matter.

   0) SA   1) A   2)   D   3) SD

07) The instructor relates different concepts presented in class to one another.

   0) SA   1) A   2) D   3) SD

08) The instructor is pleasant and tries to help students.

   0) SA   1) A   2) D   3) SD

09) The instructor answers students' questions with specific content, data and references.

   0) SA   1) A   2) D   3) SD

10) The course tests and examinations reflect what has been taught in class.

   0) SA   1) A   2) D   3) SD

11) The instructor repeats material that the students do not understand.

   0) SA   1) A   2) D   3) SD

12) The instructor is friendly to students.

   0) SA   1) A   2) D   3) SD

13) The instructor keeps the course on the planned schedule.

   0) SA   1) A   2) D   3) SD

14) The instructor reviews and discusses examination procedures and results with the class.

   0) SA   1) A   2) D   3) SD

15) The instructor is interested in whether each student understands the material.

   0) SA   1) A   2) D   3) SD

(Over)

16) The instructor explained grading and testing procedures at the beginning of the course.

   0) SA   1) A   2) D   3) SD

17) The instructor is concerned with each student as an individual.

   0) SA   1) A   2) D   3)SD

18) The instructor has adequate knowledge of the course material.

   0) SA   1) A   2) D   3) SD

19) The content of the course is organized around its objectives.

   0) SA   1) A   2) D   3) SD

20) References the instructor gives in class are current.

   0) SA   1) A   2) D   3) SD

21) The instructor asks students their opinions about the course tests and assignments.

   0) SA   1) A   2) D   3) SD

22) The instructor's presentations in class follow a logical sequence or outline.

   0) SA   1) A   2) D   3) SD

23) The instructor manages course time effectively.

   0) SA   1) A   2) D   3) SD

24) During class lectures and discussions the instructor asks the students if they understand the material being presented.

   0) SA   1) A   2) D   3) SD

25) In class presentations, the instructor stays close to the major topic of the presentation.

   0) SA   1) A   2) D   3) SD

26) Course objectives and requirements were made clear within the first two weeks of class.

   0) SA   1) A   2) D   3) SD

27) The instructor has the expertise required to answer students' questions effectively.

   0) SA   1) A   2) D   3) SD

(Over)

28) The instructor returns tests and assignments within one week.

0) SA   1) A   2) D   3) SD

29) The tests and examinations in the course are fair and impartial.

0) SA   1) A   2) D   3) SD

30) Overall, the course is well plannned and organized.

0) SA   1) A   2) D   3) SD

31) The grading procedures used in this course are fair.

0) SA   1) A   2) D   3) SD

32) The instructor's presentations are substantive.

0) SA   1) A   2) D   3) SD

From the list of 32 statements you have just read, please select three (3) statements that describe activities you think contribute significantly to the quality of the course.

In columns 33-34 put the number of one of the three statements you have just selected.

In columns 35-36 put the number of one of the three statements you have just selected.

In columns 37-38 put the number of one of the three statements you have just selected.

Questions 39-43 deal with specific materials, techniques, or procedures used in the course. For each of these questions, indicate how useful you thought each was in helping you learn the course material. Use the following code:

0 - Very Effective (VE)
1 - Effective (E)
2 - Ineffective (IE)
3 - Very Ineffective (VIE)

39) Class discussions

0) VE   1) E   2) IE   3) VIE

40) Class handouts

0) VE   1) E   2) IE   3) VIE

(Over)

41) Course text book(s)

    0) VE   1) E   2) IE   3) VIE

42) Supplementary readings

    0) VE   1) E   2) IE   3) VIE

43) Course lectures

    0) VE   1) E   2) IE   3) VIE

44) How should the amount of material covered in the course by changed (if at all)?

45) How should the pace with which the material in the course is covered be changed (if at all)?

    0) the pace should be slower 1) no change should be made
                 2) the pace should be quicker

46) Overall, how would you rate the performance of the teacher in this course?

    0) Very good   1) Good   2) Poor   3) Very poor

47) How would you rate this course overall?

    0) Very good   1) Good   2) Poor   3) Very poor

48) Please indicate your current academic status.

    0) Freshman   1) Sophmore   2) Junior   3) Senior   4)   Masters student
    5) Doctoral student   6) Graduate - special   7) Other

49) Please indicate why you took this course by circling one of the following:

    0) This course is an elective I wanted to take.
    1) This course is an elective my advisor strongly encouraged me to take.
    2) This course is required, but I would have taken it even if it were not required.
    3) This course is required and I had to take it.

50) What grade do you expect to make in this course?

    0) A   1) B   2) C   3) D   4) F

(Developed under the auspices of the Graduate Regional Studies Program, College of Education, University of South Carolina)

APPENDIX N

Sample Formats for Observational Records

OHIO OBSERVATIONAL RECORD
(Original Edition)

MEETING PUPIL NEEDS

Directions: Indicate your judgments on this form about the extent to which pupil needs were being met during the period of observation. Place checks in Column 1 beside the pupil needs which you feel were being met. If a situation arose where a need could have been met but wasn't, place a check in Column 2. Space is provided beneath each need to write in anecdotal notes to give meaning to each check mark. It is desirable to indicate how each need which was checked was met or could have been met.

	Met this Need (1)	Missed a Chance (2)
1. Need for activity		
2. Need for aesthetic satisfaction or developing appreciations		
3. Need for assurance of "growing up"		
4. Need for consumer information		
5. Need for creative experience		
6. Need for cultivating leisure-time activities		
7. Need for intelligent self-direction		
8. Need for physical and mental health		
9. Need for satisfying curiosity		
10. Need for security		
11. Need for self-assurance		
12. Need for social participation		
13. Need for social recognition		
14. Need for variety of personal interests		
15. Need for vocational orientation		
16. Need for world view and working philosophy		

THE OHIO TEACHING RECORD
(Experimental edition)

SECTION III: MEETING PUPIL NEEDS

Directions: Indicate your judgments on this page concerning the evident needs of pupils which were met or which were not met during the
period of observation. Place a check (✔) in Column 1 beside the pupil
needs which you feel were being effectively met; place a check in
Column 2 beside the pupil needs which you feel were being ineffectively
met; and place a check in Column 3 beside the pupil needs which could
have been met but which were not because the teacher missed a chance to
use or change a situation in order to do so. As in other sections space
is provided for the anecdotal notations which furnish evidence for your
judgments. Add any other needs which you believe were provided for.

Pupil Needs	Effectively met	Ineffectively met	Missed a chance
	(1)	(2)	(3)
Need for:			
1. Activity			
2. Aesthetic satisfaction or developing appreciations			
3. Assurance of "growing up"			
4. Consumer information			
5. Creative experience			
6. Cultivating leisure-time activities			
7. Intelligent self-direction			
8. Physical and mental health			
9. Satisfying curiosity			
10. Security			
11. Self-assurance			
12. Social participation			
13. Social recognition			
14. Variety of personal interests			
15. Vocational orientation			
16. Developing a working philosophy			
17. Understanding one's world and seeing relationships in it			
18. Orientation to the classroom situation			
19. "Belonging" to a group			
20. Attention			
21. Genuine "success experiences"			
22. Solving personal problems			
23. Opportunity for expression in a variety of nonverbal media			
24. Functional information			
25. Carrying through a purposeful activity completely			
26. Knowledge of status and progress			
27. Others:			
28.			

ANECDOTAL EVIDENCE (What was done to meet these needs?)
Need Numbers

Form I. ANECDOTAL OBSERVATION RECORD

<u>Directions</u>: In the column on the right,   Student_____
check the attitudes and practices ob-
served in the student teacher's work   Supervisor_____
as follows:
+ for favorable attitude or effective work School_____
- for unfavorable attitude or ineffective
  work   Grade_____
+ - for conflicting evidence
0 for lack of evidence   Subjects_____

Write in anecdotal evidence for items checked, and write in additional
illustrations of competence in teaching.

I. MEETING PUPIL NEEDS: Aids boys and girls in attaining maximum growth
   in ability to face and solve problems of living and to make a satisfactory adjustment to themselves and to others.

    a. Recognizes and as far as possible, provides for the
       fundamental general needs: such as, the need for
       activity, healthful routine, feeling of belonging,
       social recognition, success experiences, self-
       direction, creative expression, aesthetic appreci-
       ation, functional information, and carrying out
       purposes_____

    b. Understands the special needs and problems of the
       particular class_____

    c. Recognizes individual differences in learning
       ability, interests, background, temperament,
       health, work habits, and degrees of maturity_____

    d. Creates an atmosphere of security, warmth,and
       friendliness in the classroom and in relationship
       with individual pupils _____

    e. Shows a genuine interest in the best all-around
       development of pupils_____

    f. Interprets problems of conduct in terms of their
       basic factors and causes rather than in terms of
       symptoms_____

    g. Makes and uses records concerning pupils in deter-
       mining their needs, planning work, and guiding
       the learning process_____

    h. Provides for individual differences by group-
       ing within the class, differentiating assign-
       ments, evaluating work in relation to ability,
       helping improve specific skills needed, making
       study of problem cases _____

    i. _____

(Troyer, 1944)

APPENDIX O

Sample Format for Analysis of Student Problems in Practice Teaching

EVALUATION OF STUDENT TEACHER

HANDLING OF CLASSROOM INCIDENTS

Date _____

Evaluator _____ Title _____

GOOD				ADEQUATE			POOR
7	6	5	4	3	2	1	0

Description of incident: _____

_____

_____

_____

_____

_____

_____

APPENDIX P

Texts on Teaching for Objectives

Ahman, J. S. & Glock, M. *Evaluating pupil growth: Principles of tests and measurement.* Boston: Allyn and Bacon, 1971.

Bloom, B. S., Englehart, M. D., Furst, E. J., Hill, W. H., & Krathwohl, D. R. *Taxonomy of educational objectives: Handbook I: Cognitive domain.* New York: McKay, 1956.

Briggs, L. J. *Handbook of procedures for the design of instruction.* Washington, D.C.: American Institute for Research, 1970.

Briggs, L. J. *Instructional design: Principles and applications.* Englewood Cliffs, N.J.: Educational Technology, 1977.

Gagné, R. M. The analysis of instructional objectives for the design of instruction. In R. M. Glaser (Ed.), *Teaching machines and programmed learning II: Data and directions.* Washington, D.C.: National Education Association, 1965.

Gagné, R. M. & Briggs, L. J. *Principles of instructional design.* New York: Holt, Rinehart and Winston, 1974.

Krathwohl, D. R. Stating objectives appropriately for program, for curriculum, and for instructional materials development. *Journal of Teacher Education,* 1965, *12,* 83–92.

Krathwohl, D. R., Bloom, B. S., & Masia, B. B. *Taxonomy of educational objectives: Handbook II: Affective domain.* New York: McKay, 1964.

Popham, W. J. *Evaluating instructions.* Englewood Cliffs, N.J.: Prentice-Hall, 1975.

Schoer, L. A. *Test construction: A programmed guide.* Boston: Allyn and Bacon, 1972.

APPENDIX Q

Texts on Interaction Analysis

Amidon, E. J. & Hough, J. B. (Eds.). *Interaction analysis in education.* Reading, Mass.: Addison-Wesley, 1967.

Brophy, J. E. & Evertson, C. M. *Learning from teaching: A developmental perspective.* Boston: Allyn and Bacon, 1976.

Flanders, N. A. *Analyzing teacher behavior.* Reading, Mass.: Addison-Wesley, 1970.

MacDonald, W. S. & Tanabe, G. (Eds.). *Focus on classroom behavior: Readings and research.* Springfield, Ill.: Thomas, 1973.

Stanford, G. & Roark, A. E. *Human interaction in education.* Boston: Allyn and Bacon, 1974.

Westbury, I. & Bellack, A. A. (Eds.). *Research into classroom processes: Recent developments and the next steps.* New York: Teachers College Press, 1971.

APPENDIX R

Texts for Selecting Standardized Tests

Grosland, N. E. *Measurement and evaluation in teaching.* New York: Macmillan, 1967.

Mehrens, W. A. & Lehman, I. J. *Standardized tests in education.* New York: Holt, Rinehart and Winston, 1969.

Tyler, L. E. *Tests and measurements.* Englewood Cliffs, N.J.: Prentice-Hall, 1963.

APPENDIX S

Texts for Psychometric Aspects of Test Construction

Blood, D. F. & Budd, W. C. *Educational measurement and evaluation.* New York: Harper and Row, 1972.

Lindvall, C. M. *Testing and evaluation: An introduction.* New York: Harcourt, Brace, and World, 1961.

Kerlinger, F. N. *Foundations of behavioral research.* New York: Holt, Rinehart and Winston, 1973.

Thorndike, R. L. & Hagan, E. *Measurement and evaluation in psychology and education.* New York: Wiley, 1961.

Bibliography

Ainsworth, B. A. Teachers talk about inservice education. *Journal of Teacher Education*, 1976, *27*(2), 107–109.

Alkin, M. C. Evaluation theory development. *Evaluation Comment*, 1969, *2*(1), 2–7.

Altman, H. Teacher-student interaction in inner-city and advantaged classes using the science curriculum improvement study. *Classroom Interaction Newsletter*, 1970, *6*(1), 5–16.

American Association of Colleges for Teacher Education. *Cooperative structures in school-college relationships for teacher education*. Washington, D.C., 1965.

Americans have lost faith in education. *Intellect*, 1978, *106*(2396), 438.

Anderson, J. E., & Lanier, P. E. What teachers need to know and teach (for survival on the planet). *Journal of Teacher Education*, 1973, *24*(1), 4–16.

Anderson, L. *Time and school learning*. Unpublished doctoral dissertation, University of Chicago, 1973.

Anderson, L. W. Student involvement in learning and school achievement. *California Journal of Educational Research*, 1975, *26*(2), 53–62.

Anderson, L. W. *Assessing affective characteristics in school*. Boston: Allyn and Bacon, (accepted for publication.)

Arends, R., Hersh, R., & Turner, J. Inservice education and the six o'clock news. *Theory Into Practice*, 1978, *17*(3), 196–205.

Association for student teaching. *Ferment in the professional education of teachers*. Washington, D.C.: National Education Association, 1969.

Atkin, J. M. Institutional self-evaluation versus national professional accreditation or back to the normal school? *Educational Researcher*, 1978, *7*(10), 3–7.

Bell, D. *Reforming general education*. New York: Columbia University Press, 1966.

Bellack, A. A., Hyman, R. T., Smith, F. L., Jr., & Kliebard, H. M. *The language of the classroom* (Final report, USOE Cooperative Research Project No. 2023). New York: Columbia University Press, 1966.

Berkeley faculty votes to raise standards, restore requirements: Text of revised requirements. *The Chronicle of Higher Education*, April 3, 1978, p. 11.

Bestor, A. *The restoration of learning*. New York, Knopf, 1955.

Bigelow, D. N. (Ed.). *The liberal arts and teacher education: A confrontation*. Lincoln: University of Nebraska Press, 1971.

Block, J. H. (Ed.). *Mastery learning: Theory and practice*. New York: Holt, Rinehart and Winston, 1971.

Block, J. H. (Ed.). *Schools, society, and mastery learning*. New York: Holt, Rinehart and Winston, 1974.

Block, J. H., & Anderson, L. W. *Mastery learning in classroom instruction*. New York: Macmillan, 1975.

Bloom, B. S. Mastery learning. In J. H. Block (Ed.), *Mastery learning: Theory and practice*. New York: Holt, Rinehart and Winston, 1971.

Bloom, B. S. *Human characteristics and learning*. New York: McGraw-Hill, 1976.

Bloom, B. S., et al. (Eds.). *Taxonomy of educational objectives: The classification of educational goals, Handbook 1: Cognitive domain*. New York: Longmans, Green, 1956.

Bloom, B. S., Hastings, J. T., & Madaus, G. F. *Handbook on formative and summative evaluation of student learning*. New York: McGraw-Hill, 1976.

Bogie, C. E., & Bogie, D. W. Teachers' preferences toward alternative systems of salary increment. *Education*, 1978, *99*(2), 215–220.

Bonanno, D., Feigley, D., & Doughterty, N. Field placement options to prestudent teachers. *Journal of Physical Education and Recreation*, 1978, *49*(5), 71–72.

Borrowman, M. L. *The liberal and technical in teacher education: A historical survey of American thought*. New York: Teachers College Press, 1956.

Borrowman, M. L. (Ed.). *Teacher education in America*. New York: Teachers College Press, 1965.

Bosley, H. E. *Teacher education in transition: Emerging roles and responsibilities*. Baltimore: Multi-State Teacher Education Project, 1969.

Bossard, J. S. *Parent and child*. Philadelphia: University of Pennsylvania Press, 1956.

Bowman, B. Teacher training: Where and how. In B. Spodek (Ed.), *Teacher education of the teacher, by the teacher, for the child*. Washington, D.C.: National Association for the Education of Young Children, 1974.

Bradley, H. *In-service education after the White paper*. Nottingham: University of Nottingham, School of Education, 1974.

Briggs, L. J. *Handbook of procedures for the design of instruction*. Washington, D.C.: American Institute for Research, 1970.

Briggs, L. J. (Ed.). *Instructional design*. Englewood Cliffs, N.J.: Educational Technology Publications, 1977.

Brimm, J. L., & Tollett, D. J. How do teachers feel about in-service education? *Educational Leadership*, 1974, *31*(6), 521–525.

Brodbelt, S. The epidemic of school violence. *The Clearing House*, 1978, *51*(8), 383–387.

Brophy, J. E., & Good, T. L. Individual differences in student-teacher instruction patterns. In J. E. Brophy & T. L. Good (Eds.), *Teacher-student relationships*. New York: Holt, Rinehart and Winston, 1974.

Brophy, J. E., & Good, T. L. (Eds.). *Teacher-student relationships*. New York: Holt, Rinehart and Winston, 1974.

Broudy, H. S. *The real world of public schools*. New York: Harcourt-Brace-Jovanovitch, 1972.

Burdin, J. *Three views of competency-based teacher foundation: I Theory*. Bloomington, Ind.: Phi Delta Kappa Foundation, 1974.

Bush, R. N. Curriculum-proof teachers. In L. Rubin (Ed.), *Improving inservice education: Proposals and procedures for change*. Boston: Allyn and Bacon, 1971.

Calhoun, T. Throwaway teachers? *Educational Leadership*, 1975, *32*(5), 310–312.

Campbell, W. J. Some effects of affective climate on the achievement motivation of pupils. In W. J. Campbell (Ed.), *Scholars in context: The effects of environment on learning*. Sidney: Wiley, 1970.

Campbell, W. J. (Ed.). *Scholars in context: The effects of environment on learning.* Sidney: Wiley, 1970.

Carroll, J. B. Neglected areas in educational research. *Phi Delta Kappan,* 1961, *42*(8), 339–343.

Carroll, J. B. A model of school learning. *Teachers College Record,* 1963, *64*(8), 723–733.

Combs, A. W. *The professional education of teachers: A perceptual view of teacher preparation.* Boston: Allyn and Bacon, 1965.

Commons examinations bulletin. Princeton, N.J.: Educational Testing Service, 1974.

Conant, J. B. *The education of American teachers.* New York: McGraw-Hill, 1963.

Conference on Teacher Education. *New directions in teacher education.* Nairobi, Kenya: East African Publishing House, 1969.

Cronbach, L. J. The role of the university in educational improvement. *Phi Delta Kappan,* 1966, *47*(10), 539–545.

Dahllof, U. S., & Lundgren, U. P. *Project compass 23: Macro and micro approaches combined for curriculum project analysis: A Swedish educational field project.* Paper presented at the annual meeting of the American Educational Research Association, Minneapolis, 1970.

Dasgupta, A. K., & Pierce, D. W. *Cost-benefit analysis: Theory and practice.* London: Macmillan, 1972.

Daniels, P. R., & O'Connell, M. J. A floating faculty—An intensive inservice technique. *Educational Leadership,* 1976, *33*(5), 355–359.

Davies, I. K. *Competency based learning: Technology, management, and design.* New York: McGraw-Hill, 1973.

Denemark, G. W. (Ed.). *Criteria for curriculum decisions in teacher education.* Washington, D.C.: Association for Supervision and Curriculum Development, 1963.

DeVault, M., Anderson, D., & Dickson, G. (Eds.). *Competency-based teacher education.* Berkeley: McCutchan, 1973.

De Young, C. A., & Wynn, R. *American education.* New York: McGraw-Hill, 1964.

Doherty, V. W. Something new in in-service education: Portland's Carnegie program. *American School Board Journal,* 1965, *150*(5), 31.

Donley, M. O. *The future of teacher power in America.* Bloomington, Ind.: Phi Delta Kappa Educational Foundation, 1977.

Drastic change in roles of schools. *Intellect,* 1977, *105*(2384), 382–383.

Dreeban, R. *The nature of teaching: Schools and the work of teachers.* Glenview, Ill.: Scott, Foresman, 1970.

Dreeban, R. The school as a workplace. In R. M. W. Travers (Ed.), *Second handbook of research on teaching.* Chicago: Rand McNally, 1963.

DuBey, R., Endly, V., Roe, B., & Tollett, D. *A performance-based guide to student teaching.* Danville, Ill.: The Interstate Printers & Publishers, 1972.

Dunkin, M., & Biddle, B. *The study of teaching.* New York: Holt, Rinehart and Winston, 1974.

Edelfelt, R. A. In-service education of teachers: Priority for the next decade. *Journal of Teacher Education,* 1974, *25*(3), 250–252.

Edelfelt, R. A. *In-service education: Criteria for and examples of local programs.* Bellingham, Wash.: Western Washington State College, 1977.

Edelfelt, R. A.. & Orvell, T. *Teacher centers—Where, what, why?* Bloomington, Ind.: Phi Delta Kappa Educational Foundation, 1978.

Edge, D., & Fink, A. H. Taking inservice training into the classroom. *Viewpoints in Teaching and Learning,* 1978, *54*(4), 113–118.

Elam, S. (Ed.). *Improving teacher education in the United States.* Bloomington, Ind.: Phi Delta Kappa Educational Foundation, 1967.

Emmer, E. T. *The effect of teacher use and acceptance of student ideas on student verbal initiation.* Unpublished doctoral dissertation, University of Michigan, 1967.

Erickson, K. A., & Rose, R. L. In-service education. In S. E. Goodman (Ed.), *Handbook on contemporary education.* New York: R. R. Bowker, 1976.

Eye, G. G. The three-way stretch. *Journal of Educational Research,* 1974, *68*(4), 164–169.

Firth, G. R. Ten issues on staff development. *Educational Leadership,* 1977, *35*(3), 215–220.

Fishbein, M., & Ajzen, I. *Belief, attitude, intention and behavior: An introduction to theory and research.* Reading, Mass.: Addison-Wesley, 1975.

Flanders, N. A. *Analyzing teaching behavior.* Reading, Mass.: Addison-Wesley, 1970.

Fortune, J. C., Gage, N. L., & Shutes, R. E. *The generality of the ability to explain.* Paper presented at the annual meeting of the American Educational Research Association, Amherst, Mass., 1966.

Friedman, M. I., & Anderson, L. W. Evaluating to solve educational problems: An alternative model. *Educational Technology,* 1979, *19*(9), 16–23.

Furst, N. The effects of training in interaction analysis on the behavior of student teachers in secondary schools. In E. J. Amidon & J. B. Hough (Eds.), *Interaction analysis: Theory, research, and application.* Reading, Mass.: Addison-Wesley, 1967.

Gage, N. L. (Ed.). *Handbook of research on teaching: A project of the American Educational Research Association.* Chicago: Rand McNally, 1963.

Gage, N. L. Tools of the trade: An approach to enhancing the teacher's ability to make a difference. In *How Teachers Make a Difference.* Washington, D.C.: U.S. Office of Education, Bureau of Educational Personnel Development, U.S. Government Printing Office, 1971.

Gage, N. L. (Ed.). *The psychology of teaching methods.* Chicago: University of Chicago Press, 1976.

Gagné, R. M. *The conditions of learning.* New York: Holt, Rinehart and Winston, 1965.

Gephart, W. J., Ingle, R. B., & Saretsky, G. *The evaluation of teaching: National Symposium for Professors of Educational Research: 1974.* Bloomington, Ind.: Phi Delta Kappa Educational Foundation, 1976.

Gillan, R. E. Middle school certification increases dramatically. *Phi Delta Kappan,* 1978, *60*(4), 315.

Glaser, R., & Nitko, A. J. Measurement in learning and instruction. In R. L. Thorndike (Ed.), *Educational measurement* (2nd ed.). Washington, D.C.: American Council on Education, 1971.

Glidewell, J. C. The entry problem in consultation. In W. G. Bennis, K. Benne, & R. Chin (Eds.), *The planning of change.* New York: Holt, Rinehart and Winston, 1961.

Goodman, S. E. *Handbook on contemporary education.* New York: R. R. Bowker, 1976.

Gosnell, J. W. The relationship between work experience and occupational aspiration and attrition from teaching. *The Clearing House,* 1977, *51*(4), 176–179.

Gronland, N. E. *Measurement and evaluation in teaching.* New York: Macmillan, 1976.

Gump, P. M. *The classroom behavior setting: Its nature and relation to student behavior.* (Final report, Contract No. OE–4–10–107). Washington, D.C.: U.S. Bureau of Research, Department of Health, Education, and Welfare, 1967.

Guskin, A. The individual: Internal processes and characteristics which inhibit knowledge utilization. In R. J. Havelock, et al. (Eds.), *Planning for innovation through dessimination and utilization of knowledge.* Ann Arbor: Institute for Social Research, University of Michigan, 1969.

Guttman, L., & Schlesinger, I. M. Systematic construction of distractors for ability and achievement test items. *Educational and Psychological Measurement,* 1967, *27*(3), 569–580.

Hall, G., & Jones, H. *Competency-based education: A process for the improvement of education.* Englewood Cliffs, N.J.: Prentice-Hall, 1976.

Hamlin, H. M. A former colleague comments on remarks by Lee J. Cronbach. *Phi Delta Kappan,* 1966, *48*(1), 6–7.

Harris, B. M., Bessent, W., & McIntyre, K. E. *In-service education: A guide to better practice.* Englewood Cliffs, N.J.: Prentice-Hall, 1969.

Harvard weighs plans to reform college curriculum, *The Chronicle of Higher Education,* March 6, 1978, pp. 1, 15.

Harvard's report on the core curriculum, *The Chronicle of Higher Education,* March 6, 1978, pp. 1, 15–19.

Havelock, R. G. *The change agent's guide to innovation in education.* Englewood Cliffs, N.J.: Educational Technology Publications, 1973.

Havelock, R. G., et al. *Planning for innovation through dissemination and utilization of knowledge.* Ann Arbor: Institute for Social Research, University of Michigan, 1969.

Heinbach, A. *Job analysis of elementary school teachers and some implications for competency-based teacher education programs.* Unpublished doctoral dissertation, McNeese State University, Lake Charles, Louisiana, 1974.

Hickey, M. E., & Hoffman, D. H. Diagnosis and prescription in education. *Educational Technology,* 1973, *13*(10), 35–37.

Hildebrand, M., Wilson, R. C., & Dienst, E. R. *Evaluating university teaching.* Berkeley: Center for Research and Development in Higher Education, 1971.

Hilgard, E. R., & Bower, G. H. *Theories of learning.* Englewood Cliffs, N.J.: Prentice-Hall, 1975.

Hodenfield, G. K., & Stinnett, T. M. *The education of teachers.* Englewood Cliffs, N.J.: Prentice-Hall, 1961.

Hodgkinson, H. L. *Institutions in transition, A profile of change in higher education.* New York: McGraw-Hill, 1971.

Houston, W. R. (Ed.). *Exploring competency-based education.* Berkeley: McCutchan, 1974.

Houston, W. R., & Jones, H. L. *Three views of competency-based teacher education: II University of Houston.* Bloomington, Ind.: Phi Delta Kappa Foundation, 1974.

Houston, W. R., & Warner, A. R. The competency-based movement: Origins and texture. In M. B. Kapser (Ed.), *Behavioral objectives: The position of the pendulum.* Englewood Cliffs, N.J.: Educational Technology Publications, 1978.

Hunt, D. E. Matching models for teacher training. In B. R. Joyce & M. Weil (Eds.), *Perspectives for reform in teacher education.* Englewood Cliffs, N.J.: Prentice-Hall, 1972.

Hsu, T. Approaches to the construction of achievement test items. *The Researcher,* 1975, *14*(1), 31–50.

In-service education of teachers. Washington, D.C.: National Education Association Research Summary, 1966.

In-service education: Teacher opinion poll. *Today's Education,* 1976, *65*(2), 16.

Jackson, P. W. *Life in the classroom.* New York: Holt, Rinehart and Winston, 1968.

Jenkins, W. A. (Ed.). *The nature of knowledge: Implications for the education of teachers.* Milwaukee: University of Wisconsin, 1961.

Joyce, B., & Weil, M. *Models of teaching.* Englewood Cliffs, N.J.: Prentice-Hall, 1972.

Joyce, B. R., & Yarger, S. J., et al. *Preservice teacher education.* Washington, D.C.: Office of Education, Department of Health, Education, and Welfare, 1977.

Judson, A. S. *A manager's guide to making changes.* New York: Wiley, 1966.

Kapser, M. B. (Ed.). *Behavioral objectives: The position of the pendulum.* Englewood Cliffs, N.J.: Educational Technology Publications, 1978.

Kaufman, R., & Knight, M. Minimum competency testing. *Phi Delta Kappan,* 1978, *60*(4), 334–355.

Kelley, E. *Three views of competency-based teacher education: III University of Nebraska.* Bloomington, Ind.: Phi Delta Kappa Educational Foundation, 1974.

Kemble, B. (Ed.). *Fit to teach.* London: Hutchinson Educational, Ltd., 1971.

Kerlinger, F. *Foundations of behavioral research: Educational and psychological inquiry.* New York: Holt, Rinehart and Winston, 1964.

Kerlinger, F. N. *Foundations of behavioral research* (2nd ed.). New York: Holt, Rinehart and Winston, 1973.

Koerner, J. *The miseducation of the American teachers.* Boston: Houghton Mifflin, 1963.

Koerner, J. D. *Who controls American education?* Boston: Beacon Press, 1968.

Kvaraceus, W., Kenney, H. J., & Bartholomew, P. NDEA National Institute for Advanced Study in Teaching Disadvantaged Youth: 1967–1968. Project Report Two.

Lawrence, G., & Branch, J. Peer support system as the heart of in-service education. *Theory Into Practice,* 1978, *17*(3), 245–247.

Layard, R. *Cost-benefit analysis: Selected readings.* Harmondsworth, England: Penguin, 1972.

LeBaron, W. *Elementary teacher education models analyzed in relation to national accreditation standards.* Washington, D.C.: American Association of Colleges for Teacher Education, 1970.

Lee, C. B. T. (Ed.). *Improving college teaching.* Washington, D.C.: American Council on Education, 1967.

Lesourne, J. *Cost-benefit analysis and economic theory.* Amsterdam: North Holland Publishing Company, 1975.

Lieberman, M. *Education as a profession.* Englewood Cliffs, N.J.: Prentice-Hall, 1956.

Lindvall, C. M., & Cox, R. C. *Evaluation as a tool in curriculum development.* Chicago: Rand McNally, 1970.

Lohman, E., Ober, R., & Hough, J. B. A study of the effect of pre-service training in interaction analysis on the verbal behavior of student teachers. In E. J. Amidon & J. B. Hough (Eds.), *Interaction analysis: Theory, research, and application.* Reading, Mass.: Addison-Wesley, 1967.

Lorentz, J. L. *The development of measures of teacher effectiveness from multiple measures of student growth.* Paper presented at the annual meeting of the American Educational Research Association, New York, 1977.

Lortie, D. C. *School teacher: A sociological study.* Chicago: University of Chicago Press, 1975.

Lundgren, U. P. *Frame factors and the teaching process: A contribution to curriculum theory and theory on teaching.* Stockholm: Almgrist and Wiksell, 1972.

Manatt, R. P. *Developing a teacher performance evaluation system.* Des Moines: Iowa Association of School Boards, 1976.

Manatt, R., Palmer, K., & Hidlebaugh, E. Evaluating teacher performance with improved rating scales. *National Association of Secondary School Principals Bulletin,* 1976, *60*(401), 21–24.

Mann, D. The politics of in-service. *Theory Into Practice,* 1978, *17*(3), 212–217.

Mark, J. H., & Anderson, B. D. Teacher survival rates—A current look. *American Educational Research Journal,* 1978, *15*(3), 379–383.

Markowitz, S. The dilemma of authority in supervisory behavior. *Educational Leadership,* 1976, *33*(5), 367–372.

Mason, W. S. *The beginning teacher* (Circular No. 644). Washington, D.C.: Office of Education, U.S. Department of Health, Education, and Welfare, 1961.

Massanari, K. What we don't know about in-service education: An agenda for action. *Journal of Teacher Education,* 1977, *28*(2), 41–45.

Mayhew, L. B., & Ford, P. J. *Changing the curriculum.* San Francisco: Jossey-Bass, 1971.

McClellan, J. E. *Toward an effective critique of American education.* Philadelphia: Lippincott, 1968.

McGeoch, D., & Quinn, P. Clinical experiences in a teacher education center. *Journal of Teacher Education,* 1975, *26*(2), 176–179.

McLaughlin, M., & Berman, P. Retooling staff development in a period of retrench-ment. *Educational Leadership,* 1977, *35*(3), 191–194.

Miller, R. I. *Evaluating faculty performance.* San Francisco: Jossey-Bass, 1972.

Miller, W. C. What's wrong with in-service education. It's topless! *Educational Leader-ship,* 1977, *35*(1), 31–34.

Mishan, E. J. *Cost-benefit analysis: An informal introduction.* London: Allen and Unwin, 1971.

Mishan, E. J. *Cost-benefit analysis.* New York: Praeger, 1976.

Monahan, W. C. Some straight talk about teacher preparation. *Educational Leadership,* 1977, *35*(3), 202–204.

Morley, F. P. Outside curriculum resources. *Educational Leadership,* 1976, *34*(1), 31–34.

Morris, L. L., & Fitz-Gibbon, C. T. *Evaluator's handbook.* Beverly Hills: Sage Publica-tions, 1978.

Mosteller, F., & Moynihan, D. P. (Eds.). *On equality of educational opportunity.* New York: Vintage Books, 1972.

Mueller, D. L. Observing student teachers in a competency-based program. *Peabody Journal of Education,* 1976, *53*(4), 248–253.

Murphy, R. T. Assessment of adult reading competence. In D. M. Nielson & H. F. Hjelm (Comp. Eds.), *Reading and career education.* Newark, Del.: International Reading Association, 1975.

Ngaiyay, M. S., & Hanley, J. L. What teachers want from in-service education. *North Central Association Quarterly,* 1978, *53*(2), 305–311.

Nielson, D. M., & Hjelm, H. F. (Comp. Eds.). *Reading and career education.* Newark, Del.: International Reading Association, 1975.

O'Hanlon, J., & Witters, L. In-service education for all schools. *Breakthrough.* Lincoln: Nebraska State Department of Education, 1967.

O'Keefe, W. J. Some teacher centered in-service programs. *Today's Education,* 1974, *63*(2), 39–42.

Olivero, J. L. Helping teachers grow professionally. *Educational Leadership,* 1976, *34*(3), 194–200.

Olson, P. A., Freeman, L., Bowman, J., & Peipes, J. (Eds.). *The university can't train teachers: A symposium of school administrators discuss school-based under-graduate education for teachers.* Lincoln: Nebraska Curriculum Development Center, University of Nebraska, 1972.

Openshaw, M. K. Research in teaching. In E. Brooks Smith, et al. (Eds.), *Summer Workshop-Symposium on School-College Partnerships in Teacher Education. Part-nership in teacher education.* Washington, D.C.: American Association of Colleges for Teacher Education, 1968.

Palmatier, L. L. How teachers can innovate and still keep their jobs. *Journal of Teacher Education,* 1975, *26*(1), 60–62.

Park, C. B. The Bay City experiment . . . As seen by the director. *Journal of Teacher Education,* 1956, *7*(2), 101–110.

Peck, R. F., & Brown, O. H. Research and development center for teacher education. *Journal of Research and Development in Education,* 1968, *1*(4), 107–126.

Perkins, H. V. A procedure for assessing the classroom behavior of students and teachers. *American Educational Research Journal,* 1964, *1*(4), 249–260. (Also reprinted in R. T. Hyman (Ed.), *Teaching: Vantage points for study.* Philadelphia: Lippincott, 1968.)

Postman, N., & Weingartner, C. *Teaching as a subversive activity.* New York: Dell, 1969.

Power, C. N. *The effects of communications patterns on student sociometric status, attitudes, and achievement in science.* Unpublished thesis, University of Queensland, Australia, 1971.

Provus, M. *Discrepancy evaluation.* Berkeley: McCutchan, 1971.

Reavis, C. A. Clinical supervision: A timely approach. *Educational Leadership,* 1976, *33*(5), 360–363.

Reavis, C. A. *Teacher improvement through clinical supervision.* Bloomington, Ind.: Phi Delta Kappa Educational Foundation, 1978.

Regier, H. *Too many teachers: fact or fiction.* Bloomington, Ind.: Phi Delta Kappa Educational Foundation, 1972.

Reilly, V. E., & Dembo, M. H. Teachers' views of in-service education: A question of confidence. *Phi Delta Kappan,* 1975, *57*(2), 126.

Resnick, L. B. *Teacher behavior in an informal British infant school.* Paper presented at the annual meeting of the American Educational Research Association, New York, 1971.

Richey, R. W. *Planning for teaching.* New York: McGraw-Hill, 1968.

Riechard, D. E. Needed: Resident clinical supervisors. *Educational Leadership,* 1976, *33*(5), 364–366.

Rosner, B., et al. *The power of competency-based teacher education: Report of the U.S. Committee on National Program Priorities in Teacher Education.* Boston: Allyn and Bacon, 1972.

Rubin, L. (Ed.). *Improving inservice education: proposals and procedures for change.* Boston: Allyn and Bacon, 1971.

Rubin, L. (Ed.). *The in-service education of teachers: Trends, processes, and prescriptions.* Boston: Allyn and Bacon, 1978.

Sarason, S. B., Davidson, K., & Blott, B. *The preparation of teachers.* New York: Wiley, 1962.

Saretsky, G. The strangely significant case of Peter Doe. *Phi Delta Kappan,* 1973, *54*(9), 589–592.

Schein, E. H., with Kommers, D. W. *Professional education: Some new directions.* New York: McGraw-Hill, 1972.

Schmeider, A. A. Profile of the states in competency-based education. *PBTE: Performance Based Teacher Education,* 1974, *3*.

Schmeider, A. A., Mark, J. L., & Aldrich, J. L. *Competency-based education: A briefing package.* Unpublished draft, U.S. Office of Education, 1975.

Schmuck, R. A., Runkel, P. J., Arends, J. H., & Arends, R. I. *The second handbook of organization development in schools.* Palo Alto, Calif.: Mayfield, 1977.

Sherwin, S. *Teacher education: A status report.* Washington, D.C.: American Association of Colleges for Teachers Education, 1974.

Shields, J. J., Jr. Social foundations of education: The problem of relevance. *Teachers College Record*, 1968, 70(1), 77–87.

Shipman, M. D. *Inside a curriculum project: A case study in the process of curriculum change*. London: Methuen, 1974.

Silberman, C. E. *Crisis in the classroom: The remaking of American education*. New York: Vintage Books, 1971.

Smith, B. O. The liberal arts and teacher education. In D. N. Bigelow (Ed.), *The liberal arts and teacher education: A confrontation*. Lincoln: University of Nebraska Press, 1971.

Smith, B. O., Cohen, S. B., & Pearl, A. *Teachers for the real world*. Washington, D.C.: American Association of Colleges for Teacher Education, 1969.

Smith, E. R. (Ed.). *Teacher education: A reappraisal*. New York: Harper and Row, 1962.

Smith, V., & Gallup, G. H. *What the people think about their schools: Gallup's findings*. Bloomington, Ind.: Phi Delta Kappa Educational Foundation, 1977.

Soar, R. S. *An integrative approach to classroom learning*. Philadelphia: Temple University, 1966.

Soar, R. S. Optimum teacher-pupil interaction for pupil growth. *Educational Leadership*, 1968, 26, 275–280.

Soar, R., Coker, H., & Lorentz, J. *Using process product relationships as the basis of describing effective teacher behavior*. Paper presented at a meeting of the American Educational Research Association, New York, 1977.

Sorber, E. Classroom interaction patterns and personality needs of traditionally prepared first-year elementary teachers and graduate teaching interns with degrees from colleges of liberal arts. *Classroom Interaction Newsletter*, 1967, 2(2), 51–55.

Spaulding, R. L. *Achievement, creativity and self-concept correlates of teacher pupil transactions in elementary schools* (Cooperative Research Project No. 1352). Urbana: College of Education, University of Illinois, 1963.

Spodek, B. (Ed.). *Teacher education of the teacher, by the teacher, for the child*. Washington, D.C.: National Association for the Education of Young Children, 1974.

Stake, R. E. *Evaluating educational programs*. Paris: Organization for Economic Cooperation and Development, 1976.

Standards for accreditation of teacher education. National Council for Accreditation of Teacher Education. Washington, D.C.: National Council for Accreditation of Teacher Education, 1977.

Standards for state approval of teacher education. Salt Lake City: National Association of State Directors of Teacher Education and Certification, 1976. (Printed by NASDTEC, 5th ed., further revision of U.S. Circular No. 351, Proposed minimum standards for state approval of teacher preparing institutions.)

Stevens, J. T., & Smith, C. L. Supervising teacher accountability: Evaluation by the student teacher. *Peabody Journal of Education*, 1978, 56(1), 64–74.

Stiles, L. J., et al. *Teacher Education in the United States*. New York: Ronald Press, 1960.

Stone, J. C. *Breakthrough in teacher education*. San Francisco: Jossey-Bass, 1968.

Student NEA looks at accreditation. An overview of accreditation and certification with guidelines for student involvement to improve teacher education. A partnership project between the Student National Education Association and the National Education Association. Washington, D.C.: National Education Association, 1975.

Study Commission on Undergraduate Education and the Education of Teachers. *Teacher education in the United States: The responsibility gap.* Lincoln: University of Nebraska Press, 1976.

Stufflebeam, D. L., Foley, W. J., Gephart, W. J., Guba, E. G., Hammond, R. L., Merriam, H. O., & Provus, M. M. *Educational evaluation and decision-making in education.* Atasca, Ill.: Peacock, 1971.

Summer Workshop-Symposium on School-College Partnerships in Teacher Education, E. Brooks Smith (Ed.). *Partnership in teacher education.* Washington, D.C.: American Association of Colleges for Teacher Education, 1968.

Survey of high school educator opinion, 1975–1976. Columbia: South Carolina Education Association, 1976.

Taylor, H. *The world and the American teacher.* Washington, D.C.: American Association of Colleges for Teacher Education, 1968.

Taylor, P. A., & Cowley, D. M. *Readings in curriculum evaluation.* Dubuque: Wm. C. Brown, 1972.

Teacher education: Issues and innovations. Proceedings of the Twentieth Annual Meeting of the American Association of Colleges for Teacher Education, 1968. Washington, D.C.: American Association of Colleges for Teacher Education, 1968.

Tenbrink, T. D. *Evaluation: A practical guide for teachers.* New York: McGraw-Hill, 1974.

Thias, H. H., & Martin, C. *Cost-benefit analysis in education: A case study in education: A case study of Kenya.* Washington, D.C.: International Bank for Reconstruction and Development, 1972. (Distributed by the Johns Hopkins Press, Baltimore.)

Thomas, J. M., & Bennis, W. G. (Eds.). *The management of change and conflict.* Baltimore: Penguin, 1972.

Tisher, R. Verbal interaction in science classes. *Journal of Research in Science Teaching,* 1971, *8*(1), 1–8.

Travers, R. M. W. (Ed.). *Second handbook of research on teaching.* Chicago: Rand McNally, 1973.

Troyer, M. E. *Evaluation in teacher education.* Washington, D.C.: American Council on Education, 1944.

Waimon, M. D., & Hermanowicz, H. J. *A conceptual system for prospective teachers to study teaching behavior.* Paper presented at the annual meeting of the American Educational Research Association, Chicago, February 1965.

Walberg, H. J. (Ed.). *Evaluating educational performance: A source book of methods, instruments and examples.* Berkeley: McCutchan, 1974.

Walker, D. F. [Educational policy is flapping in the wind.] *Journal of Teacher Education,* 1975, *26*(1), 24–29.

Watkins, R. (Ed.). *In-service training: Structure and content.* London: Ward Lock Educational, 1973.

Watson, G. Resistance to change in the planning of change. In W. G. Bennis, K. D. Benne, & R. Chin (Eds.), *The planning of change: Readings in the applied behavioral sciences.* New York: Holt, Rinehart and Winston, 1961.

Wiegand, J. (Ed.). *Developing teacher competencies.* Englewood Cliffs, N.J.: Prentice-Hall, 1971.

Wick, W. W., & Beggs, D. L. *Evaluation for decision making in the schools.* Boston: Houghton Mifflin, 1971.

Wilen, W. W., & Kindsvatter, R. Implications of research for effective in-service education. *The Clearing House,* 1978, *51*(8), 393–396.

Wolfe, J. N. (Ed.). *Cost benefit and cost effectiveness: Studies and analysis.* London: Allen and Unwin, 1973.

Woodring, P. *New directions in teacher education.* New York: Fund for the Advancement of Education, 1957.

Worthen, B. R., & Sanders, J. R. *Educational evaluation: Theory and practice.* Belmont, Calif.: Wadsworth, 1973.

Yeatts, E. H. Staff development: A teacher-centered in-service design. *Educational Leadership,* 1976, *33*(6), 417–421.

Zenke, L. L. Staff development in Florida. *Educational Leadership,* 1976, *34*(3), 177–181.

Index

AACTE (American Association of Colleges for Teacher Education), 66, 142

Accountability, in education, 6, 84, 234–236; criticisms of, 6; and incentives for professional growth, 234–236

Accreditation standards, 65–68, 70–73. *See also* NASDTEC; NCATE

Achievement, student profile. *See* Profile, student achievement

Achievement test construction, 41, 60, 287; and instructional evaluation, 41, 60; texts for psychometric aspect of, 287

Achievement Testing, 128, 179, 187. *See also* Achievement test construction; Achievement test construction and instructional evaluation; Evaluation, instructional

Achievement tests, 187

Activities, 16, 17, 18, 221; defined, 221; at the Identifying Problems Stage, 16; at the Designing and Preparing Solutions Stage, 17; at the Testing and Achieving Solutions Stage, 18

Advisement, 112–113

Advisor, 112, 247–248. *See also* Advisement

Affective entry characteristics, 69, 74

Affective pretest, 238

Affective posttest, 238

American Association of Colleges for Teacher Education. *See* AACTE

Analysis of student problems of Teachers College of Columbia University, 206

Analyzing and certifying teaching practices, 115

Anecdotal records, 187

Anderson, Lorin W., 16, 69, 74

Aptitude, defined, 225

ASCUS (Association for School, College, and University Staffing), 139

Assessment, 229, 249; defined, 223; for overall curriculum, questionnaire, 262–264

Association for School, College, and University Staffing. *See* ASCUS

Athletic Coaching, 144–145

Attitude scale, for perception of training effectiveness, 239

Attitudes: defined, 47; desired, 48. *See also* Generic teacher competencies, desired; Data base

Attrition rate, 187, 196; in evaluating program operations, 196

Behavioral objectives, 7. *See also* Objectives

Berkeley. *See* University of California at Berkeley

Bilingual programs, 136

Case study, 187

CCSSO (Council of Chief State School Officers), 66

Certificate renewal, 8

Certification standards, 25. *See also* NASDTEC; NCATE

Checklists, 187, 241

CLEP (College Level Examination Program), 221

Cognate, 134, 143–147; defined, 134; description of sample areas, 143–147

Cognitive entry behaviors, 69, 74

Cognitive pretest, 238

Cognitive posttest, 238

College Level Examination Program, The. *See* CLEP

Competency-based teacher education: defined, 11–12; criticisms of, 12

Competency List, 29; identifying, process for, 29–34; validation, process for, 34–35; validation, purpose of, 34–35; categories and competencies, 50–60. *See also* Competency statements; Generic teacher competencies

Competency list information, 253. See also *Competency List*

Competency statements, 7

Construct validity, 191 passim

Consultant evaluation, 205. *See also* Evaluation

Content validity, 239

Context, 99–100; defined, 99; determined, 99–100; scope, 99–100

Context evaluation, 98. *See also* Context; Evaluation

Correctives, 231

Cost-benefit analysis, 19–20, 210–213

Cost effectiveness analysis, 210

Council of Chief State School Officers. *See* CCSSO

Counseling Theory and Techniques, 146

Course development procedures, 108; for instruction, 111

Course load demands, 195

Course outlines, 109–111

Course requirements, 110

Covergence technique, 210

Criterion-referenced judgment, 239. *See also* Criterion-referenced test; Evaluation

Criterion-referenced test, 240

Criterion-related evaluation, 190

Curriculum structure, defined, 178

Data base, 119, 171, 172, 178, 192; uses of, 25; development, process for, 25, 29–34, 42–49; validation, purpose of, 34–35; filtering, process for, 42–43, 65–69; filtering, purpose of, 42, 65–68; sources, professional associations, 265. *See also* Generic teacher competencies, required; Generic teacher competencies, desired; Observational Data Sources; Teacher Report Data Sources; Competency list information; General Survey Form; Data Collection Instruments

Data Collection Instruments, 255

Decision-maker, 100–102, 140, 176, 178–179, 197; role defined, 20–22

Decision-making, 103–104, 223; at the Identifying Problems Stage, 17; at the Designing and Preparing Solutions Stage, 18; at the Testing and Achieving Solutions Stage, 19

Delphi method. *See* Delphi technique

Delphi technique, 21, 210

Demonstration, 187; as a lab experience, 115

Designing and Preparing Solutions (Stage 2), 17–18; activities, 17; evaluation, 18; decision-making, 18

Desired teacher competencies. *See* Generic teacher competencies, desired

Diagnosing Readiness for Learning, 40, 59, 107, 120, 127–128, 135, 233

Diagnosis, 221, 223, 224, 229, 239; group, in planning inservice training, 96–97. *See also* Diagnostic decisions; Diagnostic discrepancy analysis; Diagnostic-prescriptive model; Diagnostic-prescriptive process

Diagnostic decisions: activities, 221; evaluation, 223; decision-making, 223

Diagnostic Discrepancy Analysis, 226

Diagnostic-prescriptive model, 221, 224; correspondence with problem-solving model, 222. *See also* Diagnosis; Diagnostic decisions; Diagnostic-prescriptive process

Diagnostic-prescriptive process, 223, 228, 234. *See also* Diagnosis; Diagnostic decisions; Diagnostic-prescriptive model

Diagnostic Techniques in Teaching Reading, 146

Diagnostic tests, 250. *See also* Evaluation; Instruments

Directed Teaching, 129

Discrepancies reduction, 119

Discrepancy, 100–101, 184; defined, 100–101; at the Program Installation Stage, 184. *See also* Discrepancy approach, evaluation

Discrepancy approach, evaluation, 171

Early Childhood, 144

Education Index, 34

Educational Anthropology, 145, 159

Educational Procedures for Integrating the Exceptional Student into the Regular Classroom, 147

Educational Resources Information Center. See ERIC

Educational Testing Service, 152

Enabling objectives, 17, 109, 121, 173, 174, 181, 186, 188, 192–194, 195, 197–198, 201, 239

Equivalence, in evaluation, 191

Equivalent forms. *See* Equivalence

ERIC *(Educational Resources Information Center),* 34

Evaluation, 228, 248, 249; defined, 223; at the Identifying Problems Stage, 17; at the Designing and Preparing Solutions Stage, 18; at the Testing and Achieving Solutions Stage, 18; instructional, 41; teacher performance, criticisms, 90; uses in planning inservice, 93; context, 98; at the Problem Identification Stage, 98–104; steps in, at the Problem Identification Stage, 99–103; of support, 102–103; curriculum, 107; at the Program Design Stage, 171–176; for program structural soundness, 172; input considerations, 173; process considerations, 173; output considerations, 173–174; questions, 175; at the Problem Installation Stage, 177–184; installation considerations, 177; installation feasibility, 178–179; of recruitment, 179–181; of student-teacher interaction, 181–182; questions for installation (inquiry procedure), 183–184; at the Program Operation Stage, 185–199; purpose, 185; of course achievement, 186–190; of student-instructor interaction, 190–192; of field experiences, 192–193; of total curriculum, 193–198; questions (inquiry procedures), 199; at the Program Effectiveness Stage, 200–209; considerations, 200–207; using learner achievement, 202–203; using teacher performance, 203–207; of teacher performance by peers, 204; of teacher performance by supervisors, 204–205; of teacher performance by consultants, 205; scheduling, 205; of teacher performance, instruments for, 205–207; using interaction analysis, 206–207; inquiry procedure, 207–208; at the Program Effectiveness Stage, 210–214; texts on scoring and, 271; of instructor performance by student, sample instruments for, 272–279; instrument for observing practice teaching, 280–283. *See also* Evaluation instruments; Instruments; Teacher supervision and evaluation; Teacher evaluation

Evaluation and Educational Planning for Mainstreamed Exceptional Individuals, 147

Evaluation instruments, 242–243; item banks, 91, 93; self-report, 93; for enabling objectives, types and uses for, 186–189; program, 200–211; examples for teacher training programs, 238. *See also* Instruments; Evaluation

Evaluator, 99–102, 176; role defined, 20–22. *See also* Evaluation; Problem-solving model

Exemplary inservice teacher education programs. *See* Inservice teacher education programs, exemplary

Exemplary preservice teacher education programs. *See* Preservice teacher education

Face validity, 191
"Facet design" approach to test construction, 241
Family Guidance, 144
Family Living Styles, A Practicum in, 144
Feedback, 232
Field-based experiences, 10, 247. *See also* Field experience; Fieldwork, Laboratory; Laboratory experience
Field experience, 109, 112; sequence and type, 115–117; evaluation of, at Program Operation Stage, 192; in exemplary preservice programs, 247. *See also* Field-based experiences; Fieldwork; Laboratory; Laboratory experiences
Fieldwork, 122, 129–133; integrating with coursework, 129, laboratory/field experiences by course, 130–131; implementing lab sections, mechanics of, 130–132
Filtering the Data Base, 43, 49; steps, 43; discussion of, 49, 66; accreditation standards, 66; state standards, 66; teacher institution specifications, 67; using standards to filter, 65–68; using a review of research, 68–75; by category, 70–73
Final examination: controversies associated with, 188; format, 188–189
Flanders Interaction Analysis Categories, 182, 268
Follow-up survey, 238
Formative evaluation, 187, 248. *See also* Formative test
Formative test, 231, 238, 240–241
Fundamentals of Teaching Reading, 120, 128, 132, 146, 233
Furman University Observational Record, The, 205–206

General education, 148–160, 247; defined, 148–149; trends in, 150; in teacher education, NASDTEC standards for, 150–151; in teacher education, NCATE standards for, 151; Harvard University and, 152–153; University of California at Berkeley, changes in, 154; in teacher education programs, 154–160; in job-related curriculum, 157–160; requirements at selected teacher education programs, 266–267
General Education Models, Project on, 148
General Survey Form, 254
Generic Competencies Examination for Teachers, 133
Generic Job Description. *See* Generic Teacher Job Description
Generic List of Teacher Competencies, 48–49. See also Generic Teacher Job Description; Generic teacher competencies; Generic teacher competencies, desired; Generic teacher competencies, required
Generic teacher competencies, 246; assessment procedures for individual practitioners, 91–95; assessment procedures for practicing staff, 95–97; organization into courses, 106; source competency lists, 256–259. *See also* Generic teacher competencies, desired; Generic teacher competencies, required
Generic teacher competencies, desired, 42–49, 119, 159; defined, 42; steps in identifying, 43; discussion of identification procedures, 43–49; data sources for identifying, 44–45; establishing categories for, 47; skills, 47–48; knowledge, 48; attitudes, 48; filtering, process for, 42–43, 65–68; filtering, defined, 67; filtering, purpose of, 42
Generic teacher competencies, required, 119, 159; identifying, process for, 24; uses for, 25–29; checklist, 35
Generic Teacher Job Description, 34–35, 36–41; limitations of, 42
Generic teaching skills. *See* Teaching skills; Generic teacher competencies, desired; Generic teacher competencies, required
Grading, 189–190. *See also* Evaluation; Scoring and evaluation
Guidance Techniques for the Classroom Teacher, 147

Harvard University, 150, 152–153
History of American Education, 124, 125
Home-School Relations, 144
Horizontal dimension of the curriculum, 121
Human Development and Teaching, 120, 124, 125

Identifying Problems (Stage 1), 16–17, 91; activities of, 16; evaluation, 17; decision-making, 17; inservice education, 91
Incentives for inservice teacher participation, 233–235
Incomplete sentence technique, 187
IEP. *See* Individualized Education Programs
Indirect observation techniques, 186
Individualized Education Programs, 147
Individualized instruction, 136
Inductive method, in identifying teacher competencies, 33
Input, 172–174, 211, 213
Inservice session, 162–163; defined, 163
Inservice teacher education, 195; criticisms of 7–8, 25, 87–90; planning, 89–91; problem identification in, 91, 93–97; teacher attitude toward, 94; instrument to measure teacher attitude toward, 260–261; organization and scheduling, 96; terms defined, 162–163; problems in designing, 161; the professional growth of, 163–164; establishing content priorities for, 165–166; alternatives for presenting, 168–170; inside-outside approach, 169–

170; exemplary, characteristics of, 249–251; teacher opinions of, questionnaire, 260–261

Inservice training, 162. *See also* Inservice teacher education

Inside-outside team approach. *See* Inservice teacher education

Installation. *See* Program installation

Instructional Aids, 127, 179

Instructional delivery systems, 111–112

Instructional design specialist, 197

Instructional objectives, 7. *See also* Objectives; Enabling objectives; Terminal objectives; Ultimate objectives

Instructional Planning and Design, 37, 52–53, 124, 126, 232–233, 250

Instructor-made instruments and scales, 186, 187

Instruments: observation of student-teacher interaction, 269; samples for student evaluation of instructor performance, 272–279; for observing student practice teaching performance, 280–283; standardized, texts for selecting, 286; construction, texts for psychometric aspects of, 287. *See also* Evaluation instruments; Evaluation; Test construction

Intended outcomes, 7

Interaction Analysis, 205–207; texts on, 284. *See also* Flanders Interaction Analysis Categories

Intern, 116. *See also* Student teacher

Internal consistency, 191

Interpersonal Skills for Teachers, 39, 56–57, 120, 124–127, 146, 187, 229, 233

Inventory, 223

Item banks, 186

Job-related curriculum, 36, 100, 119, 180, 182–183, 192, 210, 223, 231–232, 236, 245; general education in the, 157–160; relationship between professional core, teaching specialization, and general education in the, 160; open-ended questionnaires for assessing overall curriculum, 262–264

Job-Related Curriculum Project, 143. *See also* Job-related curriculum

Journal of Teacher Education, 34

Laboratory, 132–133

Laboratory experiences, 115, 129, 130–131; individualized approach, 132; approaches to, 132–133

Laboratory school, criticisms of, 135

Laboratory staff, 130–132

Learning centers, 117

Liberal arts, 149, 157. *See also* General education

Likert scale, 242

Lindvall and Cox model, The, 236

Logistics, 194, 243

Mainstreaming, 136, 147

Marking. *See* Scoring and evaluation; Evaluation; Grading

Master Teachers, 112, 164

Mastery learning, 229. *See also* Mastery learning model; Mastery level

Mastery learning model, 69, 224–225, 229. *See also* Mastery learning, Mastery level

Mastery level, 231, 240

Media Arts, 144

Merit increases, 191. *See also* Merit system

Merit system, in public education, 234–235. *See also* Accountability; Incentives; Merit increases

Methods and materials courses, in teaching specializations, 138

Michigan State College Teacher Observation Records, 206

Microteaching, 132

Minors, 144. *See also* Cognate; Teaching specializations

Model job-related curriculum. *See* Job-related curriculum

Modules, 122, 167

Multicultural Education, 144–145. *See also* Multicultural programs

Multicultural programs, 136. *See also* Multicultural education

"Musts" of Teaching. *See* Generic teacher competencies, required

NASDTEC (National Association of State Directors of Teacher Education and Certification), 106, 125, 135, 142, 149, 150, 174; defined, 66; standards, 65–68, 70–73; and general education, 158–159

National Council of Teachers of English, 67

National Council for the Accreditation of Teacher Education. *See* NCATE

National Education Association. *See* NEA

National School Boards Association. *See* NSBA

National Teacher Examination. *See* NTE

NCATE (National Council for the Accreditation of Teacher Education), 106, 114, 135–137, 140, 142, 150–151, 157, 174; defined, 66; standards, 65–68, 70–73; and general education, 158–159

NEA (National Education Association), 66, 139, 142, 168

Needs assessment, 16, 172, 178, 186; questionnaire for teacher education needs, 262–264. *See also* Problem identification; Problem-solving model

Needs identification evaluation procedures, 100–102

Norm-referenced judgment, 239. *See also* Evaluation; Norm-referenced test

Norm-referenced test, 240. *See also* Evaluation; Norm-referenced judgment

NTE (National Teacher Examination), 26, 150–151
NSBA (National School Boards Association), 66

Objectives, 118, 175, 192–193, 202, 239; as the curriculum structure, 120–122; purpose of, 173–174; texts on teaching for, 284. *See also* Enabling objectives; Terminal objectives; Ultimate objectives
Objectivity, in evaluation, 191, 202
Observation, 115, 186; as a lab experience, 115; indirect, 186
Observational Datae Sources, 252
Observational record, 193
OE. *See* United States Office of Education
Office of Education. *See* United States Office of Education
Ohio Observational Record, The, 193
Ohio Teaching Record, The, 205–206
Output, 172–173, 186, 211–213

Parental Involvement in Education, 144
Peer evaluation, 191, 204
Perseverance, defined as in mastery learning model, 224
PERT (Program Evaluation and Review Technique), 198, 210
Philosophies and Theories Applied to Education, 117, 124, 179
Placement, 220–221
Placement criteria, 221
PPBS (Program Planning and Budgeting Systems), 210
Posttest. *See* Affective posttest; Cognitive posttest
Practice teaching, sample instruments for observing, 280–283
Practicum in Family Living Styles, A. *See* Family Living Styles, A Practicum in
Practicum in Teaching Reading, A. *See* Teaching Reading, A Practicum in
Preprogrammed decisions, 182
Prescription, 225, 229, 230. *See also* Diagnostic-prescriptive model; Diagnostic-prescriptive process; Prescriptive phase
Prescriptive phase, 228. *See also* Prescription
Prescriptive Techniques in Teaching Reading, 146
Preservice curriculum, 161. *See also* Preservice teacher education
Preservice teacher education, 89, 161, 177, 178, 221, 245–249; criticisms of, 89; exemplary, characteristics of, 245–249; and teacher competencies, 246; and field-based experiences, 247; and advisement, 247–248; and evaluation, 248–249
Pretest. *See* Affective pretest; Cognitive pretest
Problem identification, 16, 164, 225. *See also* Needs assessment; Problem-solving approach; Problem-solving model; Problem-solving process
Problem-solving approach, 13, 245; rationale for, 13
Problem-solving model, the, 16, 22–23, 119, 216, 221–222, 228, 236; stages of, 16; in teacher education, application to, 22–23; correspondence with the diagnostic-prescriptive model, 222. *See also* Problem-solving approach; Problem-solving process
Problem-solving process, roles in, 20–22. *See also* Problem-solving model
Process, in evaluation, 172–174, 211. *See also* Evaluation
Professional Associations, 265
Professional development, defined, 162
Professional core, the, 119–120, 122, 231, 250–251; purpose of, 119–120; activities, 122; course sequence and overview, 122–129; role of fieldwork in, 122, 129–133
Professional coursework, 155, 246. *See also* Professional core
Profile, student achievement, 203
Program cycle, 200
Program development specialist, 179; role, 20–22, 141
Program design, 164, 171, 173–174; defined, 171; purposes, 173–174
Program effectiveness, 164
Program efficiency, 19–20
Program Evaluation and Review Technique. *See* PERT
Program installation: considerations, 177; feasibility, 178; evaluation, 182–184; fidelity, 184
Program operations: evaluation, 185; considerations, 185
Program Planning and Budgeting Systems. *See* PPBS
Program preparation, 228
Projective devices, informal, 186
Project on General Education Models. *See* General Education Models, Project on
Promotion, in education, 191
Psychology of Marriage, The, 144

Questionnaires, 46, 107–108, 260–264; use for developing data base, 46; for curriculum evaluation, 107–108. *See also* General Survey Form; Data Collection Instruments; Instruments

Rating scales, 186–187, 241
Readiness, defined, 225–226
Reading, 144, 146
Reading, A Practicum in Teaching. *See* Teaching Reading, A Practicum in
Recruitment: staff, 179; student, 180
Rehabilitation Services, 144, 146
Reliability, in evaluation, 191, 202
Remedial learning experiences, 236

Remediation, 231
Required teacher competencies. *See* Generic teacher competencies, required
Retention skills, 188
Role playing, 187

Scheduling, 194
School Guidance, 144, 146
Scoring and evaluation, texts on, 271
Selection criteria, 179, 218, 219, 220, 221, 227; enforcement, 220. *See also* Selection decisions
Selection decisions, 216–220; considerations in, 219–220. *See also* Selection criteria
Self-evaluation, 193
Self-inventories, 186
Shared teaching approach, 117, 246. *See also* Team teaching
"Shoulds" of teaching. *See* Generic teacher competencies, desired
Simulation, in education, 116, 132, 187; as a lab experience, 116
Sociology of the Family, 144
Special Education, 144, 147
Specialization. *See* Teaching specializations
Stability, in evaluation, 191
Staff development, defined, 162
Standardized measures and scales, 186. *See also* Standardized tests
Standardized tests, 186, 237, 285; in the diagnostic-prescriptive process, 237; texts for selecting, 286
Standards for State Approval of Teacher Education. *See* NASDTEC
State Department of Education, 175
Statistical analysis, 189
Student evaluation, 201–202, 204, 272–279; of instructor performance, sample instruments for, 272–279. *See also* Evaluation; Instruments
Student evaluation profile. *See* Profile, student achievement
Student-instructor interaction, 190–192
Student teacher, 116, 280–283; instruments for observing the performance of, 280–283
Student-teacher interaction, 181, 187, 199, 269; evaluating installation, 181; instruments to observe, 269
Summative tests, 248, 249, 250
Supportive coursework, in various professional programs, 156
Supportive Services, 41, 61
Supervisor evaluation, 204–205
Survey of Rehabilitation Professions, 146

Task analysis, 188, 197, 230
Teacher Center, 8, 167
Teacher competencies. *See* Generic teacher competencies; Generic teacher competencies, desired; Generic teacher competencies, required

Teacher development, defined, 162
Teacher education programs, characteristics of, 5. *See also* Teacher education
Teacher education, 7, 9, 10, 12–13, 113; criticisms of, 7, 10, 113; issues, 9; coursework apportionment, 9; humanistic approach to, 12–13. *See also* Competency-based teacher education
Teacher evaluation; criticisms of, 26–27; design of instruments based on generic teacher competencies, 27; forms, uses in identifying competencies, 33. *See also* Teacher supervision and evaluation; Evaluation
Teacher Job Description, 29, 32–33. *See also* Generic Teacher Job Description; Generic teacher competencies; Teaching skills
Teacher Report Data Sources, 253
Teacher Resource Guides, 119, 133; data included in, 133
Teacher supervision and evaluation: criteria for, 26, objectivity in, 27
Teaching as a Profession, 36, 50–51, 109, 122, 124, 133, 179, 180
Teaching, Implementing Instructional Plans, 38, 54–55
Teaching Language and Thinking Skills, 128
Teaching Multicultural Classes, 145
Teaching Reading, A Practicum in, 146
Teaching skills, 30–36; defined, 30; procedure for identifying, 31–32; identification of required skills, 32–34; categories of, 33; validation of, 34–36. *See also* Generic teacher competencies; Generic teacher competencies, required
Teaching specializations, 134–143, 246; defined, 134; considerations in developing program areas, 135–139; identifying target areas, 139–140; process for determining, 139–143; determining content and skills, 140–141; investigating recommended courses of study, 141–142; filtering through standards, 142; synthesizing findings, 143
Team teaching, 111, 116–117, 136, 170, 179; advantages, 116–117; assumptions underlying, 117; benefits, 117
Tenure, 191. *See also* Merit system
Terminal objectives, 17, 109, 120, 167, 173–175, 181, 188, 192, 194, 195, 197–199, 201, 239
Test construction, texts on, 270, 285
Testing and Achieving Solutions (Stage 3), 18–19; activities, 18; evaluation, 18; decision-making, 19
Test item banks. *See* Item banks
Time on task, 69, 74
Tutoring, 111–112

Ultimate objectives, 120, 121, 173, 175, 181, 194, 197, 200–201, 204, 207, 232. *See also* Objectives

Understanding Educational Research and Innovation, 75, 128–129, 251
Unit objectives. *See* Enabling objectives
United States Office of Education, 139
University of California at Berkeley, 150, 154
University Without Walls, 155

"Upside-down curriculum," 156
Using Instructional Aids, 40, 58, 233

Validity, in evaluation, 191, 202
Vertical dimension of the curriculum, 121
Visitation, as a lab experience, 115

Winnetka Plan, 224